MUD

RIDE

M

A MESSY TRIP THROUGH THE GRUNGE EXPLOSION

UD
RIDE

BY STEVE TURNER

WITH ADEM TEPEDELEN

CHRONICLE-PRISM

Library of Congress Cataloging-in-Publication Data

Names: Turner, Steve, 1965- author. | Tepedelen, Adem, author.
Title: Mud ride : a messy trip through the grunge explosion / by Steve Turner, with Adem Tepedelen.
Description: San Francisco : Chronicle Prism, 2023. | Identifiers: LCCN 2022051435 (print) | LCCN 2022051436 (ebook) | ISBN 9781797217222 (hardcover) | ISBN 9781797217246 (paperback) | ISBN 9781797222769 (ebook)
Subjects: LCSH: Turner, Steve, 1965- | Alternative rock musicians–United States–Biography. | Guitarists–United States–Biography. | Mudhoney (Musical group) | Grunge music–Washington (State)–Seattle–History and criticism. | LCGFT: Autobiographies.
Classification: LCC ML419.T874 A3 2023 (print) | LCC ML419.T874 (ebook) | DDC 782.42166092 [B]–dc23/eng/20221104
LC record available at https://lccn.loc.gov/2022051435
LC ebook record available at https://lccn.loc.gov/2022051436

Manufactured in China.

Design by Patrick Barber. Typesetting by Happenstance Type-O-Rama.
Typeset in Futura and Harriet Text.

10 9 8 7 6 5 4 3 2 1

Chronicle books and gifts are available at special quantity discounts to corporations, professional associations, literacy programs, and other organizations. For details and discount information, please contact our premiums department at corporatesales@chroniclebooks.com or at 1-800-759-0190.

CHRONICLE PRISM

Chronicle Prism is an imprint of Chronicle Books LLC
680 Second Street, San Francisco, California 94107

www.chronicleprism.com

CONTENTS

Part Three (2000–2022)

FOREWORD
BY STONE GOSSARD

STEVE TURNER LOVES GARAGE ROCK. HE LOVES THE UNDERDOG, the obscure-label, late-'60s, paisley-wearing, psychedelic rock band that made one record and broke up 'cause the lead guitarist—whose solos consisted of three plinky notes repeated with abandon—became an electrician. He digs the completely obscure folk duo from Northern Canada that influenced Neil Young's biggest influence.

Steve's an avid collector of records and other memorabilia, a scourer of the secondhand. He has a sheer, unkempt passion for all that is neglected, undervalued, unappreciated, and off the beaten track. You know—failures. He is also joyous, irreverent, and very, very sweet (when he's not being stubborn).

All of that, to my fifteen-year-old self, was like a drug. From the time I met Steve in 1982, I couldn't get enough of that manna.

It was intoxicating to think that life could be so much more interesting by not following the rules, your teachers, academia, or the mainstream. That you could follow the neglected story arc of the has-beens, the almost-rans, or the out-and-out rejected. Wow. Cool.

Steve's modus operandi was infectious to a pimply art school junior who had no discernible talent, passion, or ambition, other than being a smart aleck. Steve Turner taught me everything I know about punk rock, folk art, and how to find your life's course: Buy a cheap guitar and a tiny out-of-production amp, and start a band. Like a finger painter or a kid in a sandbox, go make your silly mark! I've been running with his ethos ever since.

Steve's impact on Seattle music and a huge number of artists and musicians is impressive. By God, he found the frickin' holy grail of all distortion boxes: Super-Fuzz. Talk about reverse technological innovation. Right when hard rock distortion had calcified into a ubiquitous and friendly RockMan™ sound—"More Than a Feeling" Boston, lukewarm tomato soup, no danger, no unevenness, nothing scary, just wide-leg, feathered hair FM love—he unearthed *the distortion*.

He found it in some pawn shop on the advice of some other throwback hoarder. Super-Fuzz is a pedal that makes a crappy guitarist sound brilliant, and requires only their wits, an ecstatic ambition, and this outdated, forgotten component. It was a distortion that howled again, scraped, screamed, crawled, and cackled!

Steve's playing and songwriting epitomize visceral expression in caveman style—kinda '50s, kinda '60s, kinda '80s, but without the practice. So fun! And those solos! Yes, one note!

Mudhoney are grunge. They made it up. They ruled over Green River's self-consciousness and overly complex arrangements (my fault). Mark, Steve, Danny, and Lukin set us all free. I still can't forget the feeling of euphoria from beer and seeing the crashing biplanes in the brand-new "This Gift" video cranked so loud at the Vogue—pure bliss!!

I love you, Steve. Thank you for lowering the bar for everyone.

Your old friend,

Stone

INTRODUCTION

IN 2023, PEOPLE CARE ABOUT THE SEATTLE MUSIC SCENE because of grunge.

Not metal, not punk, not hip-hop, not indie rock, even though all those genres have been well represented in the last several decades in Seattle. Nope—it's grunge.

Grunge is a silly word, I know, but at some point in the '80s, that's the word that for better or worse became attached to what was happening musically in the post-hardcore Seattle scene of the early '80s. (It might actually have been my best friend and future Mudhoney bandmate, Mark Arm [née Mark McLaughlin], who first coined the term.) I should mention, however, that at no point did anyone in this era say, "Let's start a grunge band." For musicians like me, who were trying to figure out what came next after hardcore punk, things happened organically.

I know, I know—"happened organically" is a lame platitude, but I'm using it here to indicate that there was a distinct lack of "doing this to become a rock star" ambition in Seattle. When we were all starting our first bands in the early '80s, there was absolutely no thought we were doing this to get famous, or sell a million records, or whatever. That was in no way part of the motivation for forming a band, writing songs, playing gigs—all the usual things bands do.

We wanted people to come to our gigs, have a few beers (or not, if it was an all-ages show), and hoot and holler after we finished a song. Success at this point meant playing gigs at whatever venue would have you and maybe you'd get a write-up in a local zine. That is to say, we were doing it because it was fun.

But the reality was that nobody was getting signed to a major label record deal out of Seattle. And by that, I mean that A&R reps from the music industry centers, Los Angeles and New York, weren't scouting the city for talent.

If you *were* ambitious, you sought out fame elsewhere. Local hard rockers Rail entered and won MTV's *Basement Tapes* contest in 1983, and progressive metal band Queensrÿche, around this same time, self-released their debut EP on a local label and found acclaim in the United Kingdom and Europe long before any of the major labels in the United States gave a shit about them.

There's an argument to be made that a scene such as Seattle—isolated geographically and to a certain extent, culturally—might produce music that's a little more pure and untainted by nonartistic motivations (i.e., money). Though we had access to national magazines and zines and were obviously listening to music from all over the world, we weren't channeling that into following trends or figuring out ways to make our music more appealing to labels. I mean, the music my friends and I were bashing out in the '80s, which was firmly rooted in punk, hardcore, garage rock, and noise rock—all robustly anti-commercial pursuits—had no pretense of making its proponents rich. We were playing for ourselves, each other, and for the small, supportive scene. Musically, we could (and did) do whatever we wanted to, because there was no question in our minds that what we were playing had zero commercial viability. We could mix our Killing Joke or PiL influences with a splash of Black Sabbath or

Led Zeppelin and a dash of the Stooges. I mean, why not? Getting famous or even having a career making this music, in our minds, just wasn't a possibility.

That's the setup to my story. How did we get from these humble beginnings to a world where Nirvana's *Nevermind* has sold tens of millions of copies, Pearl Jam (whose guitarist I started my first band with in 1983) are still an arena-drawing act thirty-plus years later, and Soundgarden (who recorded a song I wrote back in 1984) are played regularly on classic-rock radio? And Mudhoney, my own band, continue to be one of the flag bearers for grunge in the twenty-first century, with sold-out shows in the United States, Europe, Australia, and Asia.

Though much of my story involves my decades in Mudhoney, including the crucial years where *we* were the top of the grunge heap (years before Nirvana and Pearl Jam broke big), I want to shed as much light as I can on what gave rise to Mudhoney and what led to and fostered the explosion of million-selling bands from this unlikely locale in the Pacific Northwest. That said, I'm not a historian—my story is definitely *not* the definitive and exhaustive history of grunge, because everyone has their own perspective and take on how it all went down.

This is what *I* saw, the people I knew, and the experiences I had that capture this incredibly influential era of music. What I have to offer is an insider's insight into a time that went from homespun fun to international acclaim in a handful of years. It still seems unreal to me, because it was so unexpected. Every milestone for Mudhoney along the way—sold-out local shows, European tours, lingering on the UK charts for months, John Peel sessions, playing to tens of thouands of people at international festivals, signing a major label record deal—seemed amazing, but these were things that fell into our laps, not goals we pursued. As you'll see, any personal goals I may have had (and they were always vague) never involved a career in music. I guess I was sort of the accidental rock star.

That's not to say that I was completely passive. Mudhoney obviously said yes to the numerous opportunities we were offered, but we made decisions that weren't necessarily based on getting rich. As you'll see, it was occasionally the opposite: We made plenty of decisions that left money on the table or prevented us from reaping future monetary benefits. Sure, we wanted to sell out shows, sell records, and make a living playing music, but we didn't strive to be rich and famous (emphasis on famous, because I saw firsthand what that was like and I wanted no part of it). There's absolutely a line where bands make decisions that push them one way or the other. When a record label suggests you need to "sweeten" your guitar sound, get a singer with the "right look" and vocal range, or write something that can be played on the radio, you can either acquiesce or tell them to go fuck themselves. We always chose the latter.

Once Mudhoney realized early on that we had something special, we never felt the need to bend the knee to anyone. That attitude came predominantly from our punk rock/hardcore roots. Mark and I had been immersed in Seattle's hardcore nascence in the early '80s. Our original bassist, Matt Lukin, came from the Melvins, one of the most influential pre-grunge bands of the era. Even our young drummer, Danny Peters, was a veteran of a handful of local bands before he was of drinking age. We found our sound almost immediately after coming together in January 1988, and only messed with it as it suited *our* whims, not others'.

This approach allowed us to maintain our punk rock cred when many of our peers were forced to defend and question theirs over the years. It also put us in the unique position of experiencing both the underground world of our own making as well as the major label machinations some of our good friends were going through. Mudhoney were selling tens of thousands of albums (not bad for the underground) while we were touring arenas with Nirvana and Pearl Jam, who had already sold *millions* of albums. We led an oddly charmed life in many ways. We got to see how the "other half" lived, without having to deal with the downsides. Eddie Vedder couldn't go to the grocery store, but I could. Kurt Cobain was somehow embarrassed by or ashamed of all the gold and platinum record awards he received for Nirvana's major label debut, *Nevermind*. I had no such problem.

I obviously can't tell you about what it was like to strike it big as a Seattle musician in the grunge era. I can tell you how it all started, though. I can tell you what Seattle was like in the early '80s and how I ended up meeting and playing in bands with Jeff Ament and Stone Gossard from Pearl Jam. I can tell you how Mudhoney went from being on the cover of local fanzines like *Backlash* to being on the cover of the United Kingdom's *Melody Maker* magazine. I can tell you about some of Nirvana's first shows opening for us. I can tell you what it was like to see our once-sleepy Seattle scene become *Time* magazine cover–worthy. I can tell you what it was like to see the music we were playing become the reason why people suddenly cared about—and continue to care about—Seattle. I can tell you what happens when drugs and fame and untold wealth wreak havoc on people you know and care about.

I can tell you about grunge.

PART

2020

ONE

SOUND WAVES

EVEN THOUGH I GREW UP IN SEATTLE, I WAS BORN IN Texas, and I always tell people I'm from there because I'm proud of it. Texas has always seemed strange and exotic to me, a bit wild—like going back in time.

I was born in Houston on March 28, 1965, but I have no recollection of living there. My family moved to the Emerald City in the summer of 1967, when I was two, my sister Mary-Virginia was four, and my brother Patrick was seven. Seattle was the only city I'd known until I moved south to Portland in 2007. (But we'll get to that later.) The change in climate, scenery, and culture was no doubt a shock to my parents, who were super white-bread Texans. But for a kid, Seattle was a great place to grow up.

My parents moved the family from Texas to Seattle because my dad got a job as the director of Seattle's proposed World Trade Center. He had extensive import-export experience, focusing mainly on the Far East, so Seattle was a good fit. Seattle in the late '60s was nothing like what it is today. It was a Boeing city, as that's where the bulk of the jobs were. When we moved to Seattle, it was a much smaller, sleepy city, and was very blue collar. The high-tech industry and the pervasive wealth it brought would come twenty-five years later and would coincide, oddly enough, with the rise of the local music scene.

My father, Robert Neil Turner, was the only son of a Polish immigrant, John Peter Tuzynski, who took on the surname "Turner" when his employer at the time couldn't pronounce his last name. My mother, Patricia Jean Landers, could trace her ancestry back to the 1600s in America. There was no real ethnic heritage that I could ever find on her side, other than the fact that she was 1/32 Native American, which Boeing tried to use to its advantage (claiming her "minority" status for its hiring quotas) when she worked there in the '80s.

Because my father was an only child and my mother's dad left his family during the Great Depression and never returned, I didn't grow up near a lot of family beyond my parents and siblings. Most summers, while living in Seattle, however, we would return to Texas to see my mom's kin. My maternal grandmother, Tula "Yam" Landers, had five sisters, and we'd spend time with most of them, particularly my great-aunt Betty "Boo" Stallings, and her husband, Bob. My mom had two sisters: Rose, who we'd see in Texas, and Peg, who'd married musician Lebert Lombardo (brother of bandleader Guy Lombardo). Peg split her time between Florida and New York.

Both my parents were well educated and had college degrees. They came of age in the postwar '50s and had a straitlaced view of the world. Though they'd both been raised Catholic, they were liberal, and didn't like some of the Catholic Church's positions, like opposing birth control. (Personally, I hate the popes of the last sixty years for continuing to decry birth control, and not getting behind safe-sex education through the '80s during the AIDS crisis, when they could have saved millions of lives.)

We settled into our rented home on 18th Avenue East in the Capitol Hill neighborhood, and my older siblings were enrolled in Catholic school for the new school year. Though I'd only live at this home with my family for four years, I'd return to Capitol Hill as an adult (I bought my first home there), and this area would eventually become an enclave of Seattle's progressive cultural community.

My first memories of Seattle are of the 18th Avenue house. It was a gorgeous four-bedroom "box" with a giant porch on the front, full basement, good-sized yard, and alley in the back—a true heritage home from an earlier era. However, what captured my imagination was a weird trap door between my brother's and sister's rooms. There was a little tunnel that I loved crawling through. I have no idea why it was there. I was so enamored with this house that as an adult I pined for it and fantasized about buying it when I had money from Mudhoney's major label record deal in the early '90s. Sadly, it never went up for sale.

After four years spent getting to know Seattle and the surrounding suburbs, in the summer of 1971 my parents decided to buy their first house on nearby Mercer Island, east of Capitol Hill, across Lake Washington. Today Mercer Island is primarily known as an enclave of the well-heeled, but in the early '70s, a family home could be bought on one income for $30,000. Our new house was a 1950s split-level home, nothing fancy.

Though my parents were still young when rock 'n' roll was invented, they weren't pop music people. Elvis was just some hillbilly to them. More than that, they were completely clueless about pop culture. It simply wasn't any part of their world. Even when Mudhoney had a lot of success in the late '80s and early '90s, they had no frame of reference for what it meant to tour with Sonic Youth, play to tens of thousands of people at the Reading Festival in England, or get signed by a major label. They were always supportive, but they didn't get it. My dad had studied piano, so the few records my parents owned were mostly classical music, and we always had the local classical station, KING FM, on in the house. Outside my house, suburban ennui helped create hardcore punk rock—a faster, angrier version of first-wave punk (think the Ramones and the Sex Pistols)—and growing up on Mercer Island in the '70s would play a part in my own musical development. But the music I heard in our Mercer Island home, for the most part, didn't make much of an impact.

One of the few records I can recall my dad owning that had a connection to my musical journey was an original Capitol Records 10″ by Lead Belly, bought by my dad in his bachelor years. Lead Belly (a.k.a. Huddie William Ledbetter) was a hugely influential and iconic African American blues and folk singer whose songs were covered by Nirvana and many others.

My mom had no ear for music, but I discovered that as long as I said that whatever I was listening to was "Lead Belly," she was fine with me playing it on the family stereo. She had no clue who Lead Belly was, but since my dad owned one of his records, I guess that was the only stamp of approval needed.

The only record I can recall my mom owning was Dory Previn's first album, *On My Way to Where*, from 1970. Dory Previn had been married to André Previn, the pianist, and he left her for Mia Farrow. Dory had a nervous breakdown after André left her, and the album was about that. It's a very personal record, a beacon of the feminist movement, that's a bit psychedelic and weird at times. It's still one of my favorite albums.

There were a few other records in my parents' meager collection that also caught my ear as a kid. My dad had some Clancy Brothers albums of Irish folk music that were huge to me when I was in grade school. One album was called *Come Fill Your Glass with Us*, and it pictured the brothers sitting around a bar table wearing white turtleneck fisherman sweaters, holding steins of beer. They seemed like such *men*. To my young mind, that's what I thought men did. As unlikely as it seems, those records meant a lot to me. I still love that stuff, and in fact, on my 2004 solo EP, *A Beautiful Winter*, I recorded "The Parting Glass," which I'd first heard on a Clancy Brothers record.

My dad had a choral record of sea shanties, and I loved those songs too. The only songs I liked on the radio at the time were things like "Wreck of the Edmund Fitzgerald" by Gordon Lightfoot, or even "Brandy" by Looking Glass. I liked songs that told stories, and for some reason a lot of them seemed to be about the sea.

Mercer Island was a distinct change from Capitol Hill's urban density. There were a lot of rich people on Mercer Island—the entire waterfront is nothing but beautiful homes and fairly wealthy people—but where we lived was the definition of "suburbia," with spacious lots, plentiful parks, and green space. The whole neighborhood had been built by the same company in the late '50s. Almost none of the neighborhoods had sidewalks until you got into the downtown grid. The greenbelt behind the house had trails threading through it, and we could build tree forts anywhere we wanted in the woods. Though I'd loved the house we'd rented on Capitol Hill, life on Mercer Island was idyllic for a kid.

At six years old it was time for me to start grade school. My parents would have preferred I attend Catholic school, as my older siblings had when they were my age, but I wasn't having it. Maybe I was already exhibiting punk rock, anti-religion tendencies long before punk had even been invented, but I protested as only a six-year-old could: I had a weeklong temper tantrum. My main beef was that I didn't want to wear the school uniform, but this wouldn't be the last time I'd butt heads with my parents regarding religion. My protests worked: Unlike my older siblings, I was spared Catholic school and sent to the local public schools. Their loss, because one of the field trips we took back in elementary school was to the Olympia Brewery, something *they* never got to do. (Taking grade school kids to breweries in the '70s was A-OK. What were the teachers thinking?)

When I wasn't learning how cheap lager was made, I was taking advantage of island-living opportunities like sailing lessons. Because Mercer Island had an upscale, country club vibe, sailing and tennis were big. For team sports in school, I played soccer, which suited me, because I was a hyper kid with boundless energy, an advantage on the field. I also discovered two passions that I still have today, fascinations that would not only channel my energy but would literally define the rest of my life: skateboards and bicycles. This book is largely about my musical career, but that never would have happened had I not found these two things.

I learned to ride a bike the same as every other kid in my neighborhood did in the '70s. But my interest, or maybe obsession, went beyond cruising around the local streets. By age eleven, I was taking my bikes apart and tinkering with them. I had a sweet Schwinn Sting-Ray with a banana seat—the coolest bike you could own in the '70s—that I rode over little homemade wooden jumps. I was also a total wheelie master: I could wheelie up and down the block.

While my bicycle mania was developing, my dad, who'd quit working for the Port of Seattle and had started his own import-export business, changed my life when he brought home six crappy skateboards and a copy of *Skateboarder* magazine.

"This is a new sport down in California. Check it out," he told me as he presented me with the first boards I'd ever own.

At the time, we didn't know that skateboarding wasn't exactly new. It had been created by surfers in the '50s (to "sidewalk surf") and was popular until the mid-'60s, after which its popularity waned. In the early '70s, however, board improvements like urethane wheels provided such a drastic increase in performance that

Dressing up in our first Bellevue apartment in 1967.

Lopez Island, Washington, with Mary-Virginia and Patrick, 1968.

Mom, circa 1970, Ocean Shores, Washington.

First grade at West Mercer Elementary School. I still miss that vest.

Dad clowning around at the Port of Seattle.

Fifth grade! By this point I had firmly established my sartorial style!

skateboarding was enjoying a surge in popularity. The boards my dad brought home were *not* the best the industry had to offer. But for me, they were my first taste of not just a sport, but what would turn out to be an entire culture, a lifestyle.

Initially, skateboarding was just something fun to do on the sidewalks. The fact that we didn't have sidewalks in my neighborhood didn't stop me—I'd ride wherever I could go: in the street, on driveways, and in our carport. My favorite board my dad gave me had grippy black rubber wheels and left skid marks like my Sting-Ray did. I quickly filled the whole carport with skid marks.

Somewhat concurrently with skateboarding, I discovered BMX—bicycle motocross. Though BMX eventually became an international sport for riders of all ages, in the early '70s it was a totally new thing. Like skateboarding, it came out of California, and was spawned by young thrill-seeking bicyclists wanting to race on jump-laden motocross motorcycle dirt tracks. Once BMX's popularity caught up with me in 1976, it took over completely. It perfectly satisfied my eleven-year-old thirst for heart-pumping thrills.

I put my bike-tinkering skills to work and converted my Sting-Ray into a BMX bike: I threw on knobby tires and pseudo-motorcycle handlebars, and painted it flat black (I left the banana seat on it). The only problem was, since the sport was so new, there weren't any races in the Seattle area yet. That was OK by me—until there was an actual race in the Pacific Northwest, I'd spend my time catching air off my wooden jumps and perfecting my wheelies.

While I was immersing myself in skateboarding and BMX in the mid-'70s, a lot of my junior high school classmates had their own fascination: Kiss. Confession: I hated Kiss when I was a kid in the '70s. I'll go on record definitively stating that they weren't an influence on me. I've never even tried to learn an Ace Frehley lick. Unlike most of my musical peers (and some of my closest friends and former bandmates like Jeff Ament and Stone Gossard of Pearl Jam), I didn't see the appeal. Every other twelve-year-old was postering their room with pictures of the band, but I thought they were fucking stupid. But then, I didn't like *any* rock music. And I never went to any big rock concerts as a kid. I missed that whole scene.

Looking back, it's a wonder I ever found my way to punk rock. Nothing I'd been listening to by this point gave me any framework for the aggressive music that would speak to me in a completely new way. Punk would scratch an itch I didn't know I had.

FIX ME

I DON'T HAVE A LOT IN COMMON MUSICALLY WITH GUNS N' Roses guitarist Slash, but we have a few notable similarities: We're both the same age (within a few months), we both play lead guitar in our respective bands, and we both grew up racing BMX. I can't speak for him, but BMX was my entry-level adrenaline rush, a rush that I'd eventually replicate being onstage and playing in a band.

With my converted Sting-Ray bicycle, I was full-on into BMX when I started hanging around our local bike shop, Mercer Island Cyclery, run by Dave Gnehm and his family. Dave had been a road racer back in the day and had been a Washington State road-racing champion at some point in the '70s. His whole family were bicycle freaks. He wasn't really into BMX, but he figured it was great for the kids, so he supported it and put together a small team of riders that I joined. This is also when I got my first proper BMX bike using money from my short-lived acting career. Did I forget to mention this?

Long before I was racing BMX or skateboarding, I did a TV commercial for Pacific Northwest Bell, a regional phone company. When I was nine, my mom took my brother Patrick and me to a casting call at the Seattle Center. I don't remember much about the audition, only that I got the job and my brother didn't. The commercial shoot was on a tiny, old ferryboat moored at one of the local islands in Puget Sound, and involved a white-haired, crusty ferry-boat captain supposedly teaching us how the boat worked. I never got to see the commercial, because as far as I know it never actually aired in the Seattle area, but I did get a nice paycheck from it, which my parents banked for me. So, a few years later, when it was time to get a proper BMX bike, I went big and convinced my parents to let me spend $400 of my acting money on it, which they thought was outrageous. (It *was* outrageous because that would be about $1,600 today.) But, hey, it was my money, and they let me do it because they knew I was crazy about BMX.

BMX racing had finally arrived in Seattle, and local tracks were slowly being built around the region (some more rudimentary than others). In June 1977 I was part of the Mercer Island team that competed at the Greenwood Boys and Girls Club. It was a small, modest track, but it was still exciting to compete. This race was not only the first in our area, but it was also one of the first in the state, and it drew riders from the entire West Coast. Even with such stiff competition, our Mercer Island team took first overall, and I was the top of my age class. It was the first of many trophies I'd accumulate competing in the area over the next few years.

Not long after the Greenwood race, the Mercer Island Boys and Girls Club built a BMX track (with some help and encouragement from my BMX-riding friends and me) in a vacant lot that had once been a swimming pool that had been filled in and was sitting empty. Finally, we had BMX racing on Mercer Island! My first taste of fame was a picture of me in the *Mercer Island Reporter* hitting a jump during a race at the annual summer Mercerfair, with the headline "Turner First In."

Though I was stoked at the recognition, it didn't do much for my social game in junior high. Most of my peers had ten-speeds, and they looked at the handful of us who rode BMX bikes like we

The whole family on Mercer Island, circa 1978.

One of my early BMX trophies, 1977.

Working on my converted Schwinn
Sting-Ray, early 1977.

Well, that didn't last long!

were still riding kid's bikes, partly because they were so small. They treated me like I was the dude who still played with toys. I was still skateboarding, too, which didn't help. I was like, *These things are really popular in California!* But on Mercer Island, they weren't.

While my hobbies weren't making me particularly popular at school, they did make me more independent and willing to search out things on my own instead of doing what everybody else did. I wasn't necessarily rebelling, but I was OK with being different. This would be a recurring theme throughout my life.

Another way I asserted my independence around this time didn't sit so well with my liberal-minded but staunchly Catholic parents. I'd hated church for as long as I could remember. I didn't believe a word of what anybody said regarding religion from the get-go, and I never had the faith. By age fourteen, I'd been kicked out of catechism classes (basically Sunday school). I made two teachers cry, which isn't easy to do. I was relentlessly opposed to the lessons they tried to teach me. I wouldn't stop asking questions, wouldn't stop saying, *I don't believe any of this. Explain it to me.*

But the drama came to a head when I refused to be confirmed. The confirmation ceremony represents your first adult decision as a Catholic: confirming your faith. I didn't have the faith, so I didn't do it. This was a huge thing in my family. It was the first true rebellion my parents had dealt with and was the first crack in the veneer of their perfect, Catholic family. However, my heresy was the icebreaker.

Several years later, my older sister—who'd dutifully attended Catholic school from kindergarten through twelfth grade—got pregnant while unmarried and attending the University of Washington. Then my older brother came out as gay. To their credit, my parents handled every curveball well, but there's no denying that they had to make a lot of adjustments to the ideal Catholic family they had imagined.

Around this same time, my interest in BMX racing had started to wane. It was due to my size—at age fourteen, I still looked like I was twelve, and suddenly it seemed as if I was competing against full-grown men who outweighed me by fifty pounds. My size put me at a distinct disadvantage, because if a rider doesn't get out of the gate fast and get the "holeshot"—front position in the first turn around the course—he'll be screwed and won't place. The riders I was competing against could get off the line faster than I could. I loved riding bikes, but as far as racing, I couldn't compete anymore.

So, I became serious about skateboarding. Sometime in late 1979, I noticed that a couple of high school kids up the street had built a pair of quarter pipe skateboard ramps in their driveway. Because I was still in junior high, I didn't know these dudes (John Lee and his buddy Mike Judge), but I'd stop and watch them sometimes on my way home from school, because it looked cool and interesting. Soon I was asking to borrow their skateboards (which were better than the junk boards from my dad I was still using), and before too long I got to be as good if not better than them on the quarter pipes.

Skateboarding came naturally to me. I was fairly athletic, but I think mostly it was because I wasn't afraid. I had first gotten on a skateboard when I was young and tiny, and I was also a skilled skier—into moguls and jumps and stuff—so it wasn't terrifying to drop in and catch some air on a board. Most people who give it a go would say, *I tried skateboarding once, fell on my ass, and never touched it again*, but those of us who kept doing it were undaunted, even when we kept falling over and over. It takes a certain type.

Fortunately, I never broke anything. I had learned how to fall well in judo lessons at an early age, and I give full credit to my dad for getting me into that. He'd attained the level of brown belt in judo when he was in the service in Japan in the '50s, and he thought I'd

Going backside on John Lee's half pipe, 1980.

Going frontside on John Lee's half pipe, 1980.

enjoy the physicality of martial arts. I was the smallest kid in my judo class, so all the other kids practiced their flips on me. I learned how to fall in the very first lesson, how to spread the impact across the mat. By the time I was competing in downhill skateboard races or ripping it up on quarter and half pipes, I'd already had plenty of practice falling. The tuck and roll was second nature. This would come in handy as I continued to skate well beyond the years when young bones heal miraculously quickly.

Though skateboarding briefly lost its luster when I got into BMX, I'd continued reading issues of the revamped *Skateboarder* magazine, and I learned to do new skateboarding tricks via the photo spreads.

I also began to notice that the magazine was covering music and bands. Their music column was written by a pro surfer named Corky Carroll—the first surfer to be paid for endorsements, in fact—and by the late '70s, he was writing about the emerging new wave and punk rock world. John and Mike, my older friends down the street, started blasting punk rock records when we were skating. By this point they had built a half pipe behind John's house, and if the conditions were dry, I was there every day after school. The music they were playing appealed to me immediately—particularly the first couple of Devo records and the first two D.O.A. albums, *Something Better Change* and *Hardcore '81*. John had even gotten the first Black Flag single, *Nervous Breakdown*, not long after it was released in January 1979. Unlike Kiss and the "hits" on Top 40 AM radio at the time, this was music I could connect with.

Of course, I'm not alone in my entry into music through skateboarding. There was a generation of us that got into skateboarding around this same time, and it birthed our love of music and punk rock. Jeff Ament, my future Green River bandmate and later Pearl Jam bassist, is a perfect example. He was a skateboarder out in the middle of Montana, and *Skateboarder* and *Thrasher* magazines were his only link to the wider skateboarding world. Skateboarding was a small community at this time, and when *Skateboarder* and *Thrasher* started covering music, they found a hungry audience. You could write letters to other kids across the country and ask, "What's your skate scene like there?" It was such a small club to be in and, like hardcore and punk rock, outsiders didn't understand it. But we did. We got it.

So, alongside skating, we all started discovering music, and the music took over for quite a few of us. I embraced punk rock with the same fervor as skateboarding, and I soon learned that I could show my allegiance beyond blasting Black Flag at my buddies' half pipe. In ninth grade I decided to make a statement: I "came out" as a punk rocker. This was the tail end of '79, and straight-leg Levi's 501 jeans weren't yet "in," but I wore them because all the California skaters I saw in the skate magazines had them on. Kids at North Mercer Junior High were still mostly wearing flared-leg pants, like Brittania jeans, but I decided, *Fuck it, I'm going to wear my straight-leg jeans to school with my Vans.* And I had one of those cycling caps with the small bill, and I wrote "PUNK" in punk-type letters on the bill. You could see my ears, which meant my haircut was wrong too, because everyone still had feathered hair at that time. Short hair pissed people off so much.

That was when the last of the cool crowd abandoned me. I'd hung out with them off and on over the years, but I knew it was going to happen, because they weren't into the same stuff I was anyway. I was proto–straight edge (a hardcore scene movement started a bit later by, most notably, Minor Threat), which meant that I didn't smoke, drink, or do drugs. The cool crowd were starting to get into partying, so the gap between us grew too big.

One guy, Jim Bouvet, remained my friend, but he was also in the super-cool clique, so we would only hang out *after* school, on our own.

He really liked Devo. He was an egghead guy, and a lot of the eggheads secretly liked Devo (and especially liked when they appeared on *Saturday Night Live* in 1978). But as popular as Devo were with the skate crowd, they became a symbol of derision for anyone who somehow felt threatened by punk rockers. If you looked even remotely punk rock, the local heshers, the long-haired metal dudes, would drive by in their Camaros and yell "Fucking Devo!" or "Devo sucks!" at you as an insult. No one ever yelled "The Clash sucks!" or "Black Flag sucks!" at me. But I guess because Devo were so bizarre-looking with their flowerpot hats and matching uniforms, they were the band the heshers associated with anyone who looked weird.

This would be a pivotal time in my life in many ways. The music I liked wasn't what most kids were listening to, and in my mind, it was directly linked to skateboarding. I would carry my love of skateboarding and punk rock forward for the next four decades, and both would define who I am as a person, musician, and even parent. I had so much to learn from both pursuits that I would make them an integral part of both my personal and professional lives. I was different from the other kids—I even started cutting my own hair—but I thought I was cooler than they were. I wasn't a complete contrarian; it was just more important to me to do the things I liked to do than to be accepted by the other kids. My interests were already independent activities, so I think that kept me on my own solo path, occasionally finding like-minded souls who liked the same kinds of stuff. *The squares don't understand it*, I'd think, *but there's enough of us that do.*

Solitude didn't trouble me; it only hardened my resolve.

STREETWISE

I STARTED TAKING FOLK GUITAR LESSONS AS AN ELECTIVE in ninth grade in 1979, but I wouldn't pinpoint this as the start of my musical career. In fact, I'd never considered the thought of playing music as a career, even when I got into serious bands later on. I wasn't one of those kids standing in front of a mirror holding a tennis racket imagining I was onstage in a coliseum or at a giant festival. Funny how things work out.

Punk rock would have never crossed my radar were it not for those early skateboarding magazines. We skateboarders were led to it. *Skateboarder* covered punk bands because some of the pros were getting into them. So, we all came along for the ride. It was a whole new world.

There was also a certain amount of serendipity that the late-'70s and early-'80s skateboarding scene erupted out of Southern California, because it had a direct connection to that area's emerging hardcore punk scene. Bands like T.S.O.L. played hardcore *and* skated. (T.S.O.L.'s first 12″ EP for Posh Boy Records in 1981 is still one of my favorite hardcore records.) Even the bands that weren't necessarily known as skaters, like Black Flag (although their later singer Henry Rollins skated), became inadvertent ambassadors of the skateboarding-hardcore connection because skaters loved the raw rebelliousness of their music. For teenagers like me, who were alienated from the social scene at their junior high or high school, this was how we found our people.

Geographically, Seattle had always been at a disadvantage when it came to attracting touring bands. San Francisco, some eight hundred miles to the south, was the next closest large market. So unless you were a band with a big, guaranteed paycheck awaiting you in the Emerald City, you might skip it. That's not to say that touring bands *never* found their way to Seattle, but for most that weren't West Coast–based already, it was a significant schlep to western Washington from almost anywhere in the country.

The burgeoning West Coast hardcore scene—from Vancouver, BC, down to Los Angeles—operated on a completely different scale, touring in vans or cars towing U-Haul trailers and playing any venue that would have them. These bands would play squats, basements, universities, clubs, dives—whoever would pay them enough to get gas money to the next town. They'd sell whatever merch they had—a 7″ or an album, maybe some T-shirts—to get enough for food and maybe get some cheap beer. This was the life that Hermosa Beach hardcore quartet Black Flag were living when they rolled into town on May 2, 1980, to play at the Washington Hall on Capitol Hill. Also on the bill: Canada's Subhumans and local punks the Vains.

I desperately wanted to go to this show—my first concert of any description—but my parents didn't think sending their fifteen-year-old son into Seattle at night was a great idea. They had no idea what punk or hardcore was, so that didn't figure into the equation, but they probably sensed that it wasn't exactly going to be an evening of wholesome family entertainment. As it turned out, their intuition was spot on. What happened that night is renowned in Seattle punk lore as the "Black Flag riot show." According to two friends who were at the show (cowering behind an overturned table with Black Flag's drummer, Robo [a.k.a. Roberto Valverde]), the giant brawl was apparently instigated by some Vancouverites who'd come down to hear the band. Police were called, arrests were made, and the whole scene ended up on the front page of one of the local newspapers. My mom felt vindicated for not letting me go.

Three months later, just before I was to start attending Mercer High School as a sophomore, I finally had my chance to see Devo. They were supporting their *Freedom of Choice* album, which would soon spawn the Top 40 hit "Whip It." Devo had a lot of cachet in the skateboarding world because of their "Freedom of Choice" video, which featured some notable pro skaters of the day like Steve Olson, Jay Smith, and Eddie "El Gato" Elguera skating in an empty pool while Devo played in matching Rector knee and elbow pads.

So, when I saw they were playing at the Showbox in downtown Seattle, my friends and I knew we had to go. Despite the glamorous name, the Showbox was a jazz-era club whose luster had faded by the '80s. It was in a fairly sketchy part of First Avenue, across from the Pike Place Market, so getting my parents' permission required some finesse. A few of my skateboarding friends were already planning to stay at my place that same weekend so we could compete in a downhill contest in nearby Bellevue. Luckily there was an early show, and my parents figured that the whole "safety in numbers" thing would be justification enough to allow us to go see Devo together after the contest.

Among my motley crew were Mike "Micro" Shaughnessy, Mark "Pee Wee" Healy (apt nicknames since we were all small), and David Garrigues. David was the best skater in the area at the time, and the future bassist for 10 Minute Warning (who were hugely influential in Seattle). David showed up at my house while we were having breakfast, and my mom graciously invited him to join us at the table.

"Would you like to have some pancakes, David?" she asked. He was wearing a dirty old overcoat and was carrying his skateboard, which was a pile of junk.

"Oh, no, thank you, Mrs. Turner," he demurred. It seemed strange to me that someone who looked vaguely homeless would turn down a *Leave It to Beaver*-style breakfast. Then he added, "I brought my own breakfast," and he produced a couple of dirty carrots and a head of broccoli from inside his grubby overcoat.

So, on August 12, 1980, decked out in Bermuda shorts and Rector kneepads and clutching my skateboard, I witnessed my first punk rock show. It was my introduction to what I saw as a cool, weird, and kind of dangerous scene. Obviously not every show erupted into a riot, but punk definitely attracted a sketchy element, and was typically performed in shitty, downscale venues.

After dipping my toes in the punk rock waters at the Devo show with no obvious physical damage (no brawl at that one!), my parents decided that it'd be OK for me to *finally* see Black Flag at the same venue four nights later. This was predicated on the attendance of my older skateboarding neighbors, John Lee and Mike Judge. My mom trusted John completely, because he was a neighbor and older, and she knew him well. If I was with John and Mike, I could go anywhere.

John's stepdad owned a killer late-'60s convertible—big and white with a red interior—and John was allowed to drive it to shows in Seattle. Between the big front and back bench seats, we could easily fit six kids in the car. My skateboarder friends and I piled in and went to see Black Flag—with fingers crossed that there wouldn't be a repeat of the band's last show in town.

More so than the Devo concert, my first Black Flag gig was a revelation. I was both afraid and intrigued—afraid because the scene seemed scary and dangerous and intrigued because the members of opening band Solger were basically my age at the time; they were

Skating the Fife half pipe in 1982 with Mark "Pee Wee" Healy on the deck. Mike "Micro" Shaughnessy's legs, far left.

Mercer Island High gymnastics team. Jim Bouvet in the background, circa 1980.

At Luther Burbank Park on Mercer Island, 1981. That's my Kos Cruiser—should never have sold that one!

DEVO

AUGUST 12th
$10
IN ADVANCE
SHOWBOX
1434 1st AVENUE, SEATTLE

My first concert! 1980.

kids. Solger's MO was to play as fast as possible. They were a little rougher, more Northwest than the Southern California hardcore of the day. I think of all the punk rock from those days in Seattle as being moss-covered. Damper, darker, uglier. The scariest bands I've seen in my life were all from Seattle.

Paul Solger would go on to another influential Seattle band, 10 Minute Warning, with my skate buddy David Garrigues, but seeing him and his band opening for Black Flag was a huge eye-opener. They were kids my age. I was like, *Shit, kids have bands?*

I wasn't necessarily thinking that this was suddenly my life's calling, but it made me realize that punk was accessible to anyone who wanted to play it. You didn't have to be a virtuoso. You didn't need to have a record deal. You just needed a little bit of gear, some like-minded friends, and a desire to make a whole lot of noise. Black Flag reinforced that notion on a larger scale. They were a band putting out their own records, touring on a shoestring, and playing in whatever venue would have them. Punk rock seemed within reach, even for me. And now that I had access to what was happening in Seattle via John and his sweet convertible, I wanted more.

The arrival of hardcore in Seattle, via both touring bands and the few locals who were starting up, had a profound effect on the emerging scene and in many ways fostered the nascent grunge and "Seattle scene" the world came to know. In my mind, it all began with hardcore. This is where we all connected, developed our musical tastes, and eventually started forming our own bands.

That's not to say that there wasn't already a vital (if small) underground music scene in Seattle at the time. However, it was decidedly more new wave and collegiate, with a few punk bands riding the first wave. Those punk bands were important flag bearers, and a teenage Duff McKagan (of future Guns N' Roses fame) played in almost all of them: the Fartz and the Fastbacks (drums), the Vains (bass), the Living and 10 Minute Warning (guitar). I loved the bands he was in, and he was a great musician. So many of the future grunge musicians of the era grew up with and loved his early bands, even though the band he ultimately found fame with represented (in some people's minds) the antithesis of Seattle's anti–rock star aesthetic.

However, with the arrival of hardcore in the early '80s, there was a changing of the guard, led by a bunch of suburban teenagers like my friends and me pissing off the slightly older college kids at shows. I'd love to tell you that once I discovered this burgeoning hardcore scene, I was at shows all the time, but that was not the case, unfortunately. Because the punk scene in Seattle was still tiny, and—as noted earlier—we were a smallish and distant market for touring bands, it was still unusual to get touring bands coming through. We did get a lot of Canadian bands coming down from Vancouver (D.O.A. were practically local), but a show like Hüsker Dü and Dead Kennedys at the Showbox, for instance, was a rarity in 1981.

Also, a ton of shows were simply canceled at the last minute in the early '80s. You'd think there was going to be this rad show, and then *nope*. That happened a lot. There was a lack of venues willing to host these bands to begin with, and frequently when they did, they later regretted it because the venues would get trashed, which seemed to be a thing. If it was a rented hall, some idiot in a leather jacket would go into the bathroom and pull out the fucking sink or do something else stupid. You could always point to four or five people, like, one of *those* assholes did it.

It was a handful of troublemakers (maybe ten in the whole scene), guys who hung out on University Way (a.k.a. "The Ave") in the University of Washington's University District. Thankfully a lot of them dropped out quickly.

The U-Men, arguably one of the most prominent proto-grunge groups of this era, suffered from punk's bad rep. In '82, a string of nearly a dozen of their shows was canceled. Either the police or city officials would shut them down, or the owner of the hall would figure out, *Oh, this is gonna be a punk rock show*. It wasn't like the U-Men were inciting the bad behavior, but at the time, they drew more people to their shows than any of the other local punk bands. They were the kings; they were the coolest band in town. They were the fucking champions of the cool underground punk rock, post-punk Seattle scene.

Mr. Epp and the Calculations, another notable local band (and one that I'd have lifelong ties to), also suffered from numerous canceled shows. I'd heard their "Mohawk Man" single (which I really liked), and I'd tried repeatedly to see them, to no avail. I didn't get to see them until they played at a community hall in Seattle's Central District with Limp Richerds. (I'd eventually briefly play in both bands a bit later.)

I've gotta admit, though, that the underground nature of these shows and the music and the inherent element of danger were part of the thrill of punk. Some of the scariest bands I saw during this time were locals: the Refuzors, RPA, and Extreme Hate. In my sixteen-year-old mind, these guys were some rough people, and I knew to stay the hell away from them and stick to the back of the room at those shows. But their music was great, I think in part because of that. They were so nihilistic.

The Refuzors were one of the "leather punk" bands from the era that predated hardcore. They seemed like a biker gang to me, decked out in leather jackets and logging boots. They weren't bad people; they were just older and seemed intense. I loved their music too. They did this thing where the bass player and guitar player would come up to the edge of the stage at the same time and kick, and if you were in the way of their feet, you got kicked.

Unfortunately, as my interest in hardcore and skateboarding grew, my interest in doing schoolwork and attending class proportionately waned. Eleventh grade in 1982 was my punk rock rebellion year. My two older, skateboard-slash-punk buddies, John and Mike, had graduated and gone off to college, so I was alone. I wasn't happy in school, so I would cut class all the time. I'd go to the public library (which was right next to the high school), read books for a few hours, then go back home after school was let out. Sometimes I didn't even go home—I slept at friends' houses instead. I was still straight edge—no drinking or drugs—but I was fucking up. I flunked almost every class. I had a 1.2 grade point average. You've really gotta actively be a dick and not turn in any work to piss off the teachers and get that. I was rebellious, and I was an asshole.

My parents didn't know what the hell to do with me, so they sent me down to stay with my Texas relatives for the summer to cool my jets. Angling for any option other than returning to Mercer Island High for my senior year, I told my parents about the Northwest School, a newish private school in Seattle, founded in 1980. I knew about it because a couple of my friends were going to be attending in the fall. I suggested to my parents that it might give me a fresh start. It wasn't cheap, and it was too late to get any financial aid. But miraculously, they let me go, and bought me a second chance at a high school diploma.

But more than that, they unwittingly delivered me to my first band.

SCHOOL'S OUT

IN THE FALL OF 1982, I MET TWO PEOPLE WHO WOULD become two of my closest friends. For a brief period, we'd even play in a band together. These guys would also become cornerstones of the soon-to-be emerging Seattle music scene and remain so for the next four decades. The individual circumstances under which I met each of them, and the role each would play in my life, were very different, but I have no doubt that the story of Seattle music as we know it would have unfolded very differently—or perhaps not at all—had these connections not been made.

I know that sounds self-important, but bear with me while I connect the dots. The Northwest School, a private school where I started my senior year of high school in 1982, was the surprising nexus of all of this. It was a small school—only thirty-two students in my senior class—so as a new student, I was able to identify classmates I had something in common with early on.

I spotted Alex Shumway right away. Though he was a year behind me at school, he had the look of an obvious punk ally. He'd moved to Seattle from California with his mom and sister, and I'd probably crossed paths with him at local hardcore shows. This was an auspicious friendship to make, as he was the one who introduced me to Mr. Epp and the Calculations' guitarist and vocalist, a smart and snarky kid named Mark McLaughlin, who by then was going by Mark Arm.

Mark was a few years older than us. He'd formed Mr. Epp and the Calculations in the late '70s, while attending Bellevue Christian High School. He'd played a few Seattle-area gigs in the early '80s, and Mr. Epp had a local underground punk rock hit with "Mohawk Man" in 1982, reaching number one on "Rodney on the ROQ," the radio show of LA DJ and kingmaker Rodney Bingenheimer. After that, Mark had gone off to college at Linfield University in McMinnville, Oregon, for his freshman year, and Mr. Epp were temporarily put on hold. He returned to Seattle in 1982 when he transferred to the University of Washington (UW), and the band resumed.

Alex and I were at a concert at the Showbox in downtown Seattle in the fall of 1982 (it was either John Lydon's Public Image Ltd. or skate rock heroes T.S.O.L.) when he spotted Mark.

"Hey, Mark, I want you to meet my friend Steve," Alex said. "He's straight edge too."

Mark and I just looked at each other and rolled our eyes—me because I *was* straight edge (but didn't want to be thought of as straight edge), and Mark because he had already started experimenting with acid at that point and definitely *wasn't* straight edge.

Mark, Alex, and I became not only fast friends, but eventual bandmates. Mark's experience in the local underground punk scene, as well as his contacts at UW, would be pivotal. On a personal level, Mark and I would influence each other's tastes in music, and we'd eventually be joined at the hip through most of our decades-long careers in music.

Stone Gossard was someone else who stood out at the Northwest School. He was a year younger, and a wiry teenager like me. He wore super tight, pegged Levi's, white Capezio dance shoes, and sleeveless Iron Maiden T-shirts, and had a rooster haircut like Rod Stewart. He was a little shit and a sarcastic asshole whose personality leaned more toward "punk" than his taste in music did. When I first showed up at Northwest—a punk rock kid with a skateboard and shaved head—Stone and his metalhead friend, Jeff Covell, would flip me a lot of shit. I would flip shit back at them, and for some reason, we became friends.

Stone was a diehard metalhead when I met him, and tried to get me into Iron Maiden, but I wasn't having it. But he did turn me on to Motörhead's 1981 *No Sleep 'til Hammersmith* live album, as well as the shock rock band Alice Cooper. But while Stone was into classic Cooper hard rock albums like *Love It to Death* and *Killer*, I dug deeper into the band's weird, early, Frank Zappa label–released back catalog—*Pretties for You* and *Easy Action*. This became an ongoing theme in my musical explorations. As I discovered music and artists I liked, I always wanted to go back to the roots, the genesis of the bands or their genres, to uncover obscure and strange stuff.

Stone thought those early Alice Cooper records sucked, but he was open to listening to some of the underground stuff I was into. By late '82 or early '83, I started turning him on to punk, well before the metal and punk crowds found common ground and started "crossing over" a couple years later. Stone wasn't into the crazier hardcore stuff like Void, the Washington, DC, band that Mark and I liked. Stone's tastes ran more toward melodic Southern California punk, like Social Distortion, Agent Orange, and the Adolescents—all great stuff, but not exactly hardcore. We had found some common musical ground, somewhere between his love of metal and my love of hardcore. This would be a meaningful connection in many ways.

Even though I had taken folk guitar lessons at North Mercer Junior High, I didn't get an electric guitar until my senior year of high school, when my parents gave me a Stratocaster-style Peavey

Christmas 1982 with Patrick, Mary-Virginia, and Krinkles.

Northwest School senior
picture, September 1982.

Not the most convincing punk rocker,
1983.

for Christmas. As ungrateful as this sounds, I was horrified by it. Peavey guitars were the favorites of country musicians in Nashville in the '80s. It wasn't the kind of guitar Greg Ginn of Black Flag played, or really *any* punk band I'd ever seen. It was a shitty guitar, one I considered embarrassing, but I played it for six months or so.

It was the guitar I played when Stone and I formed the Ducky Boys in early '83, with Jeff Covell on drums and Stone playing bass. The Ducky Boys were a total garage band, the first for all of us, and we had no idea what we were doing. I'd gotten an amplifier, a Sunn Solarus combo, at a downtown pawn shop. It had a clean sound, and I couldn't figure out how to get the gnarly hardcore tone I wanted out of it. Luckily Jerry, a coworker at my job at a Bellevue Japanese restaurant, straightened me out. He happened to be a former member of the Vancouver punk band Bludgeon Pigs, and had far more musical experience and knowledge than I possessed at that point.

I was telling him about my problems getting the sound I wanted out of my amp, and he asked, "What kind of distortion box are you using?"

"Uh, what?" I had no idea what he was talking about.

He smiled.

The next day he showed up at the restaurant and said, "You should try this," and handed me a Super-Fuzz distortion pedal.

At the next practice with the Ducky Boys, I plugged in the Super-Fuzz, and it was, like, *Oohhh*.

Clouds parted.

Gabriel's trumpet sounded.

Being able to approximate that ugly, powerful, overdriven guitar sound I'd heard on those first Black Flag records, and what I was hearing from the stage from local bands like Solger, the Fartz, and the Refuzors, was a revelation.

It didn't improve the Ducky Boys at the time, though. We learned a couple covers, like the Kingsmen's "Louie Louie" and Kiss's "Calling Dr. Love" (because Stone and Jeff were really into Kiss, and I apparently couldn't escape that band). We also had an original tune called "Kissinger Killed Moro," named after a phrase that had been graffitied all over Seattle at the time. We didn't know who the fuck Moro was, or what the graffiti meant, but we didn't care. That's about as punk as the Ducky Boys got. However, it's been said that this first union of Stone, with his hard rock and metal leanings, and me, with my love of punk, became the sort of ground zero for grunge, which drew heavily from both.

Unfortunately, the Ducky Boys never played live, which was probably because our "singer" was too embarrassed to sing in front of us. He just sat on the couch in the basement, looked cool, and never touched the microphone. No wonder I can't remember his name.

Jeff Covell didn't go on to pursue a musical career, but he still lives in Seattle. Stone keeps in touch with him, and I reconnected with him at the thirtieth anniversary celebration of Sub Pop Records in 2018.

Though Mark Arm and I were hanging out, going to shows together, and immersing ourselves in Seattle's seminal punk and hardcore scene, he was steps ahead of me in a few significant ways: He was a university student, while I was still in high school. His band, Mr. Epp, had put out a record that got airplay both locally and in LA, and he had played actual gigs in local venues. I had only the Ducky Boys to my credit. One thing we had in common, though, was a ravenous appetite for discovering new music—music that went beyond punk and hardcore. We figured hardcore was eventually a dead end—you can only go so fast for so long.

We were seeing signs of this evolution within the local Seattle scene. Former members of two early hardcore bands—Solger and the Fartz—had formed 10 Minute Warning and were playing a glammed-up, semi-psychedelic version of punk rock. It was definitely not hardcore, but I thought they were great—one of my all-time favorites from this era. Several notable Seattle musicians would cycle though the band during its short existence from 1982 to 1984, including (once again) Duff McKagan, Paul Solger, Blaine Cook, Daniel House, and Greg Gilmore. Duff's next band would be Guns N' Roses (after he moved to LA), and his former 10 Minute Warning bandmates would go on to the Accüsed, Skin Yard, and Mother Love Bone, among other notable next-generation Seattle bands.

At the time, though, 10 Minute Warning were a revelation in Seattle. They were one of the first bands from the punk scene to attempt to infiltrate the local metal scene. That scene was largely based in the suburbs, and thrived by holding gigs at roller rinks, instead of the downtown clubs where the punk crowd typically went. 10 Minute Warning landed on one of these bills when ex-Fartz singer Blaine Cook was still fronting the band, so of course Mark and I went to check it out.

Blaine's bandmates got all dolled up in their rock 'n' roll finery for the gig because they were like, *OK, this is it, we're crossing over into this other world.* They looked more like rocker dudes— they had scarves and shit like Aerosmith. Blaine wasn't playing that, however. He was the same fuckin' little Blaine as he was in the Fartz. He was dancing around and exaggerating his little elfin moves, doing his little creepy thing. The other dudes were pissed, and that was the last time I saw him in 10 Minute Warning. Shortly thereafter they got Steve Verwolf on vocals, who was more of a Jim Morrison type, and Blaine went on to replace John Dahlin as the singer for the Accüsed, a band that was better suited to Blaine's hardcore style.

The U-Men, like 10 Minute Warning, were important players in pointing the local underground punk and hardcore scene in a new direction, because their sound was unlike any other band in town. We all loved the U-Men. They weren't a hardcore band, but they played with hardcore bands, so we'd see them on local bills. They didn't bend to the heavy and sexy sound that ultimately made Seattle famous, though Jim Tillman's bass was thunderous. They had a defined mod look and drew from post-punk (think Joy Division, Gang of Four, the Fall) and noise rock influences that no other bands in town were exploring. Like 10 Minute Warning, they were showing all the younger musicians who cut their teeth on hardcore a different path forward. This wasn't quite grunge, but this was a way of thinking and playing that inspired other local players and ultimately led to grunge.

Stone, Mark, Alex, and I weren't quite there yet. Mr. Epp and the Calculations had the irreverent attitude, but they'd been tagged with the unfortunately ableist "art spazz" label early on by the punks in the scene (who Epp was usually mocking anyway), because they were a bit weird like Devo and lacked the blatant aggression of hardcore. Their sound was quirky and (at least initially) fairly experimental—lots of feedback and chaos. Alex did a brief stint as the bassist for Extreme Hate, that band of very scary individuals who I avoided at all costs. Alex was not a scary individual, which is probably why he didn't last long.

After the Ducky Boys went nowhere, Stone briefly joined some of our Bainbridge Island hardcore friends in March of Crimes as a second guitarist. Stone was the oldest one in the group. The rest were barely teenagers, including Ben Shepherd, a fourteen-year-old guitarist, who would go on to fame as Soundgarden's bassist several years later. The band's founder and vocalist went by the name Munkyseeker, but he's better known today as bestselling novelist Jonathan Evison. At that time, he was already writing, doing a hardcore fanzine called *Cineplex 1* that was really funny.

This was a formative time for all of us. We were getting our toes wet in our first bands and, whether or not we realized it at the time, we were building something. The Ducky Boys weren't my ticket to stardom (not that I wanted that), but that first experience was my transition from being a *fan* of bands to *playing* in one. This wasn't a big "aha" moment where I suddenly saw my future, but looking back, it seems like certain things lined up so that fate (or whatever) was nudging me toward something.

My parents had paid an exorbitant amount to get me across the finish line of high school, so I'd felt a real responsibility to not fuck it up that year at the Northwest School. Thankfully I didn't. I did great—but it wasn't enough to get me into the University of Washington. I had fucked up too bad for two years straight while at Mercer Island High, and one good year at Northwest couldn't erase that.

Plan B turned out to be Seattle University, but it was a short-lived stint. I hated it. I was there for all of one quarter in the fall of 1983 before dropping out. My parents were, once again, incredibly understanding, so I proposed a Plan C: I promised them that I would get through college by the time I was thirty (I was eighteen at the time). I thought I was gonna be coming and going and having adventures and doing whatever I needed to make money along the way. I saw myself maybe working on archaeological digs for six months, playing music, whatever. But I knew that the classroom wasn't the place for me. They reluctantly agreed and gave me the latitude to finish my studies at a later date.

NEW

GODS

IN ONE OF THE DISTANT BRANCHES OF THE GRUNGE FAM- ily tree you'll find an obscure generic hardcore band called Spluii Numa, which are mostly notable for their weird name and the fact that Alex and I were in it together for a hot second in the summer of 1983. Legend has it that the ridiculous name came from graffiti on Alex's locker at the Northwest School. Someone had written "John Lennon Lives" (this was after Lennon was gunned down in New York), and another student had scratched out "Lives" and replaced it with "went spluii numa." Crass, yes, but somehow poetically punk rock.

Alex was playing drums for Spluii Numa before I joined for all of a month and a half. I didn't even play a show with them, although there's YouTube footage of Mark and me joining them onstage at a couple of different gigs at the Metropolis in 1983. It gave me yet a little more experience being in a band, and I was getting serious enough about playing music that I decided I needed a guitar upgrade.

My sister's boyfriend at the University of Washington had a frat-mate who was selling a baby blue 1965 Fender Mustang for $200. I thought Mustangs looked cool as hell, and Tom Price of the U-Men played one, which was all the recommendation I needed. So, in the summer of '83 I traded in the Peavey and bought the Mustang, which I owned for about seven years.

The Fender Mustang is a rinky-dink guitar, but if you overdrive the crap out of it through a clean amp, using the neck pickup, you can almost sound like Ron Asheton of the Stooges. And as far as I'm concerned, that first Stooges record has some of the greatest guitar tones on it, so I was chasing those. Ron Asheton's gear was very different (he'd played a Fender Stratocaster), but I just knew I didn't want the standard hard rock setup of a Marshall amp and Gibson Les Paul guitar. That wasn't my vibe.

Since I was finally outfitted with what I felt was proper gear, Mark invited me to join Mr. Epp and the Calculations toward the end of the summer of '83. I was thrilled. This would be the first "real" band I'd play in, even though I still didn't know how to play guitar (which wasn't a deal-breaker when it came to punk rock). Not only would I be performing in a group that had a local draw, but I'd be doing it with one of my best friends.

My first show at the Metropolis was a little terrifying. It was weird suddenly being onstage, but the band's experimental, noisy sound provided cover for my lack of skill and experience. The Metropolis had a good crowd, and Mr. Epp had a definite following. That said, there were people who loved Epp and people who did not, so when the shouts of "art spazz" poured in between songs, it was both a rallying cry and an insult, depending on which side you were on. However, the crowds that came to the Metropolis were usually on the same team, so to speak.

The Metropolis was an all-ages club in downtown Seattle's Pioneer Square neighborhood, and for the year and a half that it was open—early 1983 to summer of 1984—this was where so much of what would become the grunge scene a few years later would coalesce. It had started out in 1983 as more of a new wave dance

One of my favorite pictures of Mark and me at the Metropolis, 1983.

The family at Mary-Virginia's wedding, November 1983.

Playing guitar in Mr. Epp at the Metropolis, 1983, with the Moreys—Todd on bass and Dorothy on drums.

With Alex Shumway and Mark Arm at the last Mr. Epp show at the Metropolis. In a couple months we'd start Green River.

club, where new wave and occasionally punk groups would play. The owners quickly realized people were only showing up for the punk shows. At this point, Gordon Doucette, one of the cofounders, bailed. He played in a local new wave band called the Red Masque, didn't like hardcore, and was dissatisfied with the direction the club was going. His partner, Hughes "Hugo" Piottin, stuck it out and turned the Metropolis into an all-ages punk club, sort of a clubhouse for all of us. Hugo would also let us do a little work—sweeping, cleaning, putting up posters, whatever—to get in to shows for free sometimes. Even though no booze was served, plenty of the crowd that hung there was over twenty-one. Sub Pop Records cofounder Bruce Pavitt, who was a bit older than us, would even DJ some nights, spinning everything from Minor Threat to Run DMC.

Hugo was very supportive of the local punk scene. For every touring band that came through the club, he would put a few of the young local bands on the bill as supporting acts. Finally, we had a consistent venue where we didn't have to worry that the show would randomly be canceled or shut down by the police.

I always point to the Metropolis—as do most of us who were there—as *the* place where the first seeds of grunge were planted because there was stability and a regular place for us to gather. It provided a place for both popular touring bands of the era and influential upcoming locals to play, but it was also an important social hub. This was where suburban kids like me could come into the city to be part of the scene. It can't be overstated how important the Metropolis was to the Seattle music scene.

The Metropolis wasn't the only venue hosting bands, but it was the most reliable. There was an art gallery called Roscoe Louie, run by the U-Men's manager, Larry Reid, that hosted shows in the early '80s. He later opened Graven Image gallery, in a basement location around the corner, and the U-Men used to practice there. These were important venues because they fostered the growth of the local talent by giving them an outlet where they could perform and hone their chops, and provided a place for the small scene to gather and connect. I remember at least one night when all these venues that hosted punk shows—when the Metropolis was still open—offered a "joint cover" with more than a dozen bands playing between the three clubs. I probably knew every single person who attended—and performed—by first name. The scene was that small.

There weren't a lot of strangers at these early shows, because the few venues that hosted this music were small and the scene was very insular; there'd be maybe only a few people I didn't recognize. You can find footage of shows on YouTube where you can see a lot of us playing in our young bands—Mr. Epp, Spluii Numa, Malfunkshun, March of Crimes, Deranged Diction—or in the crowd watching the others.

Since the Metropolis was a small venue (it would look full if there were seventy-five people in the room), for most shows it was a tight crowd. But we weren't just standing there with our arms crossed—we were very active. We'd go to the edge of the stage and be right up front. We'd jump around and do a uniquely Seattle thing called "salmon diving." We all thought it was funny to flop *onto* the stage until there was a big pile of squirming bodies up there, and then slink off. There was some stage diving, too, but we thought our take on it was hilarious.

The Metropolis wasn't just the hardcore nexus for Seattle locals. Because it would bring in bands from across the United States— Hüsker Dü, Circle Jerks, the Replacements, Fang, Tales of Terror, the Dicks, Code of Honor, Agent Orange, Butthole Surfers—it also became a destination for hardcore fans from outside the city, some of whom had their own bands. This is where we first met future Nirvana bassist Krist Novoselic, as well as Mudhoney's future bassist, Matt Lukin.

Mark and I spotted Matt at a Metropolis show because he was wearing a homemade Void T-shirt. Void was a DC hardcore band that Mark and I loved, so we figured we should meet this guy. He told us he was from Montesano, a small logging town over on the coast, and that he played bass in a band called the Melvins, who we'd never heard of.

We had no idea what we were in for when the Melvins finally played in Seattle, not long after we met Matt. It's no exaggeration to say that the Melvins were the tightest, fastest hardcore band in town. They were proper hardcore, like Washington, DC, icons Minor Threat. Their music wasn't just a blur of speed—it was *musical*; you could discern what was going on with the structure and progressions. Their songs were also more complex. We were like, *Holy fuck, these guys are amazing!* At this point they still had Mike Dillard on drums. They got even better when Dale Crover took over on drums a bit later.

Malfunkshun were another band from just outside Seattle proper that became a crucial part of the scene and the transformation of Seattle's hardcore aesthetic. (They were part of the

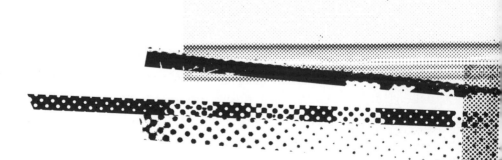

Bainbridge Island crew, like the band Stone joined, March of Crimes.) When I first saw Malfunkshun at the Metropolis, they were a noisy band that played a little bit faster—not exactly hardcore, but definitely punk. Malfunkshun were fronted by diminutive bassist/vocalist Andrew Wood (who Stone would later play with in Mother Love Bone).

Andrew was a funny guy and a great performer. He created a persona for himself, Landrew the Love God, and as the band evolved, he got more flamboyant. Early on, Landrew wore Kiss-like white face paint when he performed, and had short, spiky hair. (That would soon change, as he and the rest of the band started growing their hair out.)

Like the Melvins, they were one of the era's influential bands that started to move away from "loud fast rules," an aesthetic where speed and volume were valued over songwriting. They were on their own trip, incorporating more '70s hard rock theatrics and musical elements, but still maintaining their underground aesthetic. Landrew played the part of a rock star onstage (and he obviously wanted to be one someday), but the music Malfunkshun played was in no way commercially oriented. A lot of local musicians like myself

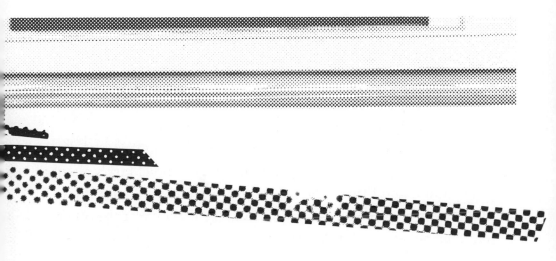

were starting to see bands like Malfunkshun, 10 Minute Warning, and the U-Men as guides toward a post-hardcore music scene.

Because those three bands were regular performers at the Metropolis, there was a gathering aesthetic and cross-pollination happening. We were all seeing these bands perform, listening to a lot of the same records, and starting to develop our own thing. That didn't mean all these bands sounded the same, or looked the same, but together we were figuring out where to go after hardcore, and we were taking slightly different routes along the way.

Not all the bands that formed the grunge scene a few years later had exactly the same DNA or influences, but we grew up playing together, starting bands together, and watching each other play. Some were poppier, some were artier, some were heavier, some were noisier, but there was something of an indefinable Seattleness to what was happening.

The Metropolis was a fitting place to play my second and final gig with Mr. Epp in early '84, which turned into a bit of a disaster. In addition to my Fender Mustang, I had bought a cheap guitar, a Kalamazoo, at a thrift store for twenty-five dollars. I'd had it jerry-rigged with duct tape, but at some point the pickups and everything fell off it, right as the show was about to start. There's a Mr. Epp CD that Epp vocalist Jo Smitty and I eventually released in the '90s with live footage, and one of the tracks, recorded at that show, is of me name-checking all the future members of Green River: "Uh, Stone or Alex, can someone go get the other guitar out of the car?" I think Stone's guitar was in the trunk, theoretically, as a spare.

I didn't know at the time, but this ill-fated gig would not only be my last, but the band's last. When I joined, I became Mark's main collaborator, and I think the direction Mark and I were unintentionally starting to take Epp didn't sit well with some of the other founding members. Smitty and drummer Dorothy Kent were into

Throbbing Gristle and experimental stuff, but Mark and I wanted to rock. So Smitty and Dorothy shut it down.

Because I hadn't gotten accepted into the University of Washington after I graduated from the Northwest School—and my brief stint at Seattle University didn't last long—I still mostly lived at home. Mark, on the other hand, was in his second year at UW and had a bunch of cool college friends. The gaggle of people he lived with in group houses in the early '80s was a fun collection of weirdos. Photographer Charles Peterson—who became known for his iconic pictures of the Seattle grunge scene—was one of his roommates for many years, as was artist Ed Fotheringham.

Mark also introduced me to his buddy Kim Thayil, who went to UW and would soon be Soundgarden's lead guitarist. I liked him right off the bat, and at that point he was just a dude with a mustache who liked the MC5. He was open-minded musically, but he wasn't a hardcore guy. I have fond memories of having friendly arguments about philosophy with Kim, who was a philosophy major.

The first time I saw Soundgarden in 1984, they were a three-piece with Chris Cornell on drums and singing. I felt like with Chris drumming and singing, they were sloppy when they first started. Bassist Hiro Yamamoto sang a few songs too, which I liked, because his songs seemed to have more of a hardcore influence. Soundgarden's early material, generally, was more influenced by post-punk bands like Killing Joke and Bauhaus, though. There was definitely this sort of artier approach to some of the other young bands in the scene—Bundle of Hiss and Death of Marat, for example—who relied a little more on guitar effects and less on pure fuzz or distortion.

Mark and I were working on our own exit strategy from hardcore. After Mr. Epp ended in early '84, we both briefly played in Limp Richerds, a punk band based in Federal Way (about fifteen miles south of Seattle), that Scott Schickler (who'd play in the

Thrown Ups and Swallow) would also cycle through. Even though Limp Richerds had been active in the Seattle scene for a few years, I never actually played any gigs with them. Though I'd only played in a handful of combos up to this point, I was getting a better sense of what kind of band I'd eventually want to form.

In my early explorations of punk rock (remember, I liked to dig deep) I stumbled across '60s garage rock, a lot of which was sort of proto-punk. I used to go to a record store called Cellophane Square on the Ave in the University District. There was a guy probably ten years older than me who worked there, Scott McCaughey, who played in a local band called Young Fresh Fellows, sort of a throwback, power pop garage band. I think Scott used to put '60s records—the local stuff like the Sonics and the Wailers—in the punk section, along with the *Pebbles* compilation albums, which were filled with obscure '60s garage rock and psych bands.

I remember looking at some of those *Pebbles* records and reading the notes on the back—some of them were really sarcastic. I figured the bands on them *must* be punk rock bands. I was trying to figure out what this stuff was, so I bought one for $3.99.

It was one of the best purchases I ever made. I discovered that the Pacific Northwest had a heck of a legacy of gnarly music from the '60s. There were the Sonics and the Wailers, but it went even deeper. One of the *Pebbles* compilations I bought had a song on it called "You Must Be a Witch" by the Lollipop Shoppe. I later realized that one of the members of that band, Fred Cole, was a current member of Portland punk band the Rats. (Cole would further cement his Northwest garage punk legacy in Dead Moon for another couple of decades.) That was a big, big deal to me, because of all the things I'd heard, that song was the closest to sounding like the Stooges. I couldn't believe it was the dude from the Rats! This song was my first inkling that there was a connection between '60s garage rock and contemporary punk.

The attitude and look of these bands also appealed to me, with their matching suits and long (for the time) haircuts. They wrote simple songs, and a lot of the lyrics were angry put-down songs about no-good chicks and whatnot. There was a pervasive rotten tone, a snotty teenaged punk rock attitude that I dug. "He's Waitin'" by the Sonics is as tough as music's gonna get.

Unsurprisingly, all this influenced my guitar playing because I was still trying to find *my* sound. The pure fuzz tone on the '60s garage stuff, not necessarily a wall of distortion (which had its time and place), really spoke to me. I discovered Davie Allan and the Arrows, who did a lot of teen rebel and biker movie soundtracks in the '60s—nothing but single-string fuzz note runs. It was like surf guitar on steroids. That was huge to me; I loved that pure fuzz thing.

I also loved the teenage garage band look, which I slowly started to emulate in my own way. I became a regular at the local thrift stores, and I only bought stuff from the '60s: a lot of paisley shirts, sweater vests, and things like that. I thought they looked cool. And the boots, the dirty off-white jeans—there was a real aesthetic. A lot of people at the punk shows were wearing '60s stuff, and this dirtier version of that fashion probably informed what people associated with the grunge look. Grunge wasn't about flannel; it was about thrift store chic, long before that was a thing.

I brought all of this—my '60s look, my garage punk aesthetic, and my fuzzed-out sound—to my first real band, Green River, with explosive results.

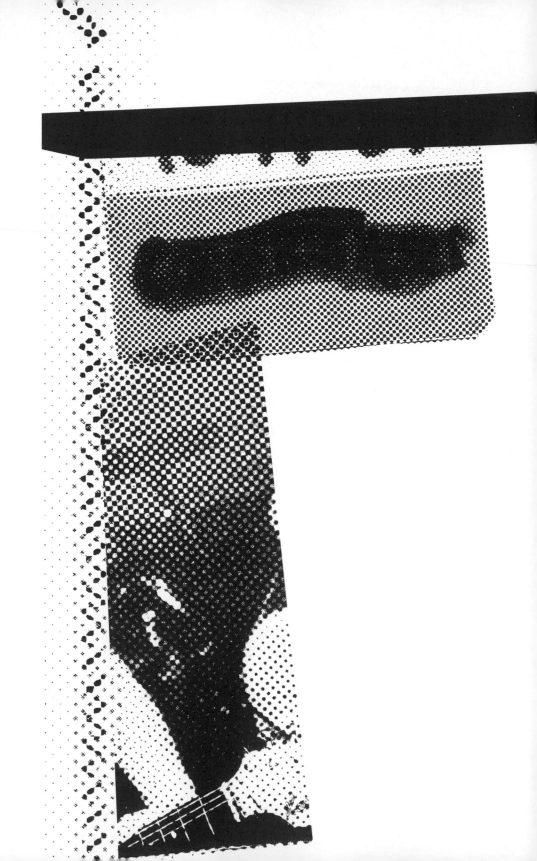

33 REVOLUTIONS

IN 1984, IT FELT LIKE HARDCORE WAS AT A DEAD END. A lot of other musicians, both locally and nationally, must have felt the same way, because the underground punk scene was transforming. We were seeing possibilities beyond the confines of hard and fast. Simply put, you couldn't go any faster, so you had to start slowing down. Fast hardcore was a phase that burned hot and then quickly cooled.

Mark and I were hanging out a lot during this time, playing records for each other, and he was a big influence on me. Because he was a few years older, he knew about bands I'd never heard of—he was the one who had first introduced me to the Stooges. There were big gaps in my knowledge, because I hadn't listened to '70s rock, so Mark acted as tastemaker and picked out some of the better material from the era for me. He'd already been a college DJ, so he'd been exposed to way more music than I had. Inevitably, the music he introduced me to influenced my playing, because the more I listened, the more guitar tones I heard and could try to match.

Being introduced to the Stooges—and chasing Ron Asheton's sound—was definitely an inspiration for my next significant musical purchases: a wah-wah pedal and Big Muff fuzz box. While wah-wah pedals have been an essential part of rock guitarists' arsenals since they were popularized in the late '60s by Eric Clapton of Cream, Jimi Hendrix, Ron Asheton, and many others, in 1984, you could barely give away a Big Muff. Big Muffs distorted the guitar sound, but not in the overdriven way that other brands of distortion pedals did (the ones responsible for the more slashing wall of sound). Big Muffs weren't good for strumming open chords; they were best suited for two-finger bar chords, or single-string riffs. It was more about "fuzz" than "crunch," and I loved it. I picked up my first one at American Music in University Village, where they had a table stacked with them and were blowing them out for twenty-five dollars each. Electro-Harmonix, the company that made the Big Muff, had gone out of business in 1982, and nobody wanted those things in 1984.

They may have been unpopular then, but that combination— Big Muff plus wah-wah pedal—was like the Big Bang of the "sound" part of the Seattle sound. And this is what I was armed with in my quest to move on from hardcore. Mr. Epp broke up in early 1984, so Mark and I had the opportunity to start a band together for the first time. We were on the same wavelength musically, listening to a lot of the same records, so it made sense. And since we were hanging out with Alex so much—and he played drums (as well as bass)—it was a given that he was going to be the drummer.

All that was missing was a bass player, and we had our sights set on Jeff Ament, who we'd seen playing in Deranged Diction. They were a straightforward hardcore quartet that arrived in Seattle from Missoula in the early '80s and instantly became part of our little scene. In early 1984, however, the band seemed to be winding down, so we wanted to nab Jeff to join our new outfit. We liked Jeff personally of course (he was a skater like me), he was super energetic onstage (his jumps were legendary), and, most importantly, he played his bass through a RAT distortion pedal.

However, it was a hard "no" from Jeff when we approached him. He didn't like Epp at all, and wasn't convinced that Mark, Alex, and I offered any reason to move on from Deranged Diction. So, we began our weird stalker-like campaign to convince him otherwise.

He worked at Raison d'Être, a local café, which was in the basement of the Terminal Sales Building (the future home of Sub Pop's offices). Jeff had mentioned that there was an opening for a dishwasher, so I had the brilliant idea of taking the job so I could butter him up/wear him down while we worked together. Mostly my "pitch" involved convincing Jeff that we were going to be a "real band," a serious band, not like the weird, experimental snark of Epp. It took a while to convince him, but after a couple months of me pestering, he relented. In the spring of 1984, Green River was born.

I had wanted Mark to play guitar in the band, as I'd always liked his playing style. However, he only wanted to sing and didn't want to be encumbered by a guitar. Early on, Alex did a lot of the songwriting. He was the master of simple, great, hardcore songs. He wrote some of our coolest early songs on bass because he'd played bass in Extreme Hate for a hot minute. Some of the simpler, two-note stuff we wrote early on, like "33 Revolutions," was Alex's. The four of us were drawing from some very diverse influences, but the music was at least initially grounded in and informed by hardcore. We definitely weren't a hardcore band, but our roots were still showing at that point, largely because of Alex's influence.

In the early '80s, Black Flag toured the United States relentlessly, exposing people across the country in music venues small and large to their gnarly, fucked-up version of punk rock. I don't know if it was a West Coast thing, but something about their sound and approach particularly resonated in Seattle. Around the same time that Green River formed, Black Flag released *My War*, a game changer of an album that had a notable impact on the Seattle

Poster from the first Green River show, July 28, 1984!

Jeff Ament's classic Green River design. He had a lot to do with the aesthetics of the early grunge scene.

Green River opened for the Dead Kennedys, October 19, 1984, at the Moore Theater. We'd never had a backstage pass before!

ROCK

The Dead Kennedys stay alive musically

by Patrick MacDonald
Times staff critic

You've got to admire the Dead Kennedys — if not for their music, at least for their guts and tenacity.

It takes guts for a band to give itself a name that virtually guarantees it will be shunned by the straight media and major record companies, even if the name does endear the band to its punker audience.

And the San Francisco-based group, which will headline a show at 9 tonight at the Moore Theater, has held onto that name, and suffered the consequences, since the late 1970s.

It's also held onto its radical political beliefs, making the Dead Kennedys virtually the only protest group left in rock. The band is uncompromising in its attacks on President Reagan, calling him a "fascist," and the overall thrust of the Dead Kennedys' message is that American culture is in collapse.

That message may fall on mostly deaf ears in this country but, not surprisingly, they love it in Europe, and in the past few years the band has spent more time, and sold more records, there. In fact, the most recent Dead Kennedys album is on an Italian label.

Anti-americanism is rampant among European rock fans, mostly because of the deployment of American missiles there. The British rock press — Melody Maker, New Musical Express, Sounds — are scathing in their attacks on anything American, but their views do not extend to the Dead Kennedys, who are hailed as heroes and bearers of truth.

However, the Dead Kennedys' deafening, thrashing, unlistenable music does not bear this out. You cannot understand the lyrics at a Dead Kennedys concert because the music is too fast and too loud. Some of the lyrics are printed on the album covers, but that only reveals how shallow they are — for instance, "All religions make me wanna throw up, they really make me sick."

What insight!

The show will be opened by a young Seattle band with an equally tragedy-charged name, Green River, and a third group whose name is so obscene we can't even print it.

Sounds like a fun evening!

Patrick McDonald's not-so-positive review of punk rock, circa 1984, in the *Seattle Times*.

hardcore scene. Released on their own label, SST Records, in March 1984, *My War* introduced a whole new dimension to their previously adrenaline-laced hardcore sound: slow, Black Sabbath–inspired heaviness. One of the vanguards of raucous American hardcore had slowed down and amped up the sludgy aspects of their sound (at least on side two of the album).

We were all blown away by *My War*, but I got the sense that a lot of people outside Seattle didn't like that record when it came out. Black Flag's crowd was bummed about it, because the band was moving away from simply blasting away full-tilt. Black Flag came through town so often that we had seen in real time how they were slowing down and mixing things up a bit and growing their hair and challenging that punk orthodoxy. We all appreciated that, because we didn't have much of that punk orthodoxy ourselves. Black Flag brought a heaviness to hardcore that seemed to make it OK for us to draw on distinctly non-punk influences like Black Sabbath and even Kiss. That's directly because of *My War*. That particular record's influence on Seattle can't be overestimated—from the Melvins to Soundgarden to Green River to Malfunkshun.

Green River's early attempts at integrating non-hardcore influences in our earliest material produced mixed results. As the only guitar player in the band at the time, I wasn't necessarily always on the same page as the other three members. *Meat Puppets II*, the second Meat Puppets album, came out on Black Flag's label a month after *My War* and blew my mind with its punk-fried country. It was a *huge* record for me (and for Kurt Cobain, who covered three songs from it while in Nirvana). It was frequently compared to Neil Young's *Zuma*, so when I saw *Everyone Knows This Is Nowhere*, Young's album from the same era (with "Cinnamon Girl" and "Down by the River") at a thrift store, I bought it and was amazed by that as well.

I also liked Minneapolis band the Replacements, who didn't necessarily have a '60s sound, but they played sloppy garage rock early on. Their 1981 album, *Sorry, Ma, Forgot to Take Out the Trash,* is still one of my favorite records. Some of the songs are awful, but I liked the tossed-off aspect of some of it. I was a fan of garage rock, and I brought that aesthetic to Green River.

On June 23, 1984, a couple months after we'd formed and before we'd played our first show, Green River went into Reciprocal Recording studio (before it moved to its more famous triangle-shaped location in Seattle's Fremont neighborhood) and we laid down our first demo with owner Chris Hanzsek. Mark and Jeff had some previous recording experience—Mark with Mr. Epp and Jeff with Deranged Diction—but this was new territory for Alex and me. I was so freaked out—I had no idea what I was in for. Being in the studio was mysterious and alien and uncomfortable, and, honestly, I wasn't interested in the technical aspects of it. I just wanted to play, record, and be done. Jeff was interested though and asked a lot of questions in the control booth.

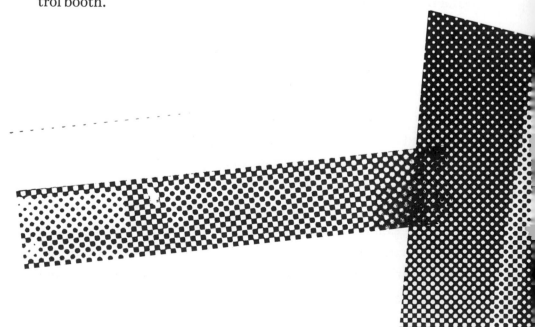

The result was a decent documentation of our first batch of songs (nine in total) that showed the musical push and pull that was happening within the band. There's the hardcore side represented by "33 Revolutions," "Means to an End," and "Take Me," and the sludgier, heavier side represented by "New God," "Tunnel of Love," and "Leech."

I'd written "Leech" not long after discovering Black Sabbath. (I didn't have strong roots in metal, so I was late to the Sabbath game.) I figured, *OK, I'll try to do a Black Sabbath song here.* (Melvins would famously "steal" this song and record it as "Leeech" for their *Gluey Porch Treatments* album in 1987, without giving us credit.) We even recorded a Mr. Epp tune, "Baby Help Me Forget." None of this was officially released at the time, but it was eventually issued by Portland label Jackpot Records as *1984 Demos* in 2018.

After the recording, everybody in Green River—except me—thought we needed a second guitar player. They wanted to "fatten up" the sound, because it was 1984 and bands were starting to get more of that *chunk-chunk-chunk* sound going. My bandmates had gotten into British metal bands Venom and Iron Maiden, and that metal-punk crossover thing that was happening at the time with bands like Slayer was captivating to them. I liked Venom, but Iron Maiden I couldn't take. (I appreciate them much more now.)

I'd gone to see Slayer in 1984 when they played the Moore Theater. I was already a snob, but I thought, *This crowd is even dumber than the punk crowd.* There were kids with their heads inside these giant subwoofer speakers thrashing away. Not my scene. I was into Billy Childish and the Replacements and Meat Puppets; I wanted things to branch out in Green River in a non-metal way. My guitar sound was getting thinner and thinner, and everyone else in Green River wanted more heft, so they brought in Stone. I love Stone, and he's still one of my best friends, but I was like, *Really?* I wasn't too keen on it at the time, but I eventually liked how it came together, the weirdness of our differing styles. Stone's addition solidified the lineup.

Green River's first live performance was July 28, 1984, at a place on Capitol Hill in what would have been the storefront of a building. A coworker friend from Raison d'Être lived in the building, and he invited us to open for his band (a psychedelic paisley pop band called P.M.A., or Positive Metal Attitude) at what amounted to a private party. Soundgarden's Chris Cornell claimed he was there, and if so, he would have been one of a few dozen who were.

This gig is notable for several reasons: Stone didn't play, because he was nervous and didn't feel ready. Also, Jeff made an impression on the small crowd (as well as the other members of Green River) when he showed up wearing a face full of white greasepaint, possibly inspired by Landrew from Malfunkshun and/or Kiss. We had no idea he was going to do this, but we rolled with it. This gig was also the first and last time I sang lead vocals in Green River. For two songs, Mark and I switched roles—I sang, and he played guitar. It was a strange start for Green River.

Our next gig, on August 11, 1984, and our first with Stone, was at a quasi-legal "club" called the Grey Door in Pioneer Square, not far from the Metropolis (which by this point had closed), and Melvins were on the bill. To put it bluntly: We sucked. We were awful. The sound was terrible, but beyond that, we didn't know what we were doing at all. It was demoralizing. I can't blame our poor performance entirely on the venue, but the Grey Door was one of the scummiest places that hosted live music during this time. It was a total pit. It had a big, open space with a one-foot stage that somebody built, a shitty PA, and a big pile of rubble in the room. And they only had a Porta Potty for a bathroom. It wasn't exactly a welcoming and friendly place, but it hosted a lot of great all-ages punk and hardcore shows (I saw Duff's band the Living there) during a crucial time in Seattle music, which I appreciated.

After Green River's catastrophically bad second show—which left me questioning if playing music was even a worthwhile pursuit—things improved. The creative tension between the rest of the band and me didn't go away, but it added some spice to what we were doing. I was able to moderate their metal aspirations.

But what's perhaps more integral to the larger story is that we were on some historic bills in those early days. Before the end of 1984, we would appear onstage with Dead Kennedys, Butthole Surfers, Black Flag, and Fang (whose song, "The Money Will Roll Right In," has been in Mudhoney's live set off and on over the years). As we were playing in front of increasingly larger crowds, we were honing and expanding our sound. It wouldn't be long before we'd head back to the studio to record a fresh batch of songs, this time with Stone, and we would each have a much clearer vision of how to leave our hardcore roots behind and chart a new path for the future.

The only problem was, the five of us wouldn't exactly see eye to eye on the specifics of that path.

COME ON DOWN

"DO YOU GUYS SMELL THAT?"

Green River were practicing at Stone's parents' house on Capitol Hill—Mark, Stone, Alex, Jeff, and I crammed into a room with all our gear, amps cranked up—when I stopped mid-song to ask if anyone else noticed what I did. Everyone sniffed.

"Yeah, it smells *horrible*," Stone replied.

There was smoke in the air—something was definitely burning. The odor, whatever it was, was growing in intensity and acridity. It smelled like the whole house was on fire. I could see a growing sense of panic on everyone's face as they realized our options for escape were limited. Alex came to this conclusion first and jumped off his drum throne, popped open the window, and leaped out. Luckily, we were on the first floor. Alex was fine, but his every-man-for-himself attitude was duly noted.

It turns out it was my Sunn Solarus amplifier that had gone up in figurative flames. The transformer had overheated and melted down, and the amp was fried. I didn't realize it at the time, but it turned out to be a bad omen for my remaining time in Green River.

It would have been more expensive to repair the Solarus than replace it, so I bought another used amp, this time an Ampeg Porta-flex B-12 from the '60s, for ninety dollars at a pawnshop in Tacoma (the Tacoma part of this is important). After I got it home and plugged it in, the first chord I hit literally blew out the speaker. I opened up the amp to examine it and found the speaker had cuts in it that had been taped up. Before fuzz boxes were popularized, this is what guitarists used to do to their speakers to get them to distort more. It looked like someone had intentionally been fucking with the speaker cone to get it to "buzz."

So, in my mind, the amp had either belonged to a member of the Sonics—Tacoma's garage rock pioneers, whom I loved—or a teenage kid from Tacoma trying to sound like the Sonics. Might not have been either, but it added a bit of mythology to the amp. I repurposed one of the speakers from the dead Solarus to replace the Ampeg's sliced up one. I still have that Ampeg, and that speaker is still in it today. It's been used on many recordings over the years.

Unfortunately, my "Sonics" amp was no match for the Marshall Half Stack that Stone had recently acquired. And this was a prime example of the growing musical schism in Green River: I was a little bit garage punk, and he was a little bit heavy metal, with only our fading interest in hardcore as common ground. Lines were starting to be drawn as we continued to write music and play shows. Our

repertoire was expanding, but instead of Alex contributing music, more of that was falling to Stone and Jeff, with some contributions from me. The creative dynamic was definitely shifting. I started to feel like *my* influences were getting outvoted, because I still saw Green River as a garage band. I was disappointed and ticked off when our escape from hardcore took a decidedly more metal turn.

Stone had obviously come to Green River from more of a metal perspective, but even Jeff, who cut his teeth playing hardcore in Deranged Diction, was starting to get into metal as well, because he liked the production—the thicker, heavier sound. But my heart was not there. Green River's songs, with Jeff and Stone largely steering the ship, were getting longer and more complicated.

This was the backdrop to the recording of what we hoped would be our debut record in December 1984, our first serious session as a five-piece, with Stone fully entrenched. We were paying for the recording ourselves with the hopes that we might find an indie label to put it out. We used Crow Studios, where the U-Men had recorded their debut 12″ EP that was released by local indie Bomb Shelter that year. If Crow was good enough for the U-Men, it was good enough for us. We brought along Chris Hanzsek to engineer the session, rather than using Crow owner John Nelson, because Chris knew what we wanted from our sound.

We recorded six songs over the initial sessions at Crow: "Come On Down," "New God," "Ride of Your Life," "Corner of My Eye," "Tunnel of Love," and "Swallow My Pride." Some of the songs we'd previously recorded before Stone was in the band, while others were fairly new. "Swallow My Pride" was the only one I wrote. It's no coincidence that it was the shortest song from the session, clocking in at barely three minutes—garage rock tunes are typically short and sweet; metal tunes, not so much. The results of the session reflected the ongoing musical battle happening in Green River, one that I was slowly losing.

It wasn't just the music—it was the approach we took to making it that put us at odds. While Stone practiced and planned his guitar solos note for note and performed them basically the same every time, that wasn't my style. As a dude who likes garage rock and punk rock, I've never planned out a guitar solo in my life (and still don't). The things that I listened to at the time, like Neil Young and Blue Cheer and the Stooges and Meat Puppets, their shit wasn't planned out either. These were the kinds of solos where you go off and see how it works out. Spontaneity sounded better to me. When I was recording my lead guitar part in "Swallow My Pride," it was all over the map. I knew that my soloing on that song wasn't very good, but I was OK with that. I think this reflected my inexperience and basic ignorance of the instrument at the time, but I still subscribe to it.

Jeff's songs in this period stood in stark contrast to my aesthetic, especially "Tunnel of Love," which we'd been kicking around since our first demo. That was Jeff's baby at the time. I thought it was awful, to be completely honest. It's seven and a half minutes long, and it had all these minor, unnecessary changes in it. It has almost the same riff for the duration, but it slightly changes for one or two measures throughout. That was Jeff's mathematic mind going or something. But I was like, *I can't figure this out at all*. I don't think I ever played it right. I managed to get through it halfway decently in our Crow session.

I don't have a lot of fond memories of the recordings. I was down about the direction the band seemed to be heading. We ended 1984 with the six tracks we'd recorded still unmixed.

Green River's first show of 1985, on January 19, was a momentous one, opening for New York noise rockers Sonic Youth (along with the U-Men) at a venue called Gorilla Gardens. This was where Mark and I first met them, and we made a real connection. They were touring in support of their soon-to-be-released third album, *Bad Moon Rising*, which was set to be issued on Homestead Records a couple months later.

I can't speak for the rest of Green River, but I was already a huge Sonic Youth fan by the time we got this gig, so meeting them and getting to play on the same bill was a big deal. In 1982 I'd seen their first self-titled album in a record store, but based on the look of the cover I was unsure of what kind of band they were. In '82, any band that had "Youth" in its name likely *was* a hardcore band, but I couldn't tell what Sonic Youth were about until *Confusion Is Sex* came out a year later. That album looked like such a shitty record that I figured, *Oh, they must be some kind of hardcore band*. I was wrong. But it is a noisy, fucked-up record, and I loved it.

I don't know if Sonic Youth initially loved Green River, though. Guitarist/vocalist Thurston Moore has been quoted as saying that we had "too many members onstage" at that gig. Nonetheless, this show is where Sonic Youth's connection to Seattle began. I think they saw that there was something cool happening there, and a year later Sonic Youth appeared on the first Sub Pop compilation album, *Sub Pop 100*.

Gorilla Gardens, at this point, had picked up where the Metropolis had left off, in that it was booking a lot of the same kinds of bands and hosting all-ages shows. And it was fairly organized. Tony Chu, the guy who ran it, had previously run an earlier iteration of it between 1980 and 1982, the Gorilla Room, which was an over-21 club that had punk shows. I never went there, because I looked like I was twelve and had no chance of sneaking into an over-21 club. When the Gorilla Room closed, he started Gorilla Gardens in the International District of Seattle.

It had two rooms for live music—one was a metal room and one was a punk room. The two live rooms shared a common entranceway and hallway, and some nights if you paid one cover charge, you could go into both. This is where a lot of the cross-pollination between the two scenes started happening in real time. This is where I saw Mike McCready (later of Pearl Jam) play in Shadow in the metal room. McCready was so tiny and skinny that his spandex pants—probably the smallest size you could buy—were still baggy on him. He was already doing all the split leaps and shit like that, and the spandex crotch was all the way down to his knees.

The dudes in Shadow were super nice guys, upbeat middle-class Seattle kids, and because Stone knew some of them already, Green River started hanging out with them as the crossover between the metal and punk crowds crossed over even more. This was an important stop in the grunge continuum, because between the two bands—Green River and Shadow—three-fifths of Pearl Jam was already friendly by early 1985.

Gorilla Gardens, arguably, was the incubator in many ways of the sound that became known as grunge a few years later. All the most important and influential bands—Green River, Soundgarden, Melvins, Malfunkshun, the U-Men, Skin Yard (featuring Matt Cameron who went on to Soundgarden and later Pearl Jam)—gathered

Seasons Greetings

Not sure why Green River had a Christmas card, but here it is!

A sticker from the first Green River record, 1985, featuring a Jeff Ament design and a Charles Peterson photo.

Green River and Melvins poster, March 30, 1985. In a few months I would be out of Green River and in the Thrown Ups.

and began shaping something new. If the Metropolis was where we all first "found" each other playing in our earliest (mostly hardcore-leaning) bands, then Gorilla Gardens is where we began to mix and mingle and develop our sound, the Seattle sound. We'd all left hardcore behind us and were bringing in different influences—including metal and '70s hard rock—that the hardcore scene in its narrow musical scope didn't "allow."

I didn't feel any rivalry with any other bands that came out of the Gorilla Gardens scene, or the Metropolis before it. There was this punk sensibility, knowing the scene was small and that nothing was that important, so why would there be? I wouldn't say Green River were any bigger than our peers' bands, as far as influencing the underground music culture in Seattle. Bands had slightly different points of view, but I think it was a group effort to grow the developing scene together. And then the crowds slowly started showing up.

One of Seattle's influential pre-grunge bands, 10 Minute Warning, had broken up not long after guitarist Duff McKagan left for Los Angeles in 1983. (The final Duff-less incarnation did make an album together before folding in '84. It was released in 2021.) In early 1985, Duff joined the newly formed Guns N' Roses, and by summer, the band embarked on an ill-fated West Coast tour (which they've since dubbed the "Hell Tour," because every transportation failure imaginable happened, with some hitchhiking thrown in).

Guns N' Roses made their way to Seattle for only their second show *ever* with a lineup that had solidified four days earlier. On June 8, 1985, we went to see Duff's new band play at Gorilla Gardens. While we were stoked to see our local boy made good, the impression I was left with was: *Duff left Seattle for* this? We had all really loved 10 Minute Warning; they had been a big deal to us, and this band seemed lesser. Let's just say that after witnessing this show, it didn't seem like success was imminent for these guys.

To be fair, Guns N' Roses were still finding their footing, and when they scored a multiplatinum hit with *Appetite for Destruction* two years later, I finally got the appeal. (And to be honest, I don't have the best instincts on what's going to hit big.)

Even though Duff was a returning hero, and the Fastbacks (one of the Seattle bands he'd drummed for) opened the show, there weren't many people at Gorilla Gardens that night. (There certainly weren't as many people as I'm sure have *claimed* they were there.) But Mark and I were, and probably all of Green River.

After Green River went back into the studio in early '85 to mix the six songs we'd recorded in December '84, we set about trying to find a label to release them. Or, I should say, Jeff took on that task. He was the business guy in Green River, and by far the most ambitious. I don't know how many tapes he put in the mail, but we received two offers: one from Homestead Records on the East Coast and the other from Enigma in LA. The potential contract Enigma sent must have been fifty pages long—it seemed insane to us—so we went with Homestead.

We were excited that Homestead wanted to put out our album. It was an easy choice, as far as I was concerned, because the U-Men had recently released their *Stop Spinning* EP on Homestead, and the label was also issuing records by Dinosaur (later Dinosaur Jr., they added the suffix to avoid legal issues), Sonic Youth, and other cool and interesting underground bands at the time. Green River's debut, titled *Come On Down*, was set for release in the fall of 1985. Along with the U-Men's Homestead EP, it would be one of the first grunge records to get a nationwide release, and it is inarguably the first true example of the style, even if it was a rough version. It felt like a little groundswell was starting. And full credit to Gerard Cosloy, who was running Homestead at the time, for taking a chance on a couple of Seattle bands.

As excited as I was that *Come On Down* was going to be released, I wasn't exactly thrilled with the material itself. I think half of the stuff on it is good, but the other half shows that we were still finding our way. I think Stone doing more of the metal *chunka-chunka* and me being a little bit weirder worked on "Swallow My Pride." I thought there was room to make the differences in our styles and sound work, but after we recorded the songs for *Come On Down*, the new material my bandmates wrote got *more* metal. It intensified and went too far, honestly. I wasn't fitting into it at all. Here's a perfect example: I bought a cheap Harmony Stratotone guitar for twenty-four dollars at a pawnshop, and I wanted to play that onstage. Jeff looked at me like, *What are you doing?* It came down to a battle of aesthetics.

Adding to the tension in the band was the fact that they wanted to go on tour in the fall once the EP was out, and I had no interest in that. It was gonna cost us money, and I didn't see the point. I'd like to say that I brought all these concerns up to my bandmates—my friends—in a mature and communicative way and we addressed them like adults, but I was twenty, and that's not how it went down. I knew I was unhappy in Green River, but I guess I didn't have the guts to express that to them, so I opted for the passive-aggressive route.

The last show I played with Green River on July 7, 1985, at Gorilla Gardens, I was being a total dick onstage. I'd just gotten a bigger amp, so I was able to match Stone's volume. I played with my back to the crowd, and I was sitting down in a chair for part of the show. I was being an asshole. When it was over, I got offstage and I felt bad. I realized I shouldn't be in the band. They all seemed to have a shared vision, and I was the odd man out. They should go in the direction they wanted to go, and I should bail out, because it was the wrong band for me. So, in August, I finally broke the news.

The hardest part was the friendship thing. Alex was so sad when I quit. Jeff and I, however, had a much better relationship because we both knew it was the right decision for everyone, so we were good *immediately* after I quit. Stone, I think, felt a little bit of guilt, like he came into the band and made me quit or something, but that wasn't the case. I just wasn't that invested in Green River anymore. Mark and I still hung out, even though he was hurt by my leaving.

Probably because I felt a little guilty leaving before our record even came out, I felt like I should find my own replacement. I suggested Jeff's former Deranged Diction bandmate, Bruce Fairweather, but it turned out they were already considering that because Bruce and Jeff were roommates. It was a good fit all around, as he led Green River back to a way better sound. He got them off the full-on metal and into more of that Aerosmith swagger and late-period Stooges thing they did on their next record, *Dry as a Bone*, my favorite Green River record. I was thrilled for them.

Most importantly, they found someone who shared their ambition. Jeff was a real working-class, small-town Montana kid, and he wanted to make a career in music. Stone did too, but his family had more money. He was going to college, so he had things to fall back on. Jeff didn't, and it was Jeff who had the drive.

At the time, I thought they were deluded. *This isn't going to go anywhere. No one makes it in music from Seattle*, especially playing the sort of music we were playing. I was sure of it. The scene was fun, but I thought that they were going to be heartbroken. None of us could have known how wrong I would be.

(Signature)

STEVE GOES TO COLLEGE

WHEN I QUIT GREEN RIVER IN AUGUST '85, I WAS SURE I was done playing in bands, period. I was through with the whole scene. I found myself at an uncomfortable crossroads.

I had made a deal with my parents that I would get a university degree before I was thirty, but I had some hard decisions to make, because whatever musical adventures I'd envisioned were no longer part of the plan. Though my parents had always been very supportive of whatever path I chose, they weren't going to remain entirely passive, since, like any parents, they had their thoughts on guiding their children into adulthood.

I'd been dating a girl named Lisa for a year. We'd been good friends at the Northwest School, but at the time I didn't have any interest in dating whatsoever. I was still a kid and liked skateboards. But about a year after we graduated, one thing led to another and we crossed over from being just friends to dating. She was a total new waver, so it was that classic cliché: punk rock boy with new wave girl.

She came from a wealthy Bainbridge Island family. She drove a 1962 red Porsche that her dad bought her and lived in a huge three-bedroom apartment on First Hill, just up the hill from downtown. Though I was "officially" living at home, I was unofficially living with Lisa. Her parents didn't know this. She had a twin bed in one of the guest rooms, which was where, she assured *her* parents, I slept.

My devoutly Catholic parents eventually found out the truth after an awkward but frank conversation. They had already dealt with my sister getting pregnant out of wedlock and my brother coming out as gay, and my coed cohabitation threw them one more curveball.

"Steve, where do you sleep when you stay over at Lisa's apartment?" my mom asked one day, with a concerned look on her face. She likely already knew the answer, so I provided confirmation.

"I sleep in the bed with Lisa. Where do you think I sleep?"

I had a good, open, respectful relationship with my parents. I had done my rebelling when I was young, and I really appreciated my folks. I didn't want to lie about normal things and saw no reason why I should. I think that the fact my parents were crazy about Lisa helped to soften the blow.

So, when I quit Green River and was wondering what came next, they decided to chime in: *Get married and have a kid.*

My response: *Hell no!*

I was twenty, and Lisa was my first girlfriend. Not a good idea!

My sister had gotten married at twenty-one, while pregnant and still attending UW, and even she was pushing for me to tie the knot, which ticked me off. Because my entire family all loved Lisa so much, they were like, *You've won the lottery here. You can't mess this up! You have to put a ring on her finger!* I had to tell them that it was going to be at least another decade before I wanted any of that.

My compromise was that I'd try college again and continue to work my full-time job in the front of house at ACT Theater, a local playhouse in the Lower Queen Anne neighborhood. My parents wanted me to grow up, obviously, but I didn't exactly feel the same urgency. I wasn't done skateboarding, and I wasn't ready to leave the skating scene that was so important to me behind. Nonetheless, I felt like I'd turned a corner in my life.

I was still hanging around with a lot of the same people at the time, including Ed Fotheringham (one of my UW friends I'd met through Mark) and one of his roommates, David Lipe (the two would form Icky Joey years later). They were my two main buddies besides Mark at this point. Ed was a skater, and I was still skating a lot. One day I rolled up to their place with two giant garbage bags full of '60s vintage clothes—probably thousands of dollars' worth—which had been my rock 'n' roll wardrobe for the last few years.

"Here, you guys can have all this," I said as I dropped the bags on the floor of their house. "I don't want it."

David looked dumbstruck at first, not really understanding what was going on. He turned to Ed and said, "He's giving away all his stuff. Is that a bad sign?"

"Are you OK?" Ed asked me.

"I'm fine, I'm fine!" I said and left them with assurances I wasn't intending to harm myself or anything.

Next, I bought two pairs of Levi's 501s, a couple of Brooks Brothers button-down collared shirts, and a pair of hiking boots, and that was my outfit for the next nine months. I enrolled at Seattle Central with the thought, *That was that. Now onward to . . . something.*

At this point I was sure I'd left my rock 'n' roll life behind. I didn't even go to very many shows. But the power of punk rock drew me back in, at least temporarily, and the irony of the show that did it is too rich to make up: the Descendents on their *I Don't Want to Grow Up* tour. I loved the Descendents and didn't want to miss them, so there I was in my GORE-TEX hiking jacket and big water-proof hiking boots, standing out like a sore thumb in the punk rock crowd. I felt very removed from the scene—like I was on a different wavelength. Shows like this used to be where I felt at home, where I would know nearly everyone in the crowd. Now I was an observer, rather than a participant.

The release of Green River's *Come On Down* EP in October 1985 was bittersweet for me. It was the first time I had played on a record, and it was being distributed nationally by an independent label that I liked. Our good friend Charles Peterson took the pictures that appeared on the cover and the insert, and Jeff contributed

Playing piano with nephew Rob Maxwell, Christmas 1986. My sister was always handing me babies, so I figured out how to hold them early on!

From my trip to Europe with my dad, fall 1986. I spent almost three weeks on my own in London—lots of shows and lots of records!

The Thrown Ups "Felch" 7", 1987. Where we learned not to take music too seriously!

to the design of the album, so it felt like an excellent achievement for a bunch of ex-hardcore Seattle kids. I may not have loved all the material on the EP, but I was still proud of having been part of it.

The tour that Green River did eventually undertake to support it turned out to be a disaster, due to numerous cancellations and other unplanned mayhem. So, my reluctance to go on tour was well founded. No other Seattle bands from our little scene were doing (or attempting to do) national tours at that point, so despite the lack of gigs Green River ended up actually *playing* on that tour, they deserve credit for giving it a go. They were promoting a record I played on, so I was rooting for them, albeit from the sidelines.

Though I was going to community college, working full-time at ACT Theater, and living a very domesticated life for a twenty-year-old, I can't say my heart was any more into the school thing than it had been in the past. I was only taking basic degree requirements like English, history, oceanography, and anthropology, though I managed to fit in some music history and a basic music theory class, as well. I hadn't lost my interest in music—just my desire to play in a band. I had a Green River hangover.

Since so many of my friends were still in the scene, I obviously stayed on top of what was going on, and I could see things continuing to develop and progress. Bands were solidifying, finding their sound, and starting to write some really cool music. In fact, several of the bands that were part of the Gorilla Gardens crowd, including Green River, went into Ironwood Studios in the late summer and fall of 1985 to record tracks for a compilation called *Deep Six* that would be released on a new local label called C/Z Records in early 1986.

Though Green River's *Come On Down* was the first definitive example of grunge, *Deep Six* offered up the debut appearances on record by Soundgarden, Melvins, Malfunkshun, and Skin Yard, as well as new tracks from Green River, and, of course, the U-Men.

These bands had wildly different approaches—the members were a mix of UW students and former hardcore kids—but there was a definite Seattleness to all of them. The music was heavy, punk- and post-punk-influenced, and like nothing else out there. It perfectly captured what was happening in Seattle, an accurate snapshot of what was going on before the crowds started showing up, when it was still just the band members and their few buddies and room-mates coming to the shows.

I realized the record was a big deal, but to be honest, at the time I was like, *Eh, whatever*. I liked the Melvins, Malfunkshun, and U-Men tracks on there, but the rest . . . well, I had quit Green River for a reason. I didn't like the slow, Zeppelin-y sounding stuff that much. The two Green River tracks on *Deep Six* were written while I was still in the band, though one, "10,000 Things," was significantly rearranged. And I didn't care for Soundgarden and Skin Yard much at the time. With early Soundgarden, I thought that Kim Thayil used way too many guitar effects, that their music got stronger the fewer he used. He liked that Killing Joke, UK post-punk sound, which was such a big influence in Seattle. (One band that should have been on *Deep Six*, however, was Feast, a long-forgotten band who, like Soundgarden, went from bass-heavy post-punk to sexy and groovy '70s rock and were in the thick of things during this era. I wish that they were better documented.) I knew this album was cool and sig-nificant at the time, but there might have been some residual hard feelings clouding my judgment. There's no denying that *Deep Six* is an amazing time capsule, and I love it now.

The release of *Deep Six* in early 1986 roughly coincided with the end of my self-imposed exile from rock. Since my social life out-side of work and school still largely revolved around my friends who lived together in the U District (Mark, Ed, and David, among oth-ers), many of whom were musicians, it was inevitable that I would get sucked back in. I didn't go looking to play in another band, but it happened anyway.

A year or so previously, I'd been at a party where a couple of local bands played: the Dwindles (a precursor to Pure Joy, which led to Flop) and the Thrown Ups. The Thrown Ups were four university students—Leighton Beezer (bass), Steve Mack (vocals), Mike Faulhaber (guitar), and Scott Schickler (drums)—who played what could best be described as arty, improvised, experimental meanderings. Basically, they made up stuff on the spot.

Early in 1985, Steve Mack moved to London and found himself fronting a new band, That Petrol Emotion, led by former members of Northern Ireland's the Undertones. Within a year, that band's debut album hit number one on the UK indie chart, and *Rolling Stone* described them as "the Clash crossed with Creedence." That would be the last we'd see of Steve in Seattle for a while.

Steve Mack's departure from the Thrown Ups left a vacancy in the vocal department, and my friend Ed somehow got the job. Ed wasn't really a "singer" as far as I knew. Luckily, fronting the Thrown Ups didn't require that. Adding Ed changed the band dramatically, as he was much more of a wild card than Steve Mack. Not long after, Mike Faulhaber left the band as well, and Ed asked if I wanted to take his place. I still had a guitar and amp, I was already hanging around them anyway, and because everything was improvised, it wasn't going to take any effort to be in the Thrown Ups. It wasn't a serious thing. And no one was telling me to get a new amp or a better guitar, like they did in Green River. Playing music, or whatever it was we were doing, was fun again.

If all your songs are improvised, there's no need to practice, which seemed like a bonus to being in the Thrown Ups. We tried practicing a couple times after I first joined, but it seemed pointless, because the goal was to always be spontaneous. During this time, Scott decided he no longer wanted to play actual drums and instead had taken to banging on pots, pans, and Tupperware. That didn't work either (no surprise), and before long Scott left, eventually moving on to one of Sub Pop Records' early bands, Swallow, with Rod Moody from Deranged Diction.

But Seattle was a small, incestuous scene, so who should come along to join the Thrown Ups on drums but Mark Arm. I'd played with Mark in Mr. Epp, Limp Richerds (briefly), and Green River, and here he was again. I thought, *God, I can't get away from Mark!* This was two years into our playing in bands, and I'm like, *Man, here we are again.* And it wouldn't be the last time.

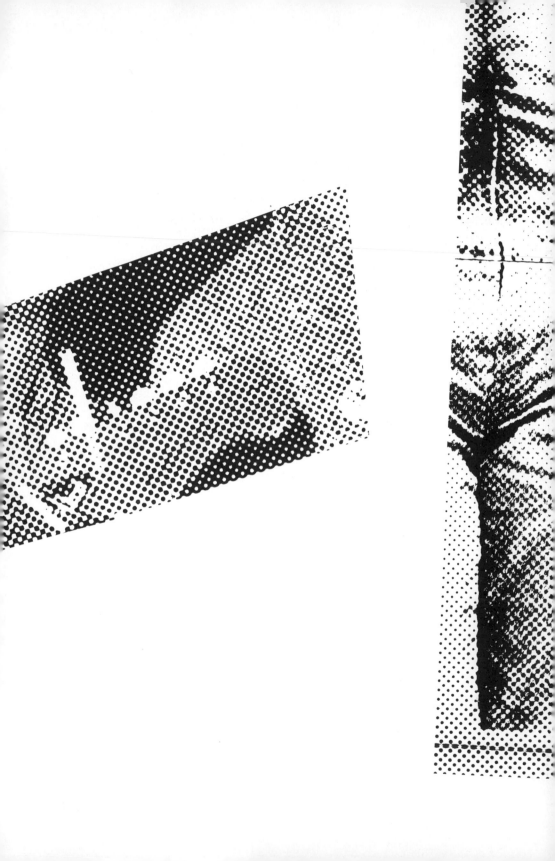

HARMONY IS ONE FRET AWAY

THE THROWN UPS WERE KNOWN, IN THE SEATTLE PAR-lance of the day, as a "fuck band." I don't know the origin of this term, but if you had a main band you were in, and then started a second, less serious band, that other band was the "fuck band." The Thrown Ups were the textbook definition of one.

Mark could moonlight as a drummer outside of singing in Green River and play music with absolutely no ambition or pressure attached. For the rest of us, playing in the Thrown Ups was primarily an opportunity to hang out, make some noise, and have a lot of laughs. This version of the Thrown Ups, with only Leighton as an original member, turned out to be dramatically different, sonically, than the original Steve Mack incarnation, and in my estimation, it's a crucial part of the grunge story.

That assertion may not seem reasonable if you've listened to any of our recordings, or even just read song titles like "Lard Butt," "Your Band Sucks," "Eat My Dump," or "The Person in My Bowel (Is Very Sad)." On the surface, it was juvenile. Well, OK, it was juvenile through and through, but beyond the toilet humor, there *was* something substantive happening. The Thrown Ups were a hugely important part of Mudhoney's initial DNA.

Mark and I had always influenced each other's musical tastes since we first became friends. Initially, it was him turning me on to a lot of stuff I hadn't been exposed to growing up, or cool stuff I'd missed out on in general. In the Thrown Ups era, the tables turned a bit. In my constant quest to dig up interesting new music, I discovered a lot of cool bands from Australia that I played for Mark when we'd get together at his place and spin records. It started with the more tuneful bands like the New Christs, and then it was all about feedtime and the Scientists (that was a big one). We also had this shared musical vibe we were into, really dirtbag punk, like Drunks with Guns and Antiseen. Those bands produced some of the gnarliest guitar sounds ever. We were gathering this aesthetic—Blue Cheer were also a big part of it, as were the Stooges—and applying it to the Thrown Ups. So, when Mark and I joined the band, the distortion and fuzz level increased substantially.

Playing together in the Thrown Ups was also where Mark and I developed our musical rapport. The Thrown Ups' MO was simple: Somebody would start making noise, and we'd all join in. And because Mark played drums and I played guitar and we had this real connection, it was so easy to come up with fake songs off the top of our heads. I think it was a mind meld for Mark and me, because we were listening to all the same music and playing together, so we could predict each other's moves. So much of it was simply making eye contact and knowing when to start and stop things, so we developed that language with each other. Leighton would start songs, and Mark and I would pile in. I'm not sure Mudhoney would have been so dialed in from the get-go were it not for the two-plus years Mark and I spent hacking improvised noise jams into "songs."

Leighton—who never wanted to be in a band that rehearsed or wrote songs—also empowered me with the best musical wisdom I ever received. It's the only music lesson that any guitarist or bassist playing in a band needs: "If what you're playing sounds awful, you're only one fret away—just move one fret in either direction." I distilled that down to "harmony is one fret away." He was right, and it was so freeing. And it works in both directions. If what you're playing sounds harmonious and you want to add dissonance, move one fret and it will sound awful. But if you're sounding awful and want to sound like you're grooving in the same world with your bandmates, move one fret in either direction and you'll most likely find a chord that you're playing together. That was his guiding principle, and it not only helped me improvise better in the Thrown Ups, but I've also carried that nugget with me through my entire musical career. This is obviously not virtuoso-level musical advice, but for anyone playing noise-based rock, it's good advice and has personally served me well.

Armed with a good musical bond with my bandmates, a developing sonic aesthetic, and a modicum of useful improvisational skills, the obvious next step was to play some gigs. Because Mark and I had the Green River connection and knew a lot of people in the scene, getting on bills right away was easy. I mean, the Thrown Ups were able to get gigs prior to Mark and me joining, but we opened some more doors. And since we didn't need to learn and rehearse a set of songs, we were ready to go right out of the gate. And this new incarnation of the band had something even more important: Ed.

Ed always had some tricks up his sleeve. Since we didn't have songs people would remember, we put on performances they would. It was all about the spectacle because people knew we were just making shit up. Luckily Ed is an amazing frontman, and I was happy to be next to him onstage, reveling in his insanity. As absurd as it sounds, we'd make a "setlist" before each show, to inspire that insanity, I suppose. We'd show up at the club, drink some beer, and start writing down the stupidest, most ridiculous song titles we could come up with on a big sheet of paper. It was free-flowing; whatever happened, happened. That was Leighton's guiding philosophy. It was chaotically democratic.

The only thing that would be planned would be the "theme" of the show. I had started going to thrift stores again and would occasionally stumble across items that would end up as our stage clothes. One time I found pale greenish tuxedos with white pants for two dollars a pop, so I bought four of those. You can see Ed sporting his on the back cover of *The Thrown Ups* LP. Usually we would give ourselves monobrows, too, and Ed would draw hair on his chest with a Sharpie.

There were several shows that were fun for the crowd but made us unpopular with the club owners. One notorious gig was the "zit show" at the Ditto Tavern, a small venue under the monorail tracks in downtown. That might have been my first show with the Thrown Ups. Ed, the genius that he was, created "zit pants." He used big black garbage bags to craft what looked like leather pants. After putting them on, he took baggies full of shaving cream and stuffed them in the legs. While we were playing, he'd stab the baggies with a pen and squirt the shaving cream everywhere. It made a mess, and the Ditto didn't love it, but it became a notorious show, probably because Charles Peterson, our photographer friend, was there documenting it.

Though we made an ungodly racket and created chaos wherever we played, the Thrown Ups weren't reviled in the music scene, and we could pull a good crowd, including plenty of our musical peers, when we played at places like the Vogue and the Central Tavern. It was no doubt due to the spectacle and absurdity of what we were doing, and not so much about the music. Some of our shenanigans may have prevented return engagements at certain clubs, but people kept showing up to see us. I think there was an

The Thrown Ups "Smiling Panties" 7", 1988.

A favorite poster. The design was still influenced by new wave, but the bands had moved far away from anything like that. 1988.

A Thrown Ups gig poster featuring a picture of my friend Dave Lipe, future singer of Icky Joey.

appreciation of the fun we were having and the fact that it wasn't a serious undertaking. There was also a sense of chaos, not all that different from what Mr. Epp had been doing a handful of years earlier. It was sloppy and noisy, but there was a sense of purpose to it. It was like a weird sonic petri dish where our developing aesthetic was growing into something a little more fully formed.

The next step was to take our insanity into the studio. In 1986 we knew producer Jack Endino (née Mike Giacondino) not for his record-making skills, but as the guitarist in Skin Yard. However, he had started working as a recording engineer at Chris Hanzsek's Reciprocal Recording and began to make a name for himself by recording both his own band and his peers. Green River had recorded its second album, *Dry as a Bone*, with him in the summer of '86, so when the Thrown Ups decided to book some studio time in the fall, he's who we went to.

Jack knew his target audience at that point—broke bands—so he was extremely budget minded. He also seemed to innately know how to capture the sounds that Seattle bands were making. I'm not sure if he was prepared for the Thrown Ups, but he was game.

I was still naive about the studio—ignorant, I guess, because I didn't know how it all worked. With the Thrown Ups, it didn't matter. There weren't going to be any overdubs; we wanted to capture pure improvisation. After the microphones were placed and the levels set, we started rolling tape, doing one piece at a time. After each "take," we would stop and laugh, maybe listen to it—then take inventory and say, *Who's going to start the next one?* That's about as much planning as we did. We also would just jam and make noise and then later try to find the good bits of noise on the recording.

That was where Jack excelled. We would do an eight-minute jam, and he could find like two minutes that sounded like something worth saving. Editing the songs involved listening to the whole take and figuring out where we could get in and get out. There was no overdubbing vocals or extra guitar parts. Whatever was there, whatever Ed was spouting off about, was what we would use. Sometimes we'd have to fade in fast. There was no Pro Tools back then to digitally construct a song with. It was like, *Where are the best two minutes?* I'm sure it was the weirdest thing Jack had done to that point, but he loved us. He still says that was one of the funnest projects he's ever worked on, which surprises me to this day. I think he saw the connection between Mark and me, and that Ed was some kind of weird genius too.

The prospect of finding an indie label to release the recording, however, seemed unlikely until Tom Hazelmyer came along. Tom was a Minneapolis musician we knew of from his first band, Otto's Chemical Lounge. He was living in the Seattle area in the mid-'80s while he was stationed in the military on nearby Whidbey Island. He briefly played bass in the U-Men and later formed Halo of Flies. U-Men vocalist John Bigley introduced me to him at some point, but Tom and I didn't become friends until shortly after the Thrown Ups' recording session with Jack, when he and I discovered a shared interest in collecting music from punk rock and noisy weird bands. Tom had recently started his own indie record label, Amphetamine Reptile Records, and had already released a few Halo of Flies 7″ singles.

I passed him a copy of our cassette to see what he thought. He might have seen us perform before, but I figured he'd at least be receptive. He actually liked it and agreed to put out our debut 7″ single, "Felch," in early 1987. I was surprised Tom wanted to release the single, because it was a little bit outside of what I thought he liked at the time.

We were the second band on AmRep (after his own band), and his roster would ultimately include some of the biggest names in noise rock, like Helmet, Cows, Boss Hog, Surgery, Lubricated Goat, Today Is the Day, Melvins, and many others. There's not much else like the Thrown Ups in the AmRep catalog to this day. Most of his bands are well rehearsed and tight—we were not. Even though he moved back to Minneapolis, his label would maintain a connection to Seattle, and he put out several more Thrown Ups releases in the next few years, as well as some Mudhoney tracks. The Thrown Ups were an anomaly for AmRep, for sure, because we were just a "fuck band," but it was somehow part of Hazelmyer's thing. He loved it.

I didn't mind being in a "fuck band." I was playing music to have fun again. There wasn't a whole lot of artistic merit to what we were doing in the Thrown Ups, but I guess we were doing that thing where you "dance like nobody's watching," because no one *was* watching Seattle. Nobody in the scene thought *any of this* mattered in the bigger musical picture. And we were making one point obvious: Anybody can be in a rock band.

SEATTLE
SYNDROME

AFTER FINISHING A YEAR AT SEATTLE CENTRAL COMMUNITY
College, I'd applied and been accepted at Western Washington University in Bellingham, about ninety miles north of Seattle and not far from the Canadian border. The plan was, however, that I'd first do some traveling in Europe with my dad in the fall of 1986, and then start at WWU in January 1987. During our time in London, I managed to connect with Steve Mack and give him a cassette of the Thrown Ups tape we'd made with Jack Endino. I didn't know Steve very well—he'd been part of that University of Washington arty music crowd—but because he was good friends with Leighton, I figured he'd want to hear it. He was obviously going in another musical direction with That Petrol Emotion at that point, but he was stoked to hear it. He and his bandmates were living in a squat in one of those tenement high-rises, which I thought was especially cool. Their first album was already out by that point, so they gave me a couple copies of it—one for me and one to take home to Leighton.

A bit later, while on tour in the States, That Petrol Emotion invited the Thrown Ups to open their show at Seattle's Moore Theater, much to everyone's regret. We kicked off our set with a song dubbed "My Cock Is the Coin to the Baby Machine," and the plan was that Ed would go out there and start it on his own, with vocals only.

"My cock is the coin to the baby machine," he wailed. He thought we were coming onstage right away, and, as a joke, we left him dying on the vine, waiting for us to come out. We finally did and bashed into the song, but it was a very uncomfortable moment—hilarious to us, not so much to Ed—where he was just singing these lyrics over and over and looking over at us in the wings.

The *Seattle Times* music critic, Patrick MacDonald, who'd done his best to ignore what was happening in the local scene, reviewed the show, and it was a hilarious summary. He loved That Petrol Emotion and was talking about lead singer Steve Mack in his tight black bicycle shorts. The only thing he wrote about us and the Squirrels, the other support band, was: "Both opening bands shall remain nameless out of kindness." I figured that must have pissed off the Squirrels to be lumped in with the fucking Thrown Ups. Their band was fun, but unlike us, they were serious about the music.

Once my dad and I returned to Seattle in December, I spent a couple weeks with my family over the holidays and then moved right up to Bellingham in January 1987 to start classes. Initially I lived in the over-twenty-one dorms, but before long I met a guy named Dave Harwell (who went on to form Earth, with Kurt Cobain's best friend, Dylan Carlson), and we lived together for a bit. That didn't last long, though, and I ended up living on my own in the equivalent of a flophouse, right across from Bellingham's main music venue, the Up and Up. Even though I'd ostensibly relocated to Bellingham for school, I was still down in Seattle a lot—playing the occasional gig with the Thrown Ups and hanging out with my friends. In a lot of ways, I still felt like my life was in Seattle, and as such, I had no interest in starting a band while I was at WWU in Bellingham.

In 1986, Bruce Pavitt issued the first vinyl release as Sub Pop Records, the *Sub Pop 100* compilation, which mostly featured artists from outside the Northwest (Sonic Youth, Naked Raygun, Scratch

Acid, Shonen Knife) but also included tracks from the U-Men, the Wipers (Portland), and Steve Fisk and Skinny Puppy (British Columbia). Pavitt had previously put out homemade Sub Pop cassette compilations that had included local Seattle bands and had written a Sub Pop music column in a Seattle music magazine called *The Rocket*, but this was his first nationally distributed effort, and it's where his larger ambitions were headed.

As a follow-up to this vinyl compilation, he agreed to release the session Green River did in the summer of 1986 with Jack Endino, as the *Dry as a Bone* EP, the label's first Seattle release and one he marketed as "ultra-loose grunge that destroyed the morals of a generation." That seems to be the first commercial/marketing use of the term *grunge*, and not surprisingly it was applied to my old band, Green River. Pavitt, who had his finger on the pulse of underground music around the world, had been witnessing what was happening in Seattle firsthand, and he saw something special, something unique to the area.

Seattle obviously wasn't the only area producing cool bands at the time. The mid-'80s American underground scene was amazing and diverse, and it seemed like most of the bands that were even sort of popular weren't trying to be *more* popular. They were making whatever racket they wanted to make. If you look at the catalogs of Homestead, Touch & Go, and SST, there was some stellar underground music being made without any mainstream notice. It was the ghetto, but it was our little ghetto. Sonic Youth playing for three or four hundred people was like, *Wow, good show!* And they were the success story! It was an inspiring time, and it didn't seem like there were any rules with it. Most of us were coming from the punk scene in one way or another, but we hadn't stayed there. Some bands did, and made great records, like Portland's Poison Idea, but I knew I didn't want to play hardcore anymore. There was a freedom in *Where*

First issue of Dawn Anderson's *Backlash*, December 1987.
It was starting to all blend together in Seattle by this point.

The Thrown Ups "Eat My Dump" 7", 1988. By this point,
the Thrown Ups were almost accidently writing songs.

do we go from here? and bands were evolving past hardcore, like Big Black using the drum machine and borrowing from krautrock and post-punk English bands. Or a bunch of the California punk bands like Dr. Know and Battalion of Saints going glammy Hollywood metal. It was a very interesting time.

We'd go see the touring bands that would come through, like SST bands, and I'd often think that the local bands on the bill were better than the bands coming from someplace else. Seattle seemed a little bit more focused. Even though a lot of the same people who'd been playing in various bands in Seattle for the previous few years were still around, new bands were forming all the time with musicians who came from the various musical strands of hardcore, post-punk, and even the paisley pop/psych crowd. It was a small enough scene that there weren't enough people to have cliques. We all went and saw each other's bands.

A lot of these musicians, many of them UW students, lived in houses together, so there was plenty of intermingling. A young drummer named Dan Peters lived in a house with Ron Nine (a.k.a. Ron Rudzitis) at the Room Nine house, just off NE 45th Street. Ron was in a paisley pop band called Room Nine, but later formed Love Battery, while Dan played drums in Bundle of Hiss, a UK post-punk-sounding band that had synth drums. But they were part of the same little world, and they held their own in the scene. My friends and I went to see those bands all the time, too, and went to the same parties. All of us were also finally over twenty-one, which was important, because a city law instituted in 1985, called the Teen Dance Ordinance, had made all-ages rock shows impossible. So, shows moved to the bars, and I started drinking beer.

We were all influencing each other musically too. There were certain touchstones that were becoming obvious. The heavy psych stuff, like the Stooges, was part of it, obviously. But then there was also some of that cleaner, jangly, and melodic stuff too. Swallow, that early Sub Pop band that Thrown Ups drummer Scott Schickler joined, played heavy power pop, but they were beefing up their guitars, adding more distortion and aggression, because so many of us were too. I think Swallow would've been poppier and more "college rock" if they'd developed someplace else. Guitarist/singer Chris Pugh's other bands were more jangly, but I think Seattle made him rockier.

Another early Sub Pop band, Blood Circus, came out of nowhere (though the guitarist had been in Extreme Hate), and we were like, *Holy shit, these guys are great!* And they were super heavy, leaning into a Motörhead vibe, which was uncommon in the Seattle underground. The singer was from Denver, and he came out of the same scene as the Fluid, another early Sub Pop band. It seemed like the bands with a heavier sound were getting more popular.

Both Soundgarden and Feast had what Sub Pop founder Bruce Pavitt called the "heavy and sexy" thing, the slow and low sound, with emphasis on the bass. When Soundgarden started, they were immensely UK post-punk influenced. Kim's guitar was all flanged and chorused and stuff, and bassist Hiro Yamamoto's playing was really heavy, and it just got heavier. So, Soundgarden morphed into being Led Zeppelin/Sabbath heavy, but still with these hints of post-punk. Feast were very much like that too, but there was a gothiness to Feast. The same with Dan's band Bundle of Hiss (which two members of Sub Pop band Tad were in at one point), which played very post-punk, UK-style stuff, like Public Image Ltd. or Gang of Four. But slowly, a lot of these post-punk-influenced bands started getting heavier. Bruce Pavitt would probably say that some of it was the drugs those guys were taking. It seemed like everybody was taking MDMA and Ecstasy. I never did any of that stuff, so it could be a little weird to be around, with everybody wanting a hug at parties.

Around this time was also when the U-Men, who were so crucial in leading the way out of hardcore, got left behind. Two years after packing them in at shows, they were not the cool guys anymore, because the difference between the music they were playing and the developing grunge was getting starker. The U-Men didn't get heavier or more distorted, or incorporate '70s rock influences, and in some regard became the odd men out. I know vocalist John Bigley was flummoxed by it. U-Men guitarist Tom Price liked what the Seattle thing was doing, and he went on to form Gas Huffer, while U-Men bassist Jim Tillman joined Ron Nine's Love Battery.

In this changing musical atmosphere, more people beyond our small, tight-knit group of musicians started attending shows. The local scene was growing, and it was getting covered with some seriousness by Dawn Anderson's upstart magazine, *Backlash*, which was crucial in spreading the word and promoting us beyond the city limits. She was reaching tens of thousands of readers in Seattle and the suburbs and turning them on to what was happening in their backyard. She was an important early promoter of the scene, and she and her writers documented the groundswell happening, in their always-humorous, *Creem* magazine–inspired way. *Backlash*'s coverage also seemed to prompt the other, larger music paper in Seattle, *The Rocket*, to step up its coverage of the local scene, rather than focusing on high-profile touring bands. It was an exciting time in Seattle, and there were a lot of good bands. It was gratifying to see the audiences getting bigger. It took years for it to build, but I think that was part of the appeal: It grew organically.

Bruce Pavitt was there to capture what was happening with Sub Pop Records. He released the Green River *Dry as a Bone* EP in 1987 and found a business partner in local promoter and DJ Jonathan Poneman to help him release Soundgarden's debut single, "Hunted Down," and their EP, *Screaming Life*, that same year.

But Sub Pop wasn't just putting out records; it was embodying what was going on in Seattle musically, aesthetically, and in attitude. Sub Pop adopted a tongue-in-cheek, corporate, world-takeover thing in its marketing efforts—magazine ads, mail-order catalog copy, photo shoots—that reflected the looseness and lack of seriousness in the music scene. The joke being that "world domination" was absurd—Seattle bands were rarely given any notice from media outside our area. And certainly, no labels were scouting Seattle for the next big thing. Sub Pop even started marketing a T-shirt with "LOSER" printed across the front, and a Sub Pop logo on the back, which summed up the self-deprecating tone. We had no aspirations beyond our local scene, because, in most of our minds, it wasn't a possibility.

In addition to the burgeoning music scene, Seattle itself was emerging from the doldrums of the previous decade right around the same time that Sub Pop started in the mid-'80s. You could buy a house cheap (not that any of us were doing that yet), rents were low, and it was easy to get a job. Seattle was growing culturally and had a healthy arts scene. The city seemed less economically depressed and more vibrant, especially compared to the early '70s, when someone had put up a billboard that said, "Will the last person leaving Seattle turn out the lights?"

One epiphany I had while attending WWU and occasionally playing in the Thrown Ups was that despite my bad ending with Green River, I *liked* making music, and it didn't necessarily have to take a lot of effort.

Right around the time I was starting my second year at WWU, I found myself at a party at Ed's house. He had instruments set up in his basement, so we went down there and started jamming with drummer Dan Peters. I didn't really know Dan, though I'd seen him play in Feast and Bundle of Hiss before. Even though the three of us were just messing around, I felt like we clicked right away, and soon I was coming down on weekends specifically to practice with them, with the intent of doing something more structured and organized than the Thrown Ups. My friend Tom Hazelmyer—without having heard a note of what we were doing—had already promised to put out a single on Amphetamine Reptile if we got some material together and recorded a couple songs.

However, regular practice and crafting songs that needed rehearsing proved to be too much for Ed. He liked the improvised Thrown Ups–style stuff. He probably came to four practices with us, but he hated it and finally bailed, saying, "I don't wanna be in a real band! It's too much effort. It's too hard." But I was digging playing with Dan and decided that I *did* want to be in a "real" band. Still, I didn't think much would come of it until I got a call on October 31, 1987, from a very drunk Mark Arm.

"Green River just broke up," he slurred. "We need to start a band."

PART

TWO

GIMME TWO YEARS

IF THE 1985 RELEASE OF GREEN RIVER'S *COME ON DOWN* WAS
a touchstone moment in the grunge continuum, the dissolution of
Green River in October 1987 was as well. I obviously wasn't in the band
at the time and can't speak to the specifics of how it all went down,
but the abbreviated version is that Mark and the more ambitious
members of the band (primarily Jeff and Stone) didn't have the same
professional goals and vision. Mark (like me) didn't think the developing Seattle music scene was commercially viable. He thought Jeff
and Stone were kidding themselves, trying to grab for something
like a major label recording contract that 1) wasn't within the realm
of possibility for their kind of music and 2) wasn't something he
was interested in, even if it were. I also thought Jeff and Stone were
setting themselves up for failure and disappointment. Still, it was
a sad day when Green River reached its end.

However, Green River's breakup turned out to be a godsend
for grunge, providing better opportunities for everyone involved.
Mark's interest in forming something new with me (even if it was
akin to a rebound relationship so soon after Green River) was perfectly timed with my own growing desire to start writing songs
instead of improvising. Ed may have decided he wasn't interested
in doing another band, but Dan was, so adding Mark to the mix was a

no-brainer. Mark and I were already playing together in the Thrown Ups and had developed a tight musical relationship. We also loved the same kinds of bands and music.

So, in November 1987, Dan, Mark, and I started rehearsing together. I insisted that if we were going to be a band, Mark couldn't just sing; he had to play guitar. One thing I didn't like about Green River was him hopping around and climbing on everything. Playing guitar would ground him to the stage. Plus, I really liked his guitar playing. Since we were into some of those dirty blues bands like feedtime, and we wanted to keep the sound sleazy and swampy, we came up with the idea that Mark should play a lot of slide guitar. And since Mark hadn't played guitar in a band for several years, we figured playing slide guitar would make it easier for him to sing and play.

The three of us rehearsed and wrote songs together in the last months of 1987. But we knew we'd need to get a bass player at some point. As luck would have it, the bassist from the Melvins had recently become available.

There had been some intrigue a few months previous with the Melvins, a band we admired from the *Deep Six* compilation album. Not long after recording their full-length debut album, *Gluey Porch Treatments* (which included a cover of Green River's "Leech"), the Melvins decided to "break up." But what actually happened was that

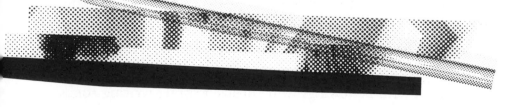

guitarist/vocalist Buzz Osbourne and drummer Dale Crover moved to the Bay Area and added Buzz's then-girlfriend, Lori Black, as their bassist. This left original Melvins bassist Matt Lukin high and dry in Aberdeen, Washington, and thoroughly pissed off. We took advantage of his availability and asked him to come up to Seattle and practice with us. He'd told us he was coming up for a concert at Seattle Center (Alice Cooper!) on December 31, and suggested we get together on New Year's Day.

January 1, 1988, was when Mudhoney officially started. After our first rehearsal with Matt that day, we knew that we had the right fit, musically and temperamentally. As for the name, it came from the title of a campy Russ Meyer sexploitation film (Mark and I were into oddball movies, B movies, and biker movies). We thought Mudhoney would be a cool name—kinda sleazy and underground, dirty and sweet.

We already had some songs together, but adding Matt pushed things along. It was instantly easy to make the music we wanted to make. And it wasn't just Mark's and my vision; we all came on board with what each person was doing almost immediately. Matt contributed a lot right away, particularly to the early material we were writing. The music to some of the early songs, like "In 'n' Out of Grace," was all Matt. It was much more precise and rhythmically challenging, more like Melvins stuff. And Dan's drumming was unique; his sound had more of a post-punk, arty, progressive rock background that was more technical than what Mark and I were into, but we liked it.

The formation of Mudhoney, however, meant that I would have to make some decisions regarding my future. Lisa and I had drifted apart when I went off to WWU, so that didn't figure into the equation. I wasn't *initially* planning to just drop out of college and start playing with Mudhoney. I figured I might continue on at WWU for another year while still in the band. That said, I was also open to whatever the universe was bringing my way. I tried to control it a little bit, but I was open. So that inevitably led to another hard conversation with my parents: I was going to choose Mudhoney over school, at least temporarily. My plea to them was simple: Gimme two years.

We all thought Mudhoney would be another short-lived project. We knew we could put out a couple singles at the very least, and that's as far as our plans went. Dan was still in Bundle of Hiss, and Matt lived a few hours away in Aberdeen at the time. I didn't see it as a career, and I didn't want it as a career. My thought was, after two years playing in Mudhoney, I'd go back and get my degree. So in early 1988, I moved into my folks' basement like a proper rock 'n' roller.

Since Dan already had his drums set up in a practice space (in a building called "the Dutchman," south of downtown), we started rehearsing there in the small, scuzzy room. After a few months we had a handful of songs, and we'd try to record them as best we could, using a boombox. Unfortunately, the room was so small, and the band was so loud, that the recordings didn't sound like anything. We put the boombox outside the door of the room to see if that would help, but the results were muffled.

Meanwhile, Mark was working at elevator music distributor Muzak, along with about half the Seattle music scene at the time: Bruce Pavitt (Sub Pop), Tad Doyle (Tad), Ron Nine (Love Battery), Grant Eckman (Walkabouts), and Chris Pugh (Swallow), among others. It was like the think tank of the nascent grunge scene.

Bruce aspired to launch Sub Pop as a full-on enterprise that spring, so Mark would bring recordings of our practices in for Bruce to hear. We thought, based on Green River's experience with the label, that he might be interested in Mudhoney. He was definitely receptive, but also somewhat befuddled by our boombox recordings.

"Man, Mark . . . I can't even tell what's going on here," he said after being subjected to one of our early rehearsal tapes. "Why don't I just pay for you guys to go do a quick, one-day demo over at Reciprocal?"

Reciprocal was affordable at the time, and that was Jack Endino's whole MO: He would record bands on the cheap. Luckily for all the Seattle bands at the time, he was also good at capturing their sound. It was a serendipitous combination, and we were fortunate to have someone like Jack who was not only an excellent engineer but also a musician and peer in the scene (in Skin Yard). So, before Mudhoney had even played a show, we went into Reciprocal in April 1988 and recorded and mixed our first demo over a couple of days, on the same 8-track machine both Green River and the Thrown Ups had previously used.

By this point, the Thrown Ups had done three sessions with Jack, including a recent one on Valentine's Day, 1988, that resulted in the "Eat My Dump" 7″, released later that year on Amphetamine Reptile. Those Thrown Ups sessions helped acclimate me to the studio, so by the time in April I went in with Mudhoney, we were focused, but still loose. I started learning a little bit about the studio too. Jack was certainly very capable and open-minded about what we sounded like. He wasn't changing anything; we were just getting some stuff down on tape and having a good time. Also, the fact that this was just a demo for Bruce kept the mood light.

During this first Mudhoney session we recorded "Touch Me I'm Sick," "Sweet Young Thing Ain't Sweet No More," "Twenty Four," "Need," "Mudride," and "In 'n' Out of Grace." Though there was no real intention to release these demo versions at the time, Tom Hazelmyer wanted to use "Twenty Four" on his *Dope-Guns-'n-Fucking in the Streets Volume One* 7″ compilation, which also featured tracks from the U-Men, the Thrown Ups, and Tom's band, Halo of Flies. That turned out to be Mudhoney's first appearance on vinyl. Jack Endino apparently noticed that our guitars were quite out of tune at the time we were recording "Twenty Four" (how could you not?), but he thought that's what we were going for. This laissez-faire attitude toward tuning was indicative of our overall approach and aesthetic; precision and well-manicured distortion were not what I was after. We used tuners so infrequently that we didn't even realize that we weren't tuned to standard E tuning but were instead dropped down a half step. We stayed with this tuning until 1991, when we shifted up to standard tuning and have kept it ever since. (We now regularly use tuners.)

From my time playing in both Green River and the Thrown Ups, I had started to develop my own distinctive sound, which was guided by my interest in both garage rock and the noisier punk I'd been soaking up. I was discovering how to get the tones I wanted to hear. On a lot of the early Mudhoney material, I'm playing my Fender Mustang guitar using the pickup positioned closest to the neck, with my Big Muff distortion pedal on super overdrive. The Big Muff was designed to allow guitarists to produce an endless sustaining note (like David Gilmour of Pink Floyd), but it can make gnarly early fuzz box sounds too. I would use different settings for different songs, but I was shooting for the-gnarlier-the-better on the early Mudhoney recordings. I listen to some of that stuff now and think, *Those are some fucked-up guitar sounds!*

Not long after we recorded our first session with Jack, Mud-honey played our first show on April 19, 1988, opening for New York band Das Damen. Like us, they had roots in the hardcore scene. They had put out records on Ecstatic Peace (Thurston Moore of Sonic Youth's label), as well as SST, so we were well matched. We didn't have a very long set at that point, so we opened the show, with Blood Circus playing after us. They were another Sub Pop band and would soon release their debut 7″ for the label.

Taken on Mudhoney's 1988 US tour with Sonic Youth. Things came together really quickly for Mudhoney, with a lot of help from Sonic Youth!

Mudhoney practice room cassette recordings, March 4, 1988. It was unlistenable so Bruce Pavitt had us record our first demo at Reciprocal with Jack Endino in April 1988.

Mudhoney show at the Alamo, June 6, 1988. Stone and Bruce from Mother Love Bone in the background.

Because all four members of Mudhoney had established reputations in the Seattle scene, we were able to get on some good bills right away—we didn't have to pay any dues. The next month we opened for another New York band, White Zombie, in both Seattle and Portland. We stayed busy in 1988, playing every couple of weeks in Seattle alone, taking any show we could. Unfortunately, ever since the Teen Dance Ordinance had been enacted, there weren't a ton of places to play. Squid Row, the Vogue, the Central, and the Ditto were all pretty small.

One place no one in Seattle seems to remember is the Alamo. It was a Mexican restaurant in Pioneer Square where we played one of our earliest shows, opening once again for Blood Circus. The Alamo didn't regularly host live shows, but the venue, in its various incarnations over the years, did have bands play sometimes. Unfortunately, the "stage" at the Alamo was in a tiny cove in the front window, so our backs were to a window where everyone walking past could watch. A friend of mine was taking pictures of the show that night and in those pictures, you can see Bruce and Stone from Green River watching from outside the window right behind us. They wouldn't even fucking pay the three bucks to get in!

After Green River broke up in late '87, Stone, Bruce, and Jeff embarked on a completely different path than Mark and me. Following a brief stint as Lords of the Wasteland (Kiss reference!) with Malfunkshun vocalist/bassist Andrew ("Landrew") Wood and drummer Regan Hager, they solidified a lineup with former 10 Minute Warning drummer Greg Gilmore (taking over for Hager) and decided to call themselves Mother Love Bone. Wood fronted the band, minus his Steinberger bass. This was the faction of Green River that was aiming high.

Because we were still friends, I knew what Stone and his new band were up to. I saw Mother Love Bone, and I thought they were terrible. It was clearly not my deal at the time. Those guys were in such a different headspace. They were dressing like the Red Hot Chili Peppers—it was another world. I was disappointed, because I loved Malfunkshun so much and I was still close with Stone and Jeff.

Mudhoney and Mother Love Bone started right around the same time, and if you listen to both bands you can hear, in no uncertain terms, where the schism was in Green River. It was quite stark. It made sense, I guess, for Stone, who didn't come from the punk background, to go in a more commercial direction, but Jeff I didn't quite get, because he was such a hardcore kid, like me.

Both bands' recorded output during this time also highlights the distinct musical division. While Jeff and Stone were aiming their new band toward the LA-based major labels and hoping to score a big deal, Mark and I were putting out our first single on Sub Pop. Mother Love Bone's music was slick, polished, and aimed at commercial success. Our music was cheaply recorded, slightly out of tune, garage-influenced punk rock with an inherently limited audience. This was an inflection point in the Seattle music scene, where certain factions strove to leave the underground while others embraced it. We were taking distinctly different approaches to making music, and it would take years before we'd once again find common ground.

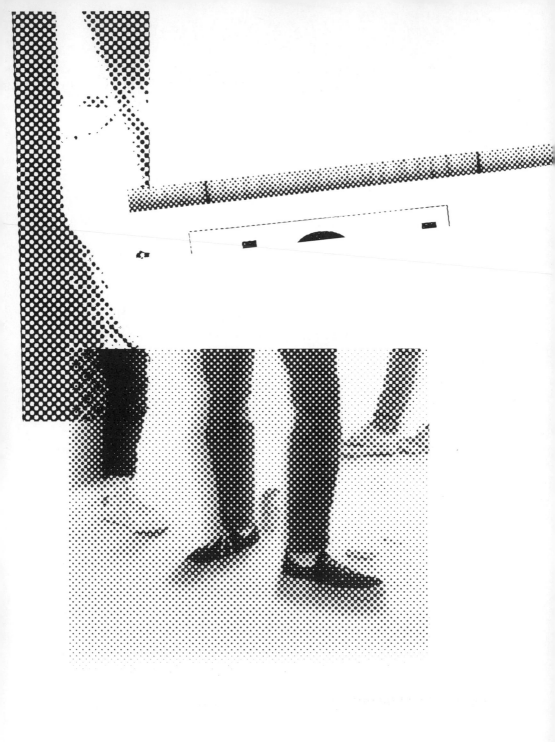

SUPERFUZZ

IT SEEMED LIKE 1988 WAS THE START OF A NEW THING IN Seattle. Part of that was my perception, because it really was the start of a new thing for me: I had moved back to town and started Mudhoncy. I was working evenings at ACT Theater and had time on my hands during the day, so I'd go into town early from my parents' place and hang out at Sub Pop's new digs in the Terminal Sales Building in downtown Seattle and package up orders. Sub Pop never paid me, but they'd often take me to lunch or an early dinner, and there was always brainstorming going on. Bruce Pavitt has credited me with coming up with the idea for the label's Singles Club series (of which Nirvana's first single, "Love Buzz," was the debut in November 1988), but I only suggested the label do a series of collectibles; they refined it into what it later became.

So, when Mudhoney were thinking about releasing some of our first recordings, Sub Pop was an obvious partner. Bruce had paid for our first demo, and we decided that the combination of "Sweet Young Thing Ain't Sweet No More" on the A side and "Touch Me I'm Sick" on the B side would be a good representation of what we were about. The two songs represented, respectively, the heavier and swampier side of the band, and our garage rock roots.

"Touch Me I'm Sick" was especially Seattle inspired. In the mid-'80s I started seeing a local garage rock band called Nights and Days, and I thought guitarist Rob Vasquez's playing was amazing. He had a nasty cheese grater sound (no distortion box, just the amp set to fry) with a cheap '60s guitar. And he would bash out chunky, full bar chords. That stuff became my aesthetic. I give credit to his style of guitar playing for the "Touch Me I'm Sick" riff: The tone knob is way up and the sustain is way down, so it gives it more of an early fuzz tone, no-sustain sound, almost like the Rolling Stones' "Satisfaction." In recording us, I think Jack Endino captured who we were perfectly, and the aesthetics of the time, that emerging sound from Seattle. Even though it got much further refined in some of the other bands, I think we were of the time and the place with those early recordings. "Touch Me I'm Sick" became our anthem.

The local excitement about the homegrown music scene was starting to build. I think that Seattleites early on understood that the local bands were really good. The entire scene was healthy and diverse; people were attending shows, and there were a lot of different sounds happening at any given show. Local media (*Backlash, The Rocket*) was supporting the scene, and Sub Pop was invested in making a big deal about the local talent. Mudhoney were in the thick of it. Bigger crowds started showing up at smaller shows; we had no idea from where. And that was awesome, because it wasn't just a couple dozen dudes in leather jackets, but also regular local folks getting into the local scene. It didn't seem fake or irritating, like, *Who are these people?* We welcomed it. We figured, *The more the merrier.*

Before Sub Pop had even released our 7″, we played a sold-out show at the Boxing Club on Capitol Hill with Swallow and Blood Circus, who were also releasing their debut 7″ singles on the label. We showed up at the gig to find a line snaking around the block. That was a big shocker because we'd just started playing shows. The explosion of excitement around the Seattle music scene took us by surprise—all the local bands at the time were astounded—and suddenly more clubs saw the viability of promoting the local talent that was playing original music (i.e., they were counting the money at the end of the night). Tuesday at the Vogue was local band night; the Central Tavern had Wednesdays; Squid Row would do weekend shows. It might have been a small thing compared to LA and New York, but the scene was growing.

Still, it surprised me that Mudhoney got popular so quickly. I think we put on a good show early on (and that probably helped), but we were still a grungy band. Whatever the reason, we were doing well locally, so Sub Pop asked us to record our debut EP, *Superfuzz Bigmuff* (named after Mark's and my distortion pedals), before we'd even released our first single.

The six songs on *Superfuzz Bigmuff* were recorded in the summer of 1988, once again with Jack Endino at Reciprocal. The difference this time was that Reciprocal had a 16-track machine, which meant twice as many tracks to put our instruments and vocals on, and a better sound overall. Because we had only formed earlier in the year and didn't have a whole lot of songs yet, it was Sub Pop's idea that we would just record an EP, like both Green River and Soundgarden had done for Sub Pop before us. I thought it was a great move at the time because I loved records like that. Underground American and English 12″ EPs were a big deal; it was a popular format. You get what the band thinks are its six strongest songs, and squeezing less music onto vinyl keeps the sound quality high as well. Plus, the EP was at a good price point ($5.99), making it more appealing for music buyers to take a chance on a band they may not have heard much from before.

Unlike the first demos, from which our Sub Pop 7″ and the AmRep compilation track "Twenty Four" would be drawn, we were definitely more confident during the sessions for *Superfuzz*. All of us

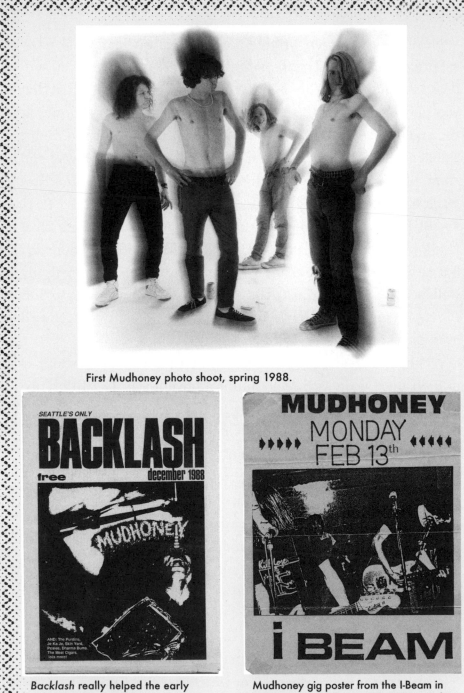

First Mudhoney photo shoot, spring 1988.

Backlash really helped the early scene come together.

Mudhoney gig poster from the I-Beam in San Francisco, February 13, 1989. We hit the road pretty hard in the first few years!

(including Jack) were getting more and more comfortable regarding what we were aiming for in the studio. We were still a new band, so it was still loose and unrefined. Jack wasn't messing with our sound at all, but if we got off track, he'd let us know if he thought we could do it better. We weren't worried about keeping perfect time because Dan often speeds up during the songs, which is the way it should be, in my mind. But if we were fucking things up, we knew it. There are obvious mistakes on some of the early material, but it didn't seem to matter because it was such chaotic, noisy music anyway. And Jack figured out in short order that *minor* details weren't an issue for us.

For the final track, "In 'n' Out of Grace," we amped up the chaos by kicking it off with a sampled rallying cry from the '60s biker movie *The Wild Angels*, starring Peter Fonda. Mark and I had watched it together at some point, and we loved Fonda's speech, so we threw it on there. I was absolutely obsessed with biker movies and their soundtracks, which featured fuzz guitar and were largely performed by Davie Allan and the Arrows—one of my biggest influences in the '80s. I remember at some point in the mid-'80s staying up every night of the week, all week, to watch all the old biker movies they were showing on late-night TV. I would be up until four in the morning every night at Lisa's house watching *Satan's Sadists* and whatever else at two in the morning.

Oddly enough, as Sub Pop was about to release our debut single and we were recording *Superfuzz*, Sub Pop finally issued Green River's posthumous album, *Rehab Doll*, several months after the band had broken up. Even stranger was the fact that it included a rerecorded version of "Swallow My Pride," a song I wrote that originally appeared on the *Come On Down* EP. Not only would Green River not be promoting the release of the album, but four of the five members who played on it were in two different new bands—Mark in Mudhoney and Stone, Jeff, and Bruce in Mother Love Bone. Both bands were active in the Seattle music scene and headed in very different directions. It was an awkward moment. That Mudhoney would find success—locally, nationally, and even abroad—so quickly and relatively easily would add tension to the relationship between the two bands.

In keeping with the idea of special limited releases, our Sub Pop debut 7″ of "Touch Me I'm Sick" and "Sweet Young Thing Ain't Sweet No More" was issued in August 1988 in an initial run of eight hundred copies pressed on toilet water–brown colored vinyl. They were packaged in clear sleeves with the song titles and band info on one side of the record label and a picture of a toilet, taken by Charles Peterson, on the other. Another two hundred were pressed on black vinyl and sent to the media and college radio stations. Much to my surprise, it became an underground hit both locally and on college radio. "Touch Me I'm Sick" has become a grunge anthem, of sorts. The initial pressing sold out quickly, and the limited run of colored brown vinyl certainly helped push the hype. What collectors at the time didn't know is that after the main run, the pressing plant also did a random run of whatever leftover bits of colored vinyl they had. So we got a handful of copies of purple, clear, red, yellow, blue—every color of the rainbow. Those are the ones that are worth the big bucks now.

The single sold so well that Sub Pop soon issued a second larger pressing with actual printed covers, with the toilet bowl picture once again prominently featured. Thurston Moore of Sonic Youth loved the early Mudhoney material and suggested that we do a split single with them for Sub Pop—they would cover "Touch Me I'm Sick" and we would cover their song "Halloween." Though our version of their song isn't my favorite Mudhoney track, you can hear Sonic Youth's influence on some of the early Mudhoney material, and it was mind-blowing to be paired up with an underground band of that stature, not to mention having them record one of our songs.

Though Green River's timing (and luck) had always been off during its three-year existence, things seemed to line up better for Mudhoney. Our debut 7″, released in August 1988, had caused a stir right away, and not long after the first pressing had sold out, we were poised to release *Superfuzz Bigmuff* in the fall. *Superfuzz* captured the spirit and the aesthetic of the tight-knit Seattle scene, in many ways beyond just the music. The photos on the record's cover and labels were shot by our friend Charles Peterson, and the lettering was done by our Thrown Ups bandmate Ed Fotheringham. It was recorded locally by Jack Endino and released on Sub Pop. Between this and our debut 7″, we took the proto-grunge that Green River and other Seattle bands were shaping at the time and put our stamp on it.

Our take on it was as much about the attitude and approach as it was the music. There was a sense of outrageous fun. We took the music seriously, but it was also a goof, trying to get a gnarly guitar sound. It was very punk rock—even the slow songs—but not in an aggro way. It was lighthearted, even though the lyrics could be dark, and there was a playfulness to it. Mudhoney shows were fun. I approached playing in Mudhoney with this attitude largely because I thought it would be another short-lived project. I thought it would be like "that was a weird thing that we did," then we'd move on to the next thing. I still didn't believe that it was possible to have a career in music. But I felt good about what we were doing.

Amazingly, before *Superfuzz* was even released, we got our first overseas show. Because Sub Pop owners Bruce and Jonathan had a distribution and licensing deal worked out with a German label called Glitterhouse, they managed to get Mudhoney booked to perform at the Berlin Independence Days Music Festival in Germany. It was a state-sponsored affair, so the band and Bruce and Jonathan were all flown over on the German government's dime. Keep in mind, the only out-of-town shows we'd done by this point were a handful of gigs in Oregon. We'd never toured the United States, much less played overseas. Though there were other bands on Sub Pop at the time, we were the "top dog" and on the brink of releasing our debut, so I guess Sub Pop wanted to show us off.

Still, I couldn't believe we were being flown over for *one* gig. I felt like we were getting away with something. In typical Mudhoney fashion, we didn't take it too seriously. Mark and I even did wacky ballet moves across the stage during the breakdown in "In 'n' Out of Grace." Our performance was professionally filmed and recorded, and it's available on YouTube, so you can see for yourself how flippantly we approached it. It's a great early snapshot of us, and I think playing in Germany gave us more confidence that we were doing the right thing. It didn't seem like a career path or anything like that; it just seemed like a wild adventure.

The trip to Germany, however, was just the beginning. Not long after we returned home to Seattle, Sub Pop released *Superfuzz Bigmuff*, and we set off on a three-week US tour to support it. Sub Pop bought a van for their bands to use for touring, and we were the first ones to christen it. We played dates in the West and Midwest—Denver, Kansas City, Kalamazoo, Lexington, and more—before heading to the East Coast. Obviously, Chicago was a big deal, because that was the home of Touch & Go Records and a lot of bands we liked.

Out there on our own, playing outside the Northwest for the first time, the crowds weren't quite what we were used to. There was definitely a buzz about us (people knew about us from our first single), but paid attendance was generally small, sometimes only twenty or thirty people.

We eventually made it to New York City, where we played at the Pyramid Club, a legendary nightclub in the East Village. While in NYC we also did our first photo shoot with photographer Michael Lavine, in the stairway of the Pyramid Club.

The tour, while an important first step forward, was little more than a warm-up for what was to come. Within days of returning to Seattle, we played one of our biggest shows yet, opening for Sonic Youth and Screaming Trees, a central Washington band featuring vocalist Mark Lanegan that became part of the Seattle scene around that time. We played at the cavernous King Street Station, and immediately embarked on a West Coast tour with the two bands.

Mark and I already felt like we had a bond with Sonic Youth going back to our Green River days, but this tour cemented that relationship. I think Sonic Youth liked being a part of the American underground scene. They weren't spearheading it, but they wanted to support the bands they liked. In the late '80s, if Sonic Youth said you were cool, you were cool. I thought it was pretty fucking amazing that Sonic Youth thought *we* were cool.

We hung out and talked with Thurston Moore because, like us, he had an interest in obscure punk. But while there was a building mutual appreciation with them musically, culturally, there was a distinct gap. Maybe it was because they were a bit older, but while we'd be staying out late, getting stupid drunk, and running around, they were soberly reading books (and being amused by us).

The shows were remarkably big—the biggest shows I'd seen Sonic Youth play. They were supporting their *Daydream Nation* album, and their notoriety was rising. The first few times I saw them at Gorilla Gardens there were three to four hundred people, but we were now playing thousand-capacity joints with them.

After being together for less than a year, I couldn't imagine things getting any better for Mudhoney. We had a single and an EP out on Sub Pop (with a split 7″ with Sonic Youth on the way), a track on an Amphetamine Reptile 7″ compilation, and now we were opening for Sonic Youth. I felt like we were at the epicenter of everything that was cool in underground music, which was all I wanted at the time.

REVOLUTION

SUB POP FIRST MADE ITS MARK ON THE UNDERGROUND music scene with the *Sub Pop 100* compilation in 1986, but when it released the three-EP box set of *Sub Pop 200*, featuring exclusively Northwest artists in December 1988, it helped kick the Seattle music revolution into high gear—particularly the interest in grunge outside the city.

The release party for the compilation, featuring ten of the twenty artists on the set, happened over two nights at the Underground nightclub in the University District. Nirvana had just released their debut 7″, "Love Buzz," via Sub Pop's new Singles Club series, and they were on the first night's bill, which included Tad, Blood Circus, Swallow, and the Thrown Ups—a grunge extravaganza. (Mudhoney had a New Year's Eve date already lined up at the Central, so we didn't play.) The compilation was a who's who of the popular bands in Seattle at the time, and it helped further establish Sub Pop's antihero aesthetic, whose "mascot" was the Loser.

Mudhoney's contribution to *Sub Pop 200* was a cover of "The Rose," a song popularized by Bette Midler in the movie of the same name. We were short on original material—after being together less than a year, we'd released almost everything we'd written to that point—so we dove into Mr. Epp's past. Mr. Epp used to perform

"The Rose" live and it was fairly legendary, because lead vocalist Jo Smitty had such a unique way about him. He was nerdy, super tall, and he spewed out lyrics in an arrhythmic fashion. Mr. Epp's version of "The Rose" was particularly mangled and fucked-up. But we all liked their version, so we decided to do an homage in our own style, with a completely messed-up guitar sound, using a new MXR Blue Box Octave Fuzz pedal I'd bought. Though "The Rose" reflected the irreverent nature of the Seattle music scene, it's not one of my favorite covers of the many we've done over the years.

Another cover on the comp I *did* like, however, was the Fastbacks' version of my Green River tune "Swallow My Pride," which Soundgarden also covered on their *Fopp* EP in August 1988. This was all Bruce Pavitt's idea. He was trying to get the song to be like the grunge "Louie Louie"—a standard or classic that a lot of bands cover. That didn't exactly happen.

Regardless, I was flattered, and since it ended up on a Soundgarden box set, *Echo of Miles*, in 2014, I still get some small royalty payments for writing it. I guess I can thank Bruce's genius for that.

One of Mudhoney's first concerts in '89 was a headlining gig at the Satyricon nightclub in Portland on January 6. For this show we brought along Nirvana, who'd yet to play outside of Washington. In fact, they'd only started playing Seattle the previous year, and I'd seen one of their first gigs in town, opening for Blood Circus at the Vogue in April '88. We'd known bassist Krist Novoselic since he was in high school, when he'd come to Seattle with Melvins, and drummer Chad Channing was another Bainbridge Island musician who'd once played in a band with Soundgarden's Ben Shepherd and had found his way into the Seattle music scene.

I was friendly with Kurt Cobain—we both played Fender Mustang guitars and were both on Sub Pop—but I can't say we were close friends. I think he looked up to Mudhoney, though. Coincidentally, he also used a Super-Fuzz distortion pedal and named *Superfuzz Bigmuff* as one of his all-time favorite records.

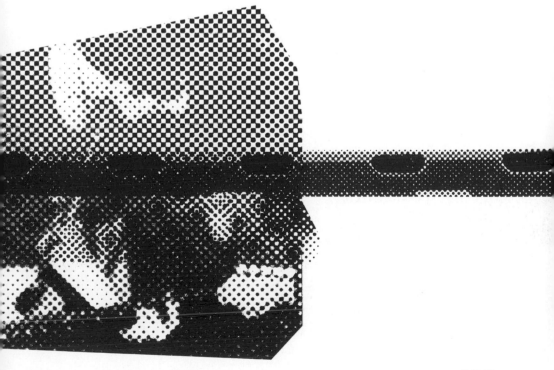

Anyway, we were happy to include Nirvana on the Oregon date. We rolled up to the Satyricon in our van and were stoked to see our band name on the marquee of the club. When Kurt Cobain arrived, though, he wasn't as thrilled with what he saw. "Nir Vona? What the fuck?!" he said with a scowl as he read how his then-unknown band's name had been mangled.

"Nirvana is *not* two fucking words, and there's no 'o' in it!" I still laugh about it. They obviously weren't a household name yet.

A few nights later, back in Seattle, I got a firsthand look at how the major labels in America were attempting to bring America's punk underground into the mainstream. Mudhoney were on a bill at the Underground opening for Danzig, a band fronted by former Misfits and Samhain vocalist Glenn Danzig, and also featuring former D.O.A. and Black Flag drummer Chuck Biscuits.

These two had been entrenched in the United States (and Canadian) punk scene since the early days, and now they were supporting an album issued by Rick Rubin's Def American label and distributed by Geffen/Warner Bros. Predictably, Danzig showed up at the Underground in a tour bus. This was a nightclub, not the Enormodome, but I guess they were already on a rock star tour. We weren't used to that yet. Backstage they were all in their outfits already, and the guitar player was sitting there on a stool doing scales for what seemed like hours. There was even a set of weights backstage that they'd brought. The whole thing seemed contrived. I didn't have much respect for Danzig at that point; the whole rock star thing turned me off.

It turned out to be a reality check for me, though, because this stuff was not just happening with other underground bands we loved—the Replacements, Soul Asylum, and Hüsker Dü all signed to major labels—it was happening close to home. A local DJ, Faith Henschel, had brought Soundgarden to the attention of A&R reps at major labels, and they signed to A&M Records and were touring in their own bus. Even Mother Love Bone were wooed by multiple labels (finally signing with Polygram). Mudhoney were on a completely different trajectory, and between Mother Love Bone's major-label ambitions and our punk rock rejection of such things, we didn't have a shared camaraderie with our former Green River bandmates. There was even an occasional war of words. I think I was quoted as calling them "careerist," which probably didn't sit well with Stone and Jeff, coming from a friend and former bandmate.

But even though Soundgarden and Mother Love Bone were signing to major labels, there was no guarantee they'd find mainstream success with the type of music they were playing. They had cleaned up some of their rough edges—Soundgarden had gone heavy and was being marketed to the metal crowd, and Mother Love Bone went '70s glam rock—but they were still weird and Seattle enough that hit records seemed unlikely.

While some of our friends hopped in bed with major labels, our own label, Sub Pop, pulled off a marketing coup that benefited the entire scene. In February '89, *Melody Maker* (England's influential weekly music magazine) flew over writer Everett True to interview and write about the bands on *Sub Pop 200*. We'd been covered in the local music press and interviewed for zines, but this was something bigger, what I would've considered mainstream press in the United Kingdom.

It turned out to be an amazing article introducing the Seattle scene to the United Kingdom. The UK music press had a reputation for being tastemakers, and getting their stamp of approval was a huge deal. The timing couldn't have been better for us, as *Superfuzz Bigmuff* had been licensed to a label in the United Kingdom, and we were scheduled to embark on a European tour with Sonic Youth in March (starting in England) that would segue into a several-week tour across Europe, mostly on our own. Our first show was in New-castle on March 17, just as Everett's story in *Melody Maker* hit the newsstands, and we didn't return home to Seattle until the middle of May. In between was all manner of bedlam, but on this tour, we established a lot of firsts for the Seattle bands of our era: We were the first to tour Europe, the first to record a John Peel BBC Radio session, the first to get our record in the UK indie charts, and the first to give Europe an up-close look at grunge.

That Newcastle show was also the first (and only) time I've seen Sonic Youth's Thurston Moore drunk. Newcastle is a rough North-ern English city where the bricks aren't red—they're black from the soot in the air. Everything there is black and gray. It looks like you're in the Middle Ages or something. It's also known for its local Newcastle Brown Ale, which Thurston imbibed with gusto with us. It was in keeping with the general insanity of the moment, though, because from the opening note of our first UK show, the crowd was going bonkers. Within the first song, Mark walked out onto the crowd, walking over their heads and shoulders. They seemed ready for whatever we wanted to do. We didn't know what to expect at all. We'd opened for Sonic Youth plenty of times down the West Coast, but this was a way wilder audience; everyone was jumping around and freaking out.

It was nuts, and it was just the beginning. From day one we did a bunch of press, and the journalists were kinda feeling us out. Seattle seemed foreign and exotic to them. Some of the mythmaking had started with Sub Pop—hyping its bands as a bunch of losers, dirt-bags, rednecks, whatever—so the UK press wanted us all to be real working class. Mark and I clearly were not, and we never claimed to be. We were longhaired but claimed to love punk rock, which was confusing to them, because in the United Kingdom, anything from ten years ago (like punk rock) was worthless trash. They also looked

Mudhoney outtake from "You Got It" 7", 1988.

Mudhoney photo shoot at the Pyramid Club, 1988.

Mudhoney on tour in NYC at the Pyramid Club, 1988.

Mudhoney in Europe, spring 1989. That's our long-suffering Dutch soundman/road manager/driver, Erik Mans.

at us funny when we talked about Motörhead (also uncool). We were very comfortable with who we were and the music we liked, and we would talk about it for hours if given the chance.

On the plus side, in England you could go into record stores and buy all these old punk singles for like a buck apiece. So, we were buying all the Buzzcocks and Sex Pistols and Clash and lesser bands we could; they were so cheap!

After a little over a week of getting hyped up in the United Kingdom opening for Sonic Youth, we went over to continental Europe and played a couple more shows with them before striking out on our own for the next several weeks, starting in Germany. Excited about the experience, I kept a tour diary and dutifully wrote a sentence or two about each gig. Revisiting it more than thirty years later, I find it's filled with stuff like:

None of us remember anything about the show. We were told it was a mess. Our clothes were filthy in the morning

Ninety people come. I drink three weizen beers and lose my marbles

Hamburg sucks. Mike from Blind Fish Promotions sucks, and we eat at McDonald's. I cut my hand the next day and get stitches

Those stitches were an ordeal. We were walking around Hamburg, and I guess I tripped as I was stepping off a curb between two parked cars. I put my hand out to grab the car that was right next to me, but it had a broken antenna, and I slit my picking hand wide open. I just kinda held it shut, and I said, "Uh, I think we have to go to the doctor's now."

We were scheduled to meet back up with Sonic Youth and play in Nijmegen in the Netherlands that evening, but after I got stitched up—with a giant bandage on my hand—it seemed unlikely that we would be able to make the five hundred-plus kilometer drive and get there in time. Plus, my bandmates decided to hit the vodka on the journey—our roadie, Erik Mans, was sober and behind the wheel—so when we *did* miraculously arrive at the venue in time to play, none of us were in great shape. Mark, Dan, and Matt were loaded, and I had to sit on the stage and play with a stitched-up paw. It was an unfortunate scenario. Mark had a meltdown, berating the audience for just standing there, and walked off in the early part of the set. We had no idea what he was doing so we kept playing. We didn't get the hint. We were like, *What's up with Mark?* He thought we were gonna follow him off, and we didn't. So, he sheepishly came back out, and we finished the set. I was in so much pain I could barely play.

The rest of the tour was alternately bizarre and fun, or boring. We were in Europe too long. We did eleven shows in the Netherlands alone (because that's where our booking agent was based), and we didn't have enough material to headline. Sometimes the crowds, even as small as a few dozen people, wouldn't let us leave until we played our set twice. Other times we would jam on the Spacemen 3's song "Revolution" for fifteen minutes. We played a festival in the Alps where most of the crowd was passed out drunk; we played a squat with a dirt floor in Italy; and we played a ton of shows in Germany where Glitterhouse Records (our German label) was based, and the crowds were excited about us. At one show in Italy, in the coastal resort town of Rimini, we were fed dinner by the family of the promoter, who owned a hotel/resort. It was the first Italian meal I'd had, and it was incredible. It was like a twelve-course meal, and food just kept coming, one delicious thing after another. We were full after the first three pasta dishes. It was one of the greatest meals of my life.

Nine weeks traveling in a tiny van full of gear is grueling, no matter how good the food or beer or crowds might occasionally be, and we collectively lost our minds at week six. So, it was only fitting that we should cap things off with a return to the United Kingdom to ratchet up the insanity that much more. The first thing on our agenda was to record a session for tastemaking BBC Radio 1 DJ John Peel's show. We recorded our four-song session a week before Soundgarden recorded theirs, giving us the honor of being the first Seattle band from our scene to do so. It was a big deal at the time. It felt like a real feather in our cap, something that none of us would've ever imagined happening. The recording session itself wasn't exactly inspiring, though we were excited to do it. The engineer was Dale "Buffin" Griffin, the former drummer of Mott the Hoople, whose first album I loved. He, however, didn't much care for us. I think he was irritated by our amateurishness. He was like a teacher who was over it. He did a fine job on the recording, but we were expected to get in, get it done, get out, and shut up. It was real workaday and done quickly—completely live, with no overdubs. And Buffin was a bitter, middle-aged guy in a white lab coat, obviously not loving it. It was kinda perfect for the BBC.

Our earlier dates in the United Kingdom were the perfect setup for the last week of shows we had scheduled there. There was so much hype about us opening for Sonic Youth that our own shows were now way bigger and sold out. And that's when they got out-of-hand crazy. The only gig Soundgarden ever opened for Mudhoney was held at the School for Oriental and African Studies in London on May 12, 1989, and it turned into a riot while we were playing. People were already amped up from our first distorted notes, and at some point, Mark invited the crowd to come onstage, and they started rushing up. But things started collapsing, because the venue had the sound monitors sitting on tables in front of the stage, and they couldn't support the weight of the crowd clamoring to get onstage. There was nonstop chaos as we urged the massive crowd to move back to the floor so that no one would get hurt. After a lot of delays, we managed to finish our set, and the show ended up as front-page news the next day. The English like big, dramatic events, ones that they can call a riot. The Jesus and Mary Chain had their riot, and we had our riot. We couldn't have asked for better publicity.

WHEN TOMORROW HITS

EVEN THOUGH WE'D GONE DOWN A STORM ON OUR FIRST
visit to the United Kingdom, with the music media falling all over
themselves to interview us, things were different back in Seattle.
We had the support of *The Rocket* (which used to run Bruce Pavitt's
Sub Pop column earlier in the '80s) and *Backlash*, but the "mainstream media," the local papers, didn't want to know about us. That
started to change, though, once they saw Mudhoney and some of
the other bands getting international coverage, like the write-up in
Melody Maker. Somehow it legitimized what was happening right
in their backyard. I guess it took someone else telling them about
it for them to think that Seattle's music scene was any good. We
had to go to England and get a lot of hype there before Patrick Mac-
Donald, the music critic at the *Seattle Times*, would mention us.
But as bands started putting records out, it was hard to continue
to ignore what was going on.

Another touchstone moment happened not long after Mudhoney returned from Europe. Sub Pop had the brilliant idea to book
the nearly two thousand–seat Moore Theater June 9, 1989, to show-
case three of its bands: Nirvana, Tad, and Mudhoney, for what it was
calling "Lame Fest," in typical self-deprecating fashion. I thought
Jonathan and Bruce were nuts to put that show at the Moore. It was

too big. Mudhoney had played very few all-ages shows at this point, so I couldn't imagine that as headliners we could fill a place of that size. It had been years since all the grunge bands that grew out of the Metropolis and Gorilla Gardens scene had played all-ages shows. We were now all twenty-one or older and had been typically playing bars, so we had no idea if younger people even knew or cared about us.

Apparently, a lot of them did! Tickets were six dollars in advance or seven dollars at the door, and it was nearly a sellout. People were going apeshit the whole time. The local press could no longer ignore us, and I don't mean just Mudhoney. Tad, Nirvana, Swallow, Blood Circus, Skin Yard, Soundgarden, Screaming Trees, the Accüsed, and yes, even Mother Love Bone all had records out or coming out, and clearly there was an appetite for the kind of music we were playing, both locally and abroad. This gig was the first significant foreshadowing of what was to come.

Mudhoney were on the upward trajectory, for sure. Once we got rolling in early '88, we were constantly busy: recording, playing locally, and touring. It felt like we had something good going. Personally, though, I felt a little conflicted. I'd never felt like this was my calling, so I always had a bit of indifference to the whole trip. I thought we were succeeding because . . . we didn't care that much about succeeding. Our indifference and lack of professionalism were somehow working in our favor. And always in the back of my mind was the promise I'd made to my parents that once I did this for a couple years, I'd go back to school. So, this felt like a lark. But our devil-may-care attitude seemed to fuel our popularity.

From my point of view, this attitude seemed to be present to some degree in the entire scene. Sure, the defining musical aspect of grunge is loud, heavy guitars coming through punk rock, but there was irreverence, too, with all the bands. Some were more serious than others, but there was always a bit of a wink to a lot of it. And I think Mark is a large part of that, because he's always had a nudge-nudge, wink-wink attitude. Not to discount his lyrics, but there's always this sensibility of, *Ah, how important is this really?* Soundgarden poked fun at the scene and their own label with the song "Sub Pop Rock City" on *Sub Pop 200*, and even though I wasn't a fan of Mother Love Bone's music, vocalist Landrew always brought a sly sense of humor to his band's overt '70s-isms.

Since Green River's split, Mother Love Bone and Mudhoney had followed somewhat parallel paths (though *definitely not* musically), both issuing EPs as our first release—ours on Sub Pop and theirs on a fake "indie" label called Stardog that was being distributed by their actual label, Polygram. Because we were working with Sub Pop before we'd even played our first show, we had a jump on things, and *Superfuzz* came out nearly six months before Mother Love Bone's EP *Shine*. In fact, we were off touring Europe when their record was released, something that I think bummed out my old bandmate Jeff. He saw Mark and me going off on all these adventures and getting some acclaim overseas, and his label wasn't offering MLB the same opportunities. Jeff was really frustrated because he just wanted to go out and play. Unlike us, they were beholden to a major label that had forked over a lot of cash to sign them. It was a tough lesson, but I think Jeff and Stone learned a lot from their first dealings with a major label that would come in handy later.

None of us in Mudhoney came back from our first European tour with a wad of cash in our pockets, but the band was generating *some* money, and between that and my job at ACT Theater, I could move out of my parents' house on Mercer Island and get a place with Dan. Our first stop was a scummy Central District basement apartment in a building owned by Russ and Janet Battaglia of Fallout Records,

Rock Mecca with Jason Finn, Bill Campbell, and a cat I don't remember having.

the cool skate shop/record store/comic shop/record label on Capitol Hill. We were only there for a couple months before rooms opened up in a group house where Ed Fotheringham lived near Lake Union, just north of downtown. We dubbed this place the Rock Mecca, and it was legendary during the late '80s and early '90s. A lot of bands that came through town stayed there: Babes in Toyland, Cows, God Bullies. It was a party house.

It was perfect for Dan and me. In this era, it was super cheap to live in Seattle, which is such a big part of why we could be bums and play in bands. My rent was $200 a month for the three years I lived at the Rock Mecca. When I was on tour, I would sublease my room to some other guy who needed a place to stay for a while. There was a rotating cast of musicians living in the house. Artist Whiting Tennis and his band, Big Tube Squeezer, preceded us, and when Dan and I arrived, Ed and Steve LaRose (another Mercer Islander like myself) from Love + Respect were living there too. In the ensuing few years, Jason Finn (ex-Skin Yard, Love Battery, and future Presidents of the United States drummer), Kevin Whitworth (ex-Crisis Party, Love Battery), and Bill Campbell (ex-Chemistry Set, Flop) would all live in the house. It was an exciting place to be for a few years. We were young, and every day had something to do with music: We were going to a show, somebody in the house was playing their own show, or we were contemplating side projects together. In fact, my first outside-Mudhoney project was playing slide guitar on the Love + Respect 7″ and album, recorded with Jack Endino and released, respectively, in '89 and '90, via Penultimate Records and Musical Tragedies (a.k.a. eMpTy Records).

My day-to-day life was a lot of fun. I bought a bike when I got home from our first European tour, and that was my main mode of transportation. I was still working at ACT Theater and would take some evening shifts every week. After having spent the better part of the spring touring, though, I wasn't as inclined to go out to shows as much as I had in the past. I also wasn't skateboarding much anymore, either. I'd brought my skateboard with me on Mudhoney's first US tour in '88 hoping to find cool places to skate along the way, but that didn't happen. The only time I got on my skateboard was when Thurston Moore and the Sonic Youth crew took us to the Beastie Boys' warehouse in Southern California, and I rode a little mini ramp they had set up there. That was the last tour I'd bring a skateboard on. Skating disappeared from my life, and music completely took over.

Living at the Rock Mecca was conducive to finishing the songs for Mudhoney's first full-length album. In those days, I used a Harmony Stratotone for songwriting, a twenty-four-dollar guitar that was a cheap '60s electric. (They're now worth hundreds of dollars.) It was the perfect guitar for writing punk and Mudhoney riffs, because it has a semi-hollow body—no f-holes or anything—just a cheap plywood body. The pick guard only has three screws holding it on, so it rattles, giving it a sort of built-in distortion effect if it's not plugged in. I used this electric guitar, played acoustically, to write a lot of early Mudhoney stuff. Songs came quickly in those days. Mark would write some riffs, Lukin brought a lot of riffs to the table, and I'd have a couple too. We were good at piecing things together—we'd just bang out a song. We didn't have to labor to come up with material, as evidenced by the fact that we had already been playing live some of the tracks that we were about to record on tour. We didn't write any differently or build it up to be anything more than the next batch of songs.

Superfuzz Bigmuff had unexpectedly become a much bigger deal than we'd ever imagined it would. It shot onto the UK Indie Rock charts and stayed there for the better part of a year. And in North

America, the original Sub Pop version sold tens of thousands of copies. So, in the summer of '89 we were faced with the task of following up our "introduction"—the first 7″ and *Superfuzz*—with a full-length album. It was a strange situation, and we were in a position that we weren't used to: Rather than trying to win people over, we were trying to show that we weren't a flash in the pan.

Naturally, we booked a week with Jack Endino and went back into Reciprocal. I'd gotten used to working with Jack—it seemed such a natural fit. He was the go-to guy for most Seattle bands at the time. In fact, one of the songs we'd track for the album, "You Got It," had been recorded with Jack previously in a different session (and Sub Pop had released it as a single). Plus, the main riff of that song was taken from an '86 Thrown Ups jam called "Bucking Retards" (I know it's terrible; talk to Ed in the mid-'80s about that) we recorded with Jack.

We didn't spend a lot of time in the studio, as we had these songs nailed down already. Some were the earliest songs we'd written, predating *Superfuzz*, so we were only in Reciprocal for maybe a week to record what would be our self-titled album, *Mudhoney*. For the most part, we had everything good to go. The timing of the session, however, turned out to be very unfortunate for me.

My mom, who was employed at Boeing, had suffered a couple of seizures while at work. After going through a battery of tests, they discovered she had a brain tumor that needed to be operated on immediately—the same week we were in the studio. The tumor was big, but fortunately it was benign. When removing brain tumors, they don't put you under; they give you a local anesthetic, saw your skull open, and remove the thing. So, just a few hours after her surgery, she was sitting up talking with us in the hospital. It was surreal. She was fine, but it was nerve-racking to think about my mom's skull being cracked open. They stapled her back together, and she recuperated at home.

In retrospect, I don't like *Mudhoney* as much as some of the other albums. We still play a lot of the songs on there, so it's not just about the material itself. Maybe because it wasn't all freshly written material, it felt a little flat to our ears. We didn't add anything to what we'd already done on *Superfuzz* (which is a more dynamic set of songs). It was just more of the same. I think it was a slightly missed opportunity to make a better album, and that's all on us as a band.

We didn't have a lot of time to reflect on how *Mudhoney* turned out before we were back on the road. The album (including a nifty limited-edition version with a gatefold front) was set for release in November, and we had the whole summer to keep the momentum going toward that.

I was more than a year into my request that my parents "gimme two years," and things were happening with Mudhoney that I'd never anticipated. Though I was keeping my parents abreast of everything going on, it didn't mean much to them, because they had no frame of reference. However, when we started to get press in the *Seattle Times* (because *Superfuzz* got on the charts in the United Kingdom in '89, and Lame Fest was a huge local phenomenon, and the *Mudhoney* album came out), *then* my parents took notice. *That* they appreciated and understood, and our success, and what we'd accomplished, started to sink in a little more with them.

After playing several shows in Washington that summer, we headed south for a short California tour with Boston trio the Lemonheads (fronted by Evan Dando) in September. The Lemonheads were another band that came from the punk scene, and not long after we played these shows with them, they signed to a major label and had some success playing mellower college rock in the '90s. The San Diego date we played with them was notable for the fact that one of the opening bands, Bad Radio, was fronted by a guy named Eddie Vedder. The next time we'd see Eddie would be in Seattle under very different circumstances, but in '89 he was just another singer in an opening band we likely wouldn't remember.

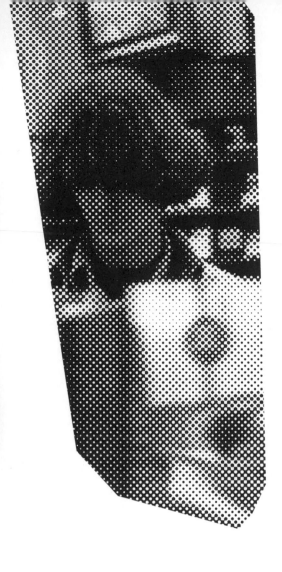

COME TO MIND

AFTER *MUDHONEY* WAS RELEASED ON SUB POP IN NOVEM-
ber, we made our *second* trip of 1989 to the United Kingdom and
Europe—which was remarkable for any underground band at the time
and definitely unheard of within the Seattle scene. One of the first
shows, at the London Astoria theater, was a redux of the Seattle Lame
Fest—same three band lineup—but this time called "Lame Fest UK"
(original, huh?). The reception was equally enthusiastic.

Tad and Nirvana had been doing their own European tour
prior to this show, so it was good to see some friendly faces when
we arrived. Though Mudhoney were still getting a lot of media attention, some journalists were starting to call bullshit on the way Sub
Pop was marketing its bands: Tad were the demented lumberjack
butchers; Cobain and Nirvana were the small-town white trash.
Some journalist called out Mudhoney for being college-educated
suburban kids. I mean, there was a definite split in the Mudhoney
ranks: Dan had a super difficult childhood and barely finished high
school; Matt was from a small logging town, where his dad was a
fireman and drove a school bus and his mom was the lunch lady.
But Mark and I never shied away from saying we're from the Seattle
suburbs (Kirkland and Mercer Island, respectively). For some reason, though, we were seen as the fakers of the Sub Pop stable, while

others, like Tad Doyle of Tad, a very educated, classically trained musician, escaped this scrutiny (though he may have once had a job as a butcher for all I know).

Our second European tour was much better and shorter than the first—only four weeks between the United Kingdom and mainland Europe. And we only played *four* dates in the Netherlands this time. The venues were bigger, and the crowds were larger and more enthusiastic. We also had more material, so we were never forced to play our entire set twice. By Christmas I was back in Seattle, and I arrived home with a fat wad of cash: $5,000 for a month's work. (Keep in mind, I was paying only $200 a month for rent.) I went to the bank to deposit it, and the teller was somebody I went to high school with. Not sure what he was thinking, but I was like, *Yeah, it's weird—I don't know, I play guitar in a band.* I think we as a band have taken a lot of what we've done in stride—the accolades, the press, whatever. I feel like our heads have always been pretty level.

It was quite clear at the start of 1990 that the promise I'd made to my parents that I'd go back to school after two years of doing Mudhoney was going to be a hard one to keep. Obviously, none of us could have predicted Mudhoney's trajectory and how quickly everything happened. And things would continue to ramp up even more in 1990, such a whirlwind year that I started to lose track of what was going on in Seattle.

We celebrated the start of Mudhoney's third year as a band with our first trip to Australia in February. Mark and I were so excited to go to the birthplace of so many of our favorite bands. The Scientists had had a profound influence on Mudhoney, and we've paid tribute to them a lot over the years; we can't hide from that one. I don't think we *sound* like the Scientists, but I think we took some of their Stooge-oid obsession from that *Blood Red River* EP and amplified it. We also tried to look like them. As it turned out, Australia had a real affinity for Mudhoney, as local label Au Go Go was licensing our records from Sub Pop and they were doing well.

This first trip to Australia was also when we recorded two songs for our next Sub Pop single: "You're Gone" and "Thorn." We did a quick session at Electric Avenue Studios in Sydney with Kent Steedman (of the Celibate Rifles), who was a good friend of ours. He came to Seattle a lot and would stay with us when he was passing through, following a guru somewhere in rural Washington.

The other song on that single, "You Make Me Die," was a Billy Childish cover we recorded the backing track for in Seattle with Jack Endino, and then had Billy put vocals on and mix in England. It was really cool to be able to work with other musicians we admired and were influenced by.

After the high of our first tour Down Under, we returned to a very dark scene in Seattle. On March 19, 1990, Andrew "Landrew" Wood of Mother Love Bone (and ex-Malfunkshun) had been pronounced dead after overdosing on heroin, just days before the band's major label debut album, *Apple*, was set for release. Sub Pop's Jonathan Poneman picked us up from the airport and broke the news. It was a sobering moment for all of us. Heroin had been quietly creeping into the scene, and this tragedy should have been a wake-up call for everyone. Sadly, it wasn't. I wasn't close friends with Landrew, but I felt terrible for my good friends Stone and Jeff, who lost a close friend and bandmate, and whose major label aspirations and ambitions were dealt a horrific blow.

Apple was released the following July, with what must have been the saddest record release party ever.

Mudhoney laid low for a few months the spring after the Australian tour because we knew the coming summer would be busy with two trips to the United Kingdom and Europe. Having learned our lesson about longer, more grueling tours the hard way, we preferred to do tours no longer than six weeks. Sandwiched between those two jaunts would be a short West Coast tour (with Billy Childish's band, Thee Headcoats) that would coincide with the release of our new Sub Pop single, which featured Billy's contributions. Though I originally figured that Mudhoney would flame out (or I'd lose interest) after a couple of years, the momentum was heading in the opposite direction. We somehow found ourselves as the leaders of a movement. Though Soundgarden had already released their major label debut and were touring with other major-label bands like Danzig, Voivod, and Faith No More, they had been pried away from any association with grunge by their label and were being squarely marketed to the metal crowd. Bassist Hiro Yamamoto had departed and was replaced by Jason Everman, who'd previously done a short stint as Nirvana's second guitarist. They were on a whole different trip.

Nirvana's popularity was also surging locally, but they had trouble keeping a solid lineup beyond bassist Krist Novoselic and Kurt Cobain. Their drummer, Chad Channing, had recently departed, so they asked Dan to record the song "Sliver" with them at Reciprocal on July 11, before Mudhoney left for a short tour with Thee Headcoats.

The highlight of Mudhoney's summer, though, was our biggest gig yet: performing at England's three-day Reading Festival, hosted by John Peel, on August 24, 1990. This was another first for bands from our scene, and it was an unbelievable experience playing to tens of thousands of people. It's hard to even describe how big the crowd seems. You look out, and it's a sea of people; it just keeps on going, over the hills and beyond. It was really fun, and the backstage area was cool, with all the bands hanging out. It seemed like the Reading organizers had a good finger on the pulse of the underground, so they got these cool bands that not a lot of people were

In my element, circa 1990! I still love searching out record stores and records.

aware of yet. Some of the smaller bands played in a little tent on the "second stage," but some, like our friends in Thee Hypnotics, played the main stage. On the day we played, the Cramps were the headliners over Faith No More, Nick Cave and the Bad Seeds, us, An Emotional Fish, and Mega City Four. We were originally scheduled to play after Jane's Addiction, who reportedly canceled because they weren't happy with the order of the lineup.

Another highlight of that show was finally getting to meet DJ John Peel, who was emceeing (or acting as compere, as the Brits would say). He was a very shy man. I was introduced to him and was probably fawning a bit too much for his liking, and he was like, *Take me back to my record booth over there.* He seemed like a very nice guy, but he didn't seem to want all the adulation; he just liked playing records. He was a huge proponent of what was going on in Seattle, so he deserves a ton of credit for playing our and other Sub Pop bands' records and introducing us to Radio 1 listeners long before a lot of people in the United States knew about us. I have to think that he was responsible in a big way for the crowds we were drawing.

We returned to Seattle at the beginning of September only to find Nirvana had lured away our drummer. Their "Sliver" single, which featured Dan on the A side, had been released by Sub Pop at the beginning of the month, and they had a gig lined up at the Motorsports Garage in Seattle with the Melvins that was going to be a big deal. Dan "joined" the band and played the show on September 22, 1990, amid rumors that Mudhoney were breaking up because I was "going back to school." This rumor wasn't 100 percent inaccurate, but it was premature, since we still had another tour of Australia booked for later in the year and were eventually planning to record another album.

What Dan didn't know was that Nirvana had Dave Grohl waiting in the wings, and he would become their permanent drummer not long after the Motorsports gig. After all of two weeks in Nirvana, they spit out Dan in favor of Grohl.

Dan wasn't the only member of Mudhoney that Nirvana had their sights set on. Not long after Grohl joined the band, I was at a party in Tacoma at Krist and his wife Shelli's house. At one point, Krist and Grohl cornered me and asked me if I wanted to be the second guitar player in Nirvana.

"What?" I responded incredulously. "No! You guys are so much better as a three-piece."

I meant it too. I'd seen them with Jason Everman as a second guitarist and I didn't think it made them any better. The second guitar didn't contribute *anything*.

"Well, Kurt wants to have some of the guitar responsibilities off him," Krist said, which I could understand. Still, I didn't know Grohl at all, and also, why wasn't Kurt asking me? Kurt might have been able to convince me, theoretically, but my point of view was it's a magical thing to be an actual ripping three-piece, and they were one of them.

Anyway, Krist didn't give me any real arguments that day as to why I should join, and from my perspective, it would have been a lateral move, or even a step down. (Looking back on it quite a few years later, that was a decision that *maybe* I should have been more thoughtful about at the time.) Adding to the awkwardness of the whole thing was the fact that they'd kicked out Dan for Grohl, and Dan was my roommate (and bandmate) at the time, so I felt loyal to him. And the fact of the matter was that I *was* enrolled back at Seattle Central Community College and intending to continue with my studies. I figured, if I'm gonna play music—and I wasn't convinced I was going to in the long term—I like playing music with Mudhoney.

Mudhoney started work in earnest on our second full-length, *Every Good Boy Deserves Fudge*, in late 1990, and this time it would be without Jack Endino behind the board. Our default as a band had always been recording with Jack at Reciprocal, but after we were less than thrilled with the results of *Mudhoney*—through no fault of Jack's—we wanted to explore different options. This search for a different sound had led to a false start the previous May when we went into the Music Source with Steve Fisk, who'd recorded Screaming Trees albums in the past, and we laid down a handful of tracks. The Music Source was a 24-track studio, and honestly I didn't like the sound of that shit either. Twenty-four tracks sounded too clean. We were changing a little bit at this time, and this sound didn't suit the direction we wanted to go in. (These recordings were forgotten by everyone involved—band, label, engineer—for decades, thanks to them being mislabeled, until they were unearthed in 2021.)

After that initial misstep with Steve Fisk at the Music Source in May, I realized I wanted to work in a studio that had *fewer* tracks. I was into lo-fi music at the time and wanted Mudhoney's next record to reflect that. I found inspiration in a record by Tacoma garage rockers Girl Trouble, who'd recorded part of their 1990 album *Thrillsphere* at Conrad Uno's Egg Studio in Seattle's Ballard neighborhood (and released it on Conrad's PopLlama label). Egg hadn't been used by the grunge crowd at all—Jack Endino at Reciprocal was the man—so when I called Conrad about Mudhoney potentially recording our next album there in the new year, his response was pretty funny.

"Hey, this is Steve from Mudhoney," I said. "We wanna come in and record at Egg with you." After a bit of a pause (maybe he thought this was a prank), he started laughing.

"Why?"

That's literally all he said: "Why?"

That was the right answer to me. I thought, *OK, this guy could be our guy.*

Egg was a modest 8-track studio. Plenty of records and demos had been recorded there, but they tended toward the garage rock and power pop crowd—Young Fresh Fellows, the Fastbacks, the Mono Men, Dharma Bums. For me, though, it wasn't necessarily about who had recorded there; it was about the aesthetic and sound we could get from the studio. Recording in a studio with only eight tracks, we would have to be a little more precise with what we were trying to do. There was something about the limitations of it that suited me. You don't get bogged down in too many possibilities. You have to think, *What is most important to this song?* There's a discipline to it that appealed to me. And I was into the simplistic, rough garage sound that you could only achieve in a small studio, so it pushed all my buttons. But before we committed to recording the whole album, we wanted to test out the sound to see if we were *all* going to be happy with it.

We booked time with Conrad in December 1990 and gave it a spin playing a bunch of punk rock covers, rather than the originals we intended to eventually record. Dan and I had been buying all these great UK punk singles every time we toured Europe, like the Jam, UK Subs, the Damned, and so many more. We learned a bunch of these songs (and other punk favorites) and spent a day blasting them out at Egg to see if we liked the sound, and if we liked working with Conrad. He's a mellow guy, with a great sense of humor. He would go with it, whatever we were doing. Conrad was very good at recording stuff, too, but he had a much more laid-back, keep-the-vibe-good approach. Like, *If that's what you want to sound like, I'll record it.*

Another thing he had dialed in was making things sound fresh, with a bit of a vintage sound to them. He knew how to make the most of the limited number of tracks in the studio, and his style suited the direction we wanted to go in. We were also more self-assured as a band when we started recording with Conrad and were aiming for more of a garage vibe that I think he got. It was perfect. This was a crucial moment for us as a band. If we made another album like *Mudhoney*, fans might have lost interest, and things might have cooled down for us. We needed to keep moving forward, and Conrad helped us do that.

INTO THE DRINK

FILMMAKER DAVE MARKEY TITLED HIS 1992 SONIC YOUTH documentary *1991: The Year Punk Broke.* For Mudhoney, it could have just as easily been the year that we almost broke up. This was the year a lot of shit went crazy for us, our friends, and Seattle in general.

Even though we were sort of unofficially on hiatus while I was at school, we set aside a little bit of time early in the year to record our second Sub Pop album, *Every Good Boy Deserves Fudge*, with Conrad Uno. Because I was attending classes at Seattle Central Community College, we weren't playing any gigs or touring for the first half of the year. There were definite questions about our long-term future, largely because I wasn't necessarily committed to making Mudhoney *my* long-term future. With things up in the air, Dan started playing drums for Screaming Trees, whose major label debut, *Uncle Anesthesia*, was released on Epic Records at the end of January. He'd recorded a couple of cover tunes with them at Egg that they'd used on a promo single, and in March he embarked on their two-month-plus tour of the United States.

When the tour wrapped up in May and he returned to Seattle, Dan called me out on my ambivalence regarding Mudhoney. He told me flat out that he wanted clarity about what I planned to do. He made it clear that Mudhoney were *his* priority, but if it wasn't going to be mine, he was going to continue to play with Screaming Trees. I didn't want this to be the way Mudhoney ended. We'd recorded an album with Conrad Uno that I loved (and is still one of my favorites), and it seemed like a bad idea to bail on the band at this point. I'd gotten into Mudhoney thinking it was a short-term thing, but I was constantly challenged to reassess this stance. Even if I thought what we were doing wasn't going to be a career, there was no reason I couldn't ride it out and see where it took us. In two-plus years, we'd already been to the United Kingdom, Europe, and Australia multiple times, and it didn't seem like our star was fading. I'd had a blast, and it seemed like there were more adventures to be had on the horizon. So, this was when Mudhoney became my full-time job and sole source of income for the next decade.

Unfortunately, I wasn't the only one in the band whose commitment was in question. Mark had been using heroin, all the way back to his Green River days, after I'd left the band. I had been alerted to his drug use in '86 by a mutual friend who was concerned about him. Even though Mark and I were close friends, I had no idea he was using—I was naive about drugs. I didn't talk to him about it at the time; we were young and not very good at heavy issues. But it started to become problematic in Mudhoney.

For the most part, he wouldn't use when we were on the road (although he did overdose once in New York), but when we were home, he would disappear. We didn't have the same hang-out-and-play-records-together thing anymore. He slept a lot, and he had this other crowd of people that did drugs. Our lives were different. I was young, living in a group house with a bunch of fun people, and riding my bike all around the city. Mark just seemed like he was holed up in his apartment. He would sometimes call, but it was impossible to have a phone conversation with him, because it felt like minutes in between words sometimes. He was literally nodding out, and since I never did drugs, I couldn't spot when people were high.

It also affected our songwriting. It affected *how* songs got written. Because Dan and I lived together, sometimes we would play around and put together song ideas on our own. This was a creative time for me, and I was writing a lot. (I even wrote an entire album of folkie songs that I was singing, which has been lost to the ages.) Mark wasn't really writing and when it came to recording sessions, he was always the last guy to get there. It was also getting harder and harder to go on tour, because he would get dopesick and go into withdrawal at the beginning of every tour. We went on tour with him when he was not doing well a couple times, and I would throw him in the back of the van where he would sleep.

We finally did something of an intervention before going on tour at that time—tried to get him to clean up *before* we left, so we didn't have to deal with all that drama on the road. I didn't want to tell him what to do, but my feeling was: *If you want to be a junkie, you can be a junkie, but it's gonna change how we operate and what happens. We can either go on tour or not go on tour, but it's up to you.* He agreed to go into detox, but not rehab—so I don't think he was completely ready to give up heroin yet.

Though heroin use became associated with the grunge scene at some point, it definitely wasn't part of the backdrop for the mainstream movie *Singles*, which was Hollywood's portrayal of what was happening in Seattle. Written and directed by Cameron Crowe (husband of Heart's Nancy Wilson), *Singles* featured cameos by Tad Doyle, Pearl Jam, Alice in Chains, and others in the Seattle music scene. Though it was released in late 1992—*after* Nirvana, Soundgarden, and Pearl Jam had already had massive success—it was actually being filmed in the summer of 1991, right as we were releasing *Every Good Boy Deserves Fudge* and before things went completely bonkers in Seattle. The irony for me about a movie being made that was set in the grunge scene was that I was already starting to feel *over* the grunge hype (*before* all those bands hit it big later in the year). You can clearly hear this on *EGBDF*, which was way less grungy, more garage rock-inspired, and even featured a Farfisa organ and harmonica on it.

Anyway, we'd seen the *Singles* film crews around town, and we'd heard the scuttlebutt about the movie, but no one involved had reached out to us, even though the fictional band in the movie, Citizen Dick, had a song called "Touch Me I'm Dick," a parody of our first single. So, we took matters into our own hands. We went with Bruce Pavitt to Cameron Crowe's office and said, "Mudhoney needs to be on the soundtrack." He agreed, and we gave him "Overblown," a song that reflected what we saw happening to the Seattle grunge scene. Even before Nirvana, Pearl Jam, et al. went to number one, Seattle was getting a lot of attention, and we were one of the bands at the forefront. Also, our pushiness in getting Mudhoney on the *Singles* soundtrack eventually resulted in the first gold record the members of Mudhoney ever received, after it sold more than five hundred thousand copies in the United States.

When *Every Good Boy Deserves Fudge* was released in the summer of '91, it rapidly became our bestselling album. We were doing pretty well for an indie band. In fact, we temporarily saved Sub Pop's bacon because of the brisk sales. They had "overextended" themselves and owed a lot of people a lot of money. This became a running joke in Seattle (not exactly funny to the people who were owed money) to the degree that Sub Pop had T-shirts printed that said, "What part of 'we don't have any money' don't you understand?"

The Rocket ran a cover story on Sub Pop's financial woes with the headline of "Sub Plop." The label was selling a lot of records,

Mudhoney's *Every Good Boy Deserves Fudge* Music Source demo, 1990. One song came out several years later on a flexi-disc in a magazine. The "instr[umental] for [Steve] Fisk to fuck" was issued on the 2021 *EGBDF* reissue as "Flowers of Industry."

With Ed Fotheringham at the Rock Mecca.

Mudhoney tour poster with Superchunk and Gas Huffer, September 18, 1991. A very fun tour!

but Bruce and Jon were apparently also spending a lot of money, and they didn't seem to be keeping very good track of how much was going out versus what was coming in. It was a tightrope act they were doing at the time. I know the money we were bringing in helped them keep going, but we also thought they should be paying us more frequently than they were. We would often have to go down to Sub Pop and demand our royalty checks. We were very forgiving of them, because they were the perfect label for us, and because we were friends with them. They helped immeasurably in getting us going, but the cracks in their business were starting to show.

My own personal interest in grunge, the music Sub Pop had built their empire on, was starting to waver. Which was ironic, as it was about to become bigger than anyone could have imagined. I was continuing to discover other music (especially folk), and I was into the early '90s garage rock scene. I felt most at home at the smaller shows. It was a fun thing to do.

I was also playing in the Sad and Lonely(s) with Ed and drummer Joe Culver (from Big Tube Squeezer), and in the summer of '91, we recorded an EP with Conrad Uno at Egg, with Dan "producing."

Mark and I also had the idea of making a record with Tim Kerr (of Poison 13 and the Big Boys), one of our musical idols we'd met while in Austin, Texas. Together we formed the Monkeywrench, with me playing bass, Mark singing, Tim on guitar, drummer Martin Bland (from Australian weirdos Lubricated Goat), and Tom Price (former U-Men guitarist who was also in Gas Huffer). We recorded an album, *Clean as a Broke-Dick Dog* (which Sub Pop released in 1992) and even managed to play a couple shows in Seattle when everyone was in town. Even though Mudhoney were selling better than ever, riding the grunge craze, my attention was being drawn elsewhere.

Still, Mudhoney had an album to promote, and that meant more touring. Before we headed back over to the United Kingdom, we played one of our strangest concerts ever, opening for '80s Canadian hard rocker Aldo Nova at a free "Pain in the Grass" concert at the Seattle Center's Mural Amphitheater. This would be the first time my parents saw me play with Mudhoney. It was a free gig, outside during the daytime, so they didn't have to go into some seedy nightclub late at night. I'm quite sure they didn't like the music, but they got a good sense of how popular we were. The thousands who had assembled for the show were clearly *our* crowd, not Aldo Nova's, as evidenced by the fact that most left after we finished.

The opening band for our UK tour was Courtney Love's band, Hole. We were both still on independent labels, and we both had ties to the Northwest, so it was a good fit in a lot of ways. They weren't *our* choice for the tour, but we got to be friends with all of them and we had a great time.

Courtney was a tireless self-promoter. I'd met her previously at a Hole show in Seattle, and I got her complete resume in the first five minutes. She knew who I was, and she gave me a very prepared backstory of her life: how she'd worked as a stripper in Japan and Alaska, how her dad worked for the Grateful Dead, getting her first guitar from Fred and Toody of Dead Moon, and her connection with Kat Bjelland of Babes in Toyland.

I liked Courtney, but she was *a lot*. I came home one day to the Rock Mecca house (after the tour), and there was a note taped to the wall, scrawled on the back of a ragged piece of cardboard ripped from a Schmidt beer Sport Pack. It said, "Steve, Courtney Love called today and asked if she and her band can stay here next weekend. No. Love, Ed."

Not long after we returned from our UK dates, we embarked on a North American tour to support *Every Good Boy*. It was during this time that records from three Seattle bands were released within weeks of each other: Pearl Jam's *Ten* (August 27), Nirvana's *Nevermind* (September 24), and Soundgarden's *Badmotorfinger* (October 8). The Seattle explosion began in earnest. We weren't there to witness the initial local reaction, but grunge's mainstream popularity—as well as our own rising star—was manifesting itself in other ways.

Even though we'd played LA plenty of times before, our October 4, 1991, show at the Hollywood Palace, a large LA venue, was particularly notable. We were filming a promotional video for our song "Who You Drivin' Now" with Dave Markey, the director behind *1991: The Year Punk Broke*. Adding to the merriment, we had two former Black Flag vocalists, Keith Morris (also of Circle Jerks) and Dez Cadena, who had individually jammed with us on Black Flag covers in the past, but never both at the same show. There were also a bunch of record label people there, because that was when all the movers and shakers wanted to see us and potentially sign us.

Backstage was a zoo, and in that crowd was our fellow (ex-) Seattleite Duff McKagan, whose band Guns N' Roses had just released two double albums, *Use Your Illusion I* and *II*, in September. He was with this very Sunset Strip–looking girl, and he had a bottle of vodka in his hand. He was a happy, hammered drunk.

Plotting our encore backstage (all of us intoxicated by this time), we figured that since both Keith and Dez were there at the show, maybe they'd want to sing Black Flag's "Fix Me" together with Mark.

"I wanna play!" Duff chimed in.

That was fine by us. Mark's guitar was available, so we ushered him onstage and gave him the guitar. Mark's amp was on the side of the stage with Matt's. Duff put on Mark's guitar, made some noise, and turned to Matt.

"What key is it in?" Duff asked him.

"What's a key?" Matt responded, totally deadpan.

Before they could sort that out, we wailed into the song, and Duff was all fucked up, trying to figure out what was going on. I don't think he played a lick, because the song's only like a minute long. The song ended, and he was looking around all confused, like *What happened?* Which was the same reaction that every hair metal musician in Los Angeles had when grunge hit the mainstream and made them, and their scene, irrelevant nearly overnight.

SUCK YOU DRY

NIRVANA HITTING NUMBER ONE ON THE *BILLBOARD* charts on January 11, 1992, seemed like an overnight phenomenon to music fans outside of Seattle, but it was the culmination of a musical movement that had been building locally for several years. By the time the world learned the word *grunge*, the Seattle musicians who were its primary instigators were over it.

When I was home, I was more focused on all the other, more underground projects I was working on, including playing bass in the Fall-Outs, a local garage rock band who'd been around since the mid-'80s. There was revitalized interest in garage rock during this period—both in the Northwest and elsewhere—and I was soaking it in. I liked the garage rock scene that the Fall-Outs were involved in; it was a nice change from the more serious Mudhoney endeavors. Caryn Palmier (my girlfriend at the time) and I loved going to see the little scrappy, shitty local bands at the Lake Union Pub, the Storeroom, and the Crocodile Cafe. I recorded an album (playing bass) with the Fall-Outs during this time, even though we didn't have a label. We just did it on the cheap at Egg and figured we'd be able to find an indie label to release it at some point.

Mudhoney, on the other hand, would be releasing our next record on a major label. Though we hadn't sought it out, as the band leading the grunge charge for the previous four years, we were inevitably courted by major labels, who saw that there was some money to be made. Also, Sub Pop forced our hand. *Every Good Boy Deserves Fudge* was selling well, but they couldn't pay us. They owed us a lot of royalties, and we were afraid they were going to go out of business, and we wouldn't get paid. (Nirvana's success—because Sub Pop got royalties from sales of *Nevermind*—would eventually bail them out.) So, things were getting a little tense with Jonathan and Bruce. They would stretch the truth at times to keep the whole thing going—it was a real house of cards. We didn't *want* to sign to a major label, because we'd heard horror stories, but the other indie labels we liked—Touch & Go, Caroline, Amphetamine Reptile—wouldn't have been a step up from where we already were.

There were a lot of major labels that wanted to talk to us, including Madonna's newly formed Maverick Records, but we quickly narrowed it down. Reprise, a subsidiary of Warner Brothers (and Neil Young's original label), was the one label that we connected with, via their young A&R rep David Katznelson.

At twenty-one, David was the youngest A&R guy at Warner Brothers. When Nirvana hit, and then Pearl Jam a little later, the major labels collectively had a bit of a panic attack, because they didn't know why people were liking this stuff, or what to do about it. They thought they'd lost control of the whole thing. And so overnight, they were hiring people like David. They needed kids to tell them what kids liked.

During one of our meetings with the president of Reprise, Lenny Waronker (who'd been in the biz a long time), we got the sense that even if they didn't get the music, he and the label at least understood and appreciated where we were coming from. We told him we'd recorded our last record at an 8-track studio, and he's like, *So? Some of the best records were recorded on 8-track.* He wasn't fazed.

The offer they made us was: *We'll give you the help that you ask for. We won't be pushing things on you, like outside producers, big-time studios, or changes to your sound.* They also didn't care that we were involved in outside projects. Reprise was the most chill of the labels we met with. At that point, they still had a lot of old-timers working there. And they seemed to have a track record of working with artists who weren't necessarily expected to get huge right away. They kept their artists around. That was all that we needed to hear, so in early 1992 we went to LA and signed our contract with Reprise. We were one of the last of our grunge "graduating class" to take this step, so we'd seen the pitfalls and knew how to steer clear.

Our former Green River bandmates Jeff and Stone were now in Pearl Jam and were supporting their blockbuster debut *Ten*, which had been released on Epic Records. They'd gone from the sorrow of Mother Love Bone's demise to this hopeful new endeavor, which included former Shadow guitarist Mike McCready and a new singer, Eddie Vedder, from San Diego. I'd seen Pearl Jam's first show (when they were called Mookie Blaylock), and I thought they were better than Mother Love Bone, but it still wasn't my thing. Mark and I weren't necessarily estranged from Jeff and Stone, but our career paths were very different. And to be honest, I'd been so busy with Mudhoney for the last few years—touring all over the world, making records—that I wasn't keeping close track of what they were up to.

Because things were starting to get ridiculous in Seattle, with every kind of mainstream media wanting to cover the grunge scene, we were contacted by our buddy, LA photographer Chris Cuffaro, who was doing a photo shoot in Seattle for *Entertainment Weekly* magazine. He'd spent the day taking pictures around the city and photographing some bands, and he wanted Mudhoney to be part of it. We invited him over to the Rock Mecca to do the shoot, and Chris brought along an assistant who was only introduced to us as

Mudhoney on tour with Gas Huffer in Montreal, 1990.

Grunge Jam? With your host TAD? Gig poster for the Fall-Outs at the Swan, March 10, 1992.

Early '90s in Los Angeles. Courtney Love was something else.

"Eddie." We spent several hours drinking beer and taking pictures with Chris and Eddie in our house.

After we'd finished up and were sitting around talking, Eddie leaned over and casually mentioned that he was the singer in Stone and Jeff's band, Pearl Jam. I'd obviously seen him play that first gig, but none of us had ever met Eddie, and I didn't really know what he looked like. It was clever of him to not open with the fact that he was in Pearl Jam, because we got to know and really like him as a person before we had any preconceived notions of what he was about. I think when he first arrived in Seattle in 1990, he was a little self-conscious about not being a Seattle guy, so he stealthily ingratiated himself. He's a really sweet guy, and we personally liked the Pearl Jam guys, even though we may not have been the biggest fans of their music at that point.

One thing we discovered during this era of craziness was that Seattle's music scene had not only caught the attention of record buyers (or CD buyers, as was the case at the time) but also other bands—some of the biggest bands in rock. Soundgarden were asked to tour with Guns N' Roses, and when Metallica rolled into town in May 1992, they wanted to hang with some of the Sub Pop crowd. Mark, Krist from Nirvana, and I met up with the group, along with some Sub Pop people, at the Raison d'Être Café. We had lunch together, and then we were all invited to the Metallica show at the arena at Seattle Center. They had this area called the Snake Pit in the middle of their stage, from which their VIP guests could watch the show. We were all in the Snake Pit when the show started, but after about three songs, my girlfriend Caryn wasn't loving it. She was just there because I had wanted to go. We knew that Beat Happening were playing the OK Hotel that night, so I said, "Let's just fucking skip out and go see Beat Happening. I love Beat Happening."

Apparently, Metallica guitarist Kirk Hammett noticed that we had bailed early on and cornered Mark backstage after the show.

"I saw Steve leave after the first few songs," Kirk said. "Was he not into it?"

"No, no, no, I, uh . . . think you played all his favorite songs," Mark said, trying to cover for me. I felt bad when Mark told me about the conversation. Those guys in Metallica were serious music fans. I don't know how much of Seattle they knew, but they seemed very familiar with Mudhoney, which I thought was super cool.

Since Reprise had given the members of Mudhoney the freedom to do outside projects, I sought a way to release two recent records I'd played on: the Sad and Lonely(s) and the Fall-Outs. I went to Sub Pop and tried to convince Bruce to put them out, but he wasn't feeling it. He suggested I start my own record label, and he offered to press and distribute them. And that's how I started Super Electro Recordings. It came together really quickly since the first two records had already been recorded, and we were doing cheap black and white covers and limited vinyl pressings due to the smaller market for that kind of music. Before I knew it, I had two records out and my sights set on a third one, the debut record from the Night Kings, fronted by Rob Vasquez of the Nights and Days, the guy who'd been a big inspiration to my own playing early on.

I guess that since I'd played on two of our first few releases, Super Electro was sort of a vanity project, but I saw it more as a way to support this new garage rock scene in Seattle that was percolating in the looming shadow of grunge. I just wanted to put out (mainly) local bands I thought were cool. And I wanted to put out things that maybe weren't getting attention elsewhere. It was good to have a completely different creative outlet outside of Mudhoney. I didn't initially have any big aspirations for where it would go; I just wanted to keep it self-sustaining—to make enough from each record to be able to put out the next one.

Mudhoney had a similarly frugal approach when we signed with Reprise. We got a relatively small signing advance, and we were OK with that. Advances from record labels are loans against royalties, and we didn't really need their money. Our tours—where we made money—were doing well without any label support. We all had money in the bank. Major labels would offer bands tour support (giant tour buses, etc.) because the label could write it off. But we didn't need it; we did just fine. I mean, the fanciest we got on the US tours was having *two* vans: one for the gear and a couple of the crew members, and one for us.

But in general, we didn't need much from the label. When it came to our recording budget for our first major label album, *Piece of Cake*, we once again did it on the cheap with Conrad at Egg. Conrad had upgraded Egg to a 16-track studio, but it retained the same vibe, and since Reprise was good with us going there, that's where we wanted to record. Reprise really didn't understand us, but I guess they trusted us since we'd already been putting out records for four years. We did what we wanted and delivered the tapes, and that was that.

We had the backing of a big label with unlimited resources and excellent distribution, but unfortunately, what we delivered to Reprise, at a moment when all eyes and ears were on Seattle, wasn't our best effort. It's called *Piece of Cake* because we thought we could do it in our sleep. Mark was still using and was somewhat compromised during the writing and recording. It was hard to get things done with him around at that time, and that was a shame. I think we all agree that it affected *Piece of Cake*, and he totally owns that.

We could've worked harder and maybe taken it a little more seriously. It's not that we thought we were gonna get big, but I wish we had made a better record, because that one doesn't really hold up. It feels a bit half-baked. It wasn't just Mark; it was all of our attitudes. Its saving grace is the song "Suck You Dry." I think that's the perfect Mudhoney song. Bruce Pavitt had a great quote about that: "Any record's only as good as its best song."

We were invited back to play at the Reading Festival in England in August 1992, two years after our first appearance there. You could really see the effect that Seattle had had on the music world in the intervening years. On the Sunday that we played, Nirvana headlined, we played third, and both Screaming Trees and Melvins were on the bill. Los Angeles band L7 (sort of honorary members of the Seattle scene), who put out an EP, *Smell the Magic*, on Sub Pop in 1990, were also part of the mix.

The weather was predictably soggy, and the crowd showed their appreciation by, fittingly, pelting us with mud. This was also the year that journalist Everett True pushed Kurt Cobain onstage in a wheelchair (Kurt's idea, as there were rumors swirling that he was too sick to play) at the start of the band's set. Kurt and Courtney were married by this point, and Courtney had just given birth to their daughter, Frances Bean. Because of Nirvana's fame, their lives had become tabloid fodder, which was unfathomable to us. They lived under constant intense scrutiny, when all Kurt wanted to do was make music.

Prior to the release of *Piece of Cake*, we were in LA doing press interviews to promote it. Kurt and Courtney had a rental house in LA, so we stopped in to visit them. Nirvana had sold a lot of records by this point—many millions—and, as evidence, Kurt had a stack of gold record awards leaning up against a wall.

"You can have one, if you want," he offered. We all thought he was joking and laughed it off. He wasn't. He was literally giving away his gold records to anyone who wanted one.

"Go ahead," he encouraged us. "I mean, what am I gonna do with all those, hang them on my walls? Sometimes I take them out to the backyard and shoot 'em with a shotgun."

Stupidly, I didn't take one, because I didn't want to haul it home on the plane. But Dan, Matt, and our manager all took Nirvana gold records from Kurt, awards that had his name engraved on the plaques. That these meant nothing to him was a clear indication of his mental state and how disturbed he was by his band's success. It was a problem we didn't have.

When *Piece of Cake* was released, it sold well, at least for us. It was our first album to hit the *Billboard* 200 chart, and it peaked at 189. We didn't earn gold or platinum sales awards for that one (obviously), but we sold a hundred and fifty thousand copies. It was also cool to see our buddy Ed Fotheringham's illustrations on the cover of a major label release. We got some good reviews and press as well.

It was at this point that I think my parents, who had always been supportive, but not really clear about what I was getting up to, started to get excited. Once we were signed to Reprise and we were in *Rolling Stone*, it finally meant something to them. They were thrilled when *Rolling Stone* called me the "Eric Clapton of grunge," because they'd *heard* of Eric Clapton. That Christmas, they gave me the Eric Clapton biography as a present. I don't know if it was their way of saying "we approve" or "now we get it," but it did feel like a validation. I'd veered far afield from what they'd hoped I'd do after high school, but at least they now seemed to understand why.

OVERBLOWN

I CAN'T REALLY SAY THAT I DIDN'T ENJOY AND APPRECIATE
what the grunge explosion brought my way. I didn't reap the same
level of financial rewards that my friends in Nirvana, Pearl Jam,
and Soundgarden ultimately did, but there were plenty of other
benefits. And why shouldn't I have enjoyed myself? I may not have
approached Mudhoney with career aspirations, but we all put in
a lot of hard work, and leading the charge in the early days definitely helped prime the pump for "the year that punk broke." By
1993, I was in a unique position, in that I could experience a lot
of the highs without all the intense scrutiny. Mudhoney weren't
"Smells Like Teen Spirit" or "Alive" big, but we were playing to
good-sized crowds wherever we went—Europe, the United Kingdom, Japan, Australia—and having a lot of fun along the way.

Australia was (and still is) one of my favorite places to tour.
They love us down there, and we love Australia. We've been to Australia many times. It's a bit of a home away from home. If I could
move to Melbourne, I'd do it in a heartbeat. I love that city more than
almost any other city in the world. It's like half Seattle, half London,
but in a smaller format. And unlike some cities in Australia, it has
seasons, because it's in the south.

Our Australian tour at the beginning of 1993, where we were part of the "Big Day Out" (sort of their version of Lollapalooza), was one of my favorites we've ever done. It was an outdoor festival, and the same lineup would travel to different cities: Melbourne, Sydney, Fremantle, and Adelaide. They also brought along a skateboarding half pipe, so they had all these pro skaters on the tour causing a lot of trouble. (Unfortunately, I wasn't skating at this point.)

I was digging the star-studded lineup of cool bands, including Nick Cave and the Bad Seeds, Sonic Youth, Iggy Pop, and the Beasts of Bourbon, who were good friends of ours from Australia. Jerry A, lead singer of Portland hardcore legends Poison Idea, was even down there doing a guest appearance with Australian punks the Hard-Ons. I loved watching all the bands every night, because everybody was at the top of their game. It was probably the craziest tour we were ever on, and we had a blast. As longtime fans of the Stooges, to be able to play on the same bill with ex-Stooges vocalist Iggy Pop was awesome. For Mark it was a little traumatic: Before he met Iggy, he had to go in the bathroom and hide for a while to collect himself.

Between all the touring we'd been doing and signing our major label deal, we all had some money and were able to buy our first houses in 1993. The house Mark bought in West Seattle is where Mudhoney have rehearsed to this day, since he renovated and soundproofed the basement for us. We respectfully end our practices at 10 p.m. sharp so we don't piss off the neighbors, and so far, it hasn't been a problem.

I bought a house on Capitol Hill with a view of Lake Union, and Caryn and I moved in there together. It was a two-bedroom house, but it was just the two of us, with a full basement and a yard, so we had room for touring bands to stay when they were in town. Caryn, who'd worked briefly in the accounting department at Sub Pop, had left her job. Despite the influx of money at the label from sales of *Nevermind*, it was still too chaotic for her liking—so we concocted the plan to make my record label, Super Electro, something a little more serious that we could do together.

I put out the first few Super Electro albums with Sub Pop's help, but with Caryn on board, we figured we could handle all the production ourselves and get a little assistance from Sub Pop with distribution, while also working with other indie distributors. I would do the A&R (i.e., find the bands) and facilitate the recording sessions, and Caryn would do the rest.

I liked the creativity involved with running a label; I liked making shitty punk rock record covers. I still do. I worked on a lot of the record covers with designer Art Chantry, who had not only been the art director at *The Rocket*, but he'd also designed dozens and dozens (maybe hundreds) of 7″ and album covers for many different labels.

Super Electro was a labor of love for both Caryn and me, and I was making enough money to pay for everything. After my experience in Mudhoney, recording for Sub Pop, one thing I wanted to do was pay the bands right off the bat. That's why I paid in advance for a lot of the releases we put out rather than royalties after the fact. As soon as I could, I would pay the artists. And I'm sure I didn't deduct things I should've deducted from their royalties. But it didn't seem like an issue, and I wanted to get some money in their pockets. We kicked things off with a 7″ single, "Sleeveless," by Wellwater Conspiracy, a band that featured former Monster Magnet guitarist John McBain (who'd relocated to Seattle), as well as Soundgarden members Ben Shepherd and Matt Cameron. We followed that up with more 7″ singles from local bands like the Statics, the Calabros, and even one from Eddy & the Back Nine, which was Ed Fotheringham basically fronting Flop and singing golf-themed punk songs. While I was on tour (which was a lot), Caryn held down the Super Electro fort.

For all the perks I was enjoying from Mudhoney's fame, there's no denying that Seattle was no longer the city it had been five or six years previously. Things had gotten weird. Everyone wanted a piece of Seattle. The population surged, bands and musicians moved there in droves, and the mainstream media—a good three or four years late to the genre's *actual* renaissance—wanted to know everything about grunge. They'd come to town and interview anyone directly (or even vaguely) related to the scene. *Time* magazine put Eddie Vedder on the cover with the headline "All the Rage." *New York Times* reporter Rick Marin called Sub Pop to find out what the grunge "lexicon" was and totally got punked by Sub Pop publicist Megan Jasper, who brilliantly made up a bunch of grunge "slang" on the spot. The list they printed is hilarious and completely nonsensical (e.g., lamestain = uncool person) and false. Nobody in Seattle ever uttered any of those things.

In the summer of '93, Ron Reagan Jr. (son of former Republican president Ronald Reagan) came to Seattle on assignment for a new Fox Network newsmagazine called "Front Page," to get the dirt on grunge (and all the other Seattle clichés du jour). Jasper was also interviewed for this and assured Reagan on camera that when ordering an espresso, he should get a "double tall latte with nonfat milk and a shot of almond" (said no self-respecting grunge musician ever).

As part of his reporting, Ron Jr. took Mudhoney to a bowling alley in the Greenwood neighborhood and plied us with a bunch of beers—big mistake. He was a super nice guy, but I don't think he appreciated me asking him if he knew how many angry punk rock songs were written about his father in the '80s. He got uncomfortable in a hurry, and that exchange obviously didn't make the final cut in the eleven-minute segment. This segment also showed Seattle's then-mayor Norm Rice admitting that he'd never heard of Mudhoney. Dang.

Rock Mecca in the early '90s. This seemed totally normal to me at the time.

With Krist Novoselic at Mark's wedding, 1994.

In my bedroom at Rock Mecca, circa 1992. This was for a guitar magazine, so I'm holding my cheapest guitar, a Harmony Stratotone!

That year, we ended up recording a song with another famous Seattleite who'd also probably never heard of Mudhoney. The producers of the movie *Judgment Night* (starring Emilio Estevez, Cuba Gooding Jr., and Jeremy Piven) had the brilliant idea of pairing rap artists with rock bands for their soundtrack, and we were hooked up with local legend Sir Mix-a-Lot, who already had a platinum-selling album and a number one hit single with the song "Baby Got Back." I was really stoked to be working with a local guy. "Baby Got Back" had just recently been a hit for him, and he used some of the lyrics from "Baby Got Back" in the song we did with him, "Freak Momma." He was recycling the theme a little bit. But at the start of the process, he came to our practice room in West Seattle with his little digital recorder to see what we had. I showed him a couple riffs that I'd written—some garage punk licks—that he then recorded and took home to arrange.

He was a real studio guy, like a lot of hip-hop artists. When it came time to record our track in the studio, he directed us live, like when to change the riff from which to which, and he was singing live in the room with us. It was much more organic than I thought it was gonna be. I thought it was gonna be more studio trickery, but he just went with it. When it came time to take a break in the session, Mudhoney went to get some beers and food; Mix and his crew took a break to go buy . . . I wanna say it was a Lamborghini. All we got from the session was a nice chunk of money and another gold record when the soundtrack eventually sold more than five hundred thousand copies in the United States.

In the fall of '93, Mudhoney were offered the opening slot for a short stint on Nirvana's first headlining arena tour in the United States. The previous week, Nirvana's third album, *In Utero*, had gone straight to number one and seemed poised to do as well as the band's 1991 breakthrough, multimillion-selling *Nevermind*—maybe even better. What should have been a fun, celebratory run with our friends (and former Sub Pop label mates) was anything but. It was miserable. We'd played with Nirvana plenty of times since that first time they'd opened for us in Portland, but once they hit big, they seemed ill-equipped to deal with everything. Success was overwhelming them, and I saw it firsthand on that arena tour.

I get it—they were big shows, and Nirvana were under a lot of pressure at the time, but they weren't handling it well. Everybody was walking on eggshells, and people were getting fired all the time. It was a terrible work environment for Nirvana's crew and everybody else. Their manager, Danny Goldberg (who also managed Sonic Youth) was even trying to keep alcohol away from Krist.

"One of the conditions of Mudhoney being on this tour is that you can't have any alcohol backstage," he told us. "No beer, no booze, nothing."

He wasn't joking, even though the idea of it was absurd.

"No, that's silly," I told him. "We respect the fact that you're trying to keep Krist sober, but we're going to drink beer and carry on as we always do."

And we did, lucky for him. The first show was in Phoenix, Arizona, and by the end of Nirvana's set, Danny Goldberg was in our dressing room trying to drink our beer.

In the Nirvana camp on that tour, it seemed *everybody* was being an asshole. For a band that was so strident about its punk rock ethos, they had completely taken their hands off the wheel and were letting management and others steer the ship. Rather than take advantage of the leverage they now wielded as a successful, moneymaking band, they were like deer in the headlights.

And even though both bands were signed to major labels, Kurt made a point of taking shots at Pearl Jam early on for being "corporate." But that whole argument of who was more punk, Nirvana versus Pearl Jam . . . it was like, *Who's in charge of their own destiny here?* Pearl Jam stopped doing interviews and took other measures to mitigate their exposure when things got out of control. And as far as punk cred, I don't think anybody in either of those bands has more than Pearl Jam bassist Jeff Ament. So, while we still cared about our old friends in Nirvana, we were definitely puzzled about what the hell was going on with them.

"Why are they so pissed off about their success?" I asked Mark while we were having a preshow beer in our dressing room. "They should be happy. For the life of me, I can't understand why they're so miserable. It doesn't make sense."

"I dunno, maybe they got bigger than they expected to," he said. "But, Jesus, deal with the situation!"

Kurt, specifically, seemed to disdain his band's major label success. Which was weird because nobody forced him to sign that contract.

"We aren't some corporate band, like Guns N' Roses," Kurt had famously said, but the DGC logo on Nirvana's albums, CDs, and cassettes said otherwise. Nirvana actively pursued a major label deal back in 1990, behind Sub Pop's back. I remember Bruce and Jon at Sub Pop being pissed off when they found out about it.

A month after our awkward and unpleasant October dates with Nirvana, we were invited to do a short run of dates with Pearl Jam, opening shows on *their* headlining US arena tour. Like Nirvana, they were supporting their own number one album, *Vs.*, but the contrast in atmosphere between the Nirvana camp and the Pearl Jam camp was like night and day. Even though there had been a few years where we weren't really hanging out much—both bands had been on the road nearly nonstop—Stone and Jeff and I had mended fences, and Mudhoney were happy that those guys offered to bring us along for these dates. In contrast to the Nirvana tour, it was a lot of fun. It was really easy and nice, and everybody was cool.

"Hey, Steve, did you bring a skateboard?" Jeff asked when we met up with them for the start of the tour, a three-day run in Boulder, Colorado. I figured he'd scoped out a skatepark where we could ride during our downtime.

"No, I got out of the habit. I rarely have the time to do that on tour, and no one else in the band skates," I replied. "Do you have some place you want to go here in town?"

"Nope, I brought my own skatepark," he said. "I have everything we need in our gearboxes—skateboards, pads, helmets, and I even had some ramps and a little half pipe built. Since we're playing bigger venues on this tour, we can ride backstage." I was stoked.

Pearl Jam were genuinely happy to be where they were, and people weren't getting fired right and left. (They still today have some of the same crew members they had when we did this first trip with them.) They had good management; everybody was on the same page. Nobody was being an asshole. It was a revelation to us to see that you could be a success and still stay grounded. It doesn't have to suck to be a huge rock star.

In fact, while on this tour with Pearl Jam in late November, we had a giant Thanksgiving meal, all of us together—the crew and everybody, like fifty people. It was so fun being on tour with them at the time (and it still is today). I was happy for them and for their success.

CHECKOUT TIME

ONE OF THE SAD LEGACIES OF THE SEATTLE MUSIC SCENE is its association with drugs—heroin, specifically. Some people overdosed, and some became long-term junkies. There were some who survived and others who didn't. Mudhoney were fortunate that we weren't one of the casualties from the era, but it could have been otherwise. Even though we'd demanded that Mark clean up his act before we went on tour back in 1991, he didn't stay clean. It was no secret that Kurt and Courtney, who were friends of ours, were both using heroin at that time. Because of this, I lost touch with them. I wasn't doing drugs, and I didn't hang out with people who did hard drugs. It was uncomfortable for me.

Mark, however, *did* spend time with them when they were in Seattle or when we were in LA, and he would succumb to his worst impulses while in their company. Fortunately for all of us, Mark stopped using not long after an overdose in a Seattle hotel, thanks to an ultimatum by his then-girlfriend, now-wife, Emily. She just said, "If you ever touch dope again, I'm gone." Still, I was very nervous for him during his first year of sobriety, because too many die on that first shot after falling off the wagon.

After the great experience we'd had on our November '93 tour with Pearl Jam, it was a no-brainer when they invited Mudhoney to open more shows, this time on the East Coast, five months later in early April 1994. There were no drug-related issues with Pearl Jam, and they were solid guys; they really seemed to be a well-oiled machine. As a bonus for this jaunt, one of the "tour dates" in the first week was going to be a private tour of the White House, occupied by Bill Clinton at the time. Pearl Jam initially got the White House invite, scheduled for the day after our show on April 8 in nearby Fairfax, Virginia, and they, in turn, brought us along. We've never been a political band, but who wouldn't want to get a behind-the-scenes tour of the White House? Our trip to DC, however, turned out to be memorable for all the wrong reasons.

The morning of the Fairfax show, Mark and I were in the hotel room we shared, getting ready to check out. Someone knocked on our door, and I figured it was our manager telling us to get going.

"Yeah, what?" I said impatiently as I opened the door. It wasn't our manager. It was Dan, and he looked pale.

"Kurt's dead."

It didn't immediately register who he was talking about, though in hindsight it should have been obvious.

"What?" I managed to stammer.

"Kurt Cobain. My wife just called me from Seattle. They found his body at his house. It looks like suicide."

He was clearly shaken—he'd played in Nirvana briefly—and as his words finally started to make some sense to me, I could feel the shock of it reverberate. I couldn't believe it, and yet it really wasn't surprising. The last time I saw Kurt in Seattle (not long before his death, in fact), I thought, *Fuck, he looks like hell*. Frumpy overcoat, all hunched over. Hat and gloves. He was by himself, walking up Madison Avenue, toward Piecora's Pizza on Capitol Hill. I remember thinking, *I wonder if he literally just escaped from his house*, because he lived down the hill from there, and people were trying to do interventions and get him into rehab at the time. There'd been an incident in Italy a few months previous that seemed like a suicide attempt.

We were numbed by the news of his death as we tried to process it while checking out of the hotel. These kinds of things don't sink in right away. And we still had a show to play that night with Pearl Jam, who also knew Cobain (though maybe they didn't always see eye to eye with him), and they would be equally affected by the news.

"This doesn't seem real," Stone said. "It seems like the kind of thing that happens to other people in other scenes."

Stone and Jeff had previously dealt with the grief of losing Andrew Wood, their Mother Love Bone singer, to a heroin overdose in 1990, so that made this event feel more raw.

"Do we even want to play tonight?" I asked.

Eddie Vedder, whose arms showed bruises and cuts from the explosion of grief he unleashed on his now-trashed hotel room when he first heard the news of Kurt's death that morning, finally weighed in.

"I think we have to. It'll be good for us, good for the fans," he offered quietly.

We collectively decided to play the show.

Though we were all saddened, Mark chose not to mention Kurt onstage that night, as far as I can remember. We weren't being callous; we just didn't want anything we said in a public forum to be grabbed onto by the media and exploited. Remember, even before Kurt's death, Seattle was under a mainstream media microscope. We also instructed our tour manager not to grant any interviews. I remember being really glad that we were on tour and not in Seattle for those next few days.

The White House trip we had scheduled for the next day (we didn't cancel) was a welcome distraction. It was a little surreal that

With Jeff Ament, on stage with Pearl Jam (Stone and Mark in the background). Clearly the healing had commenced.

With my favorite rose bush—Orangey we called her—at my house on Capitol Hill, circa 1993 or '94.

Mudhoney and Tad on the cover of *The Rocket*, 1995.

such a privilege—a VIP tour—was extended to Pearl Jam and us. Normally it's Super Bowl or World Series champions who get the star treatment, but I guess when your city is pumping out number one albums in rapid succession, you no longer belong to your scene; you've ascended to another level. People want to get close to you. They want a piece of you. Even the president of the United States, apparently.

I was very happy that I wasn't at the level of Pearl Jam or Nirvana, dealing with personal troubles from the fame. Pearl Jam got so big, they were prisoners of it, in a way. Eddie had a stalker for a long time who eventually died by suicide in front of his house. That's the sort of thing that stays with a person permanently.

I spent a lot of time with Eddie during Pearl Jam's skyrocketing fame. My girlfriend Caryn was best friends with Eddie's then-wife Beth. Eddie and Beth had two rental properties on Capitol Hill where they would hide out, and one of them was two blocks from the house Caryn and I shared. The four of us whiled away a lot of evenings drinking red wine and hanging out. I recognized the benefits of the wealth Pearl Jam gained from their success and all that, but I *liked* going to the grocery store. Eddie literally couldn't.

Eddie did, however, get a personal audience with President Bill Clinton at the White House that day in April. The rest of us, not so much. I don't even think the other Pearl Jam guys got to go into that inner sanctum. In that meeting, Clinton actually asked Eddie's opinion on whether he, the president, should address the nation in some way regarding Kurt Cobain's suicide. *That's* the impact that Seattle's music scene had on the country in 1994. Ten years previously, the thought of a lead singer from *any* local band having a one-on-one with the president of the United States would have been ridiculous.

Not surprisingly, my own experience at the White House was very different from Eddie's (although I did get a photo of Bill Clinton and a box of presidential peanut M&Ms, which I still have). Don't get me wrong—it was great, but it was just two Secret Service guys showing the eight of us around (Mudhoney, plus our merch person, sound person, stage guy, and road manager).

"Shit, can these guys arrest people?" Matt whispered when he saw the men in black. You could smell the paranoia on him. "I smoked a joint in the van on the way over here, and I might still have a little pot on me."

"You should definitely eat whatever you have left, the first chance you get," said Bob, our manager. "These guys will do a cavity search if they suspect you're holding." Bob never missed a chance to fuck with us, especially Matt.

We did eventually get a really interesting trip through places the public wouldn't normally be allowed to go (this was pre-9/11, when things were a bit more lax), like into the basement and all sorts of strange rooms. We got a fancy tour—a special VIP tour, behind the ropes—but we didn't get the *Pearl Jam–level* fancy tour. Still, it was a big deal going to the White House.

Kurt Cobain's death cast a pall on the entire country, and maybe even the world. It also felt like it had irreparably altered grunge's meteoric ascendancy. When grunge escaped Seattle and went international, it was as revolutionary as the birth of hardcore a decade before. But when Kurt died, it was, in a way, the beginning of the end for Seattle's musical supremacy. It was our city's own "The Day the Music Died" moment. It wasn't the final nail in the coffin, but from that day forward, things would be different for everyone.

A few months after Kurt died, I ran into Courtney at a show at Neumo's, a Seattle club. She told me she was hurt that we hadn't reached out to her after Kurt had died. She and I exchanged phone numbers, since we both had new places—my little two-bedroom house on Capitol Hill, and her mansion on Lake Washington. Not long after, she called and asked me to come over and take one of Kurt's guitars as a gift. I tried to demur, but Courtney—being Courtney—was not taking no for an answer. She sent a car to pick me up and take me to their house, the house where Kurt had died.

It was a bizarre visit. The house was full of people. There was the baby, Frances; two nannies; and Kurt's mom. Everyone would disappear for long stretches of time, leaving me alone, or with the bodyguard drinking coffee in the kitchen. I sat in the living room, by myself, for more than an hour going, *I'm stuck here. I want to leave.*

Finally, Courtney led me into a room filled with instruments.

"Here are Kurt's guitars; take whatever you want," she said. I was stunned.

"No, you should have these . . . your kid should have these," I said.

She had prototypes for the Kurt Cobain signature Jag-Stang guitar that Kurt had designed for Fender, and she really wanted to give me one of those. That would be like a $200,000 guitar now.

"No, I'm not taking one of those!" I protested. "These are too special. I'll take that dusty thing that doesn't even have strings on it, as a token."

It was some cheesy '60s guitar that didn't even play, a cool looking old cheapo guitar. It had no real personal link to him.

Back in the living room, I noticed there were a bunch of books and records piled up all over the place. In looking through them I found a book that was a history of rare early Canadian punk rock records. "Oh my God, this is cool! I've never seen this before," I blurted out as I was thumbing through it.

"Take that, too," she said.

I was more excited about the book than the guitar, to be honest, but mostly I just wanted to get the hell out of there.

GENERATION SPO

RATION

SPOKESMODEL

IN TYPICAL MUDHONEY CONTRARIAN FASHION, WE decided to go back to recording with Jack Endino for our next Reprise record, *My Brother the Cow*. Though the great work Jack did recording all the seminal grunge releases in the late '80s and early '90s raised his profile beyond Seattle—he'd even go on to produce a solo album by Iron Maiden vocalist Bruce Dickinson, of all people—there was starting to be something of a grunge backlash in certain quarters. Grunge had definitely lost a bit of its shine, probably as much due to overexposure as anything else, and there was a portion of the underground that hated what had happened to the Seattle scene. There was so much resentment that seemed misplaced to me. Seattle bands were still putting out good records, but it seemed like there was an inevitable shift happening in the music world, as different musical styles tend to go in and out of favor after a period of time.

Recording with Jack again, after our personal disappointment with *Piece of Cake*, made sense at the time. He knew our band, he knew our aesthetic, and he was a pro. We were also into the fact that the studio he was working out of, The Ranch, was located below a dive bar called the Storeroom Tavern, which hosted a lot of cool garage and punk bands. So, we'd be recording downstairs, and come up and drink some beer at the Storeroom, maybe see some friends or even stay late and see a show or something. I have good memories of making that record; it was a really fun recording process, and I think the album holds up. I wish we hadn't called it *My Brother the Cow*, but what are you gonna do?

Another positive for me during this time was the fact that I reconnected with both Jeff and Stone. I wasn't hanging out with Jeff as much, because he had decamped to Montana (and still lives there in an awesome place outside of Missoula), but I was regularly hanging out with Stone. We had a standing dinner date about once a month. Despite Pearl Jam's megafame, he was fine; people didn't hassle him. Eddie Vedder seemed to be the focus of everyone's attention. It was a little easier for Stone and Jeff to find ways to be in the world at a level they were comfortable with. Even though Jeff is in Montana, he's always going skating with friends and doing whatever. And I swear, no one recognizes Stone. In all the times I've been out with him, no one's clocked him—or if they did, they left him alone. He looks like a suburban dad. He looks like me.

Rekindling our personal relationships with our former Green River bandmates led to some amazing opportunities over the ensuing years. No matter Mudhoney's fortunes, we were frequently asked to join Pearl Jam on their travels. In early 1995, just before the release of *My Brother the Cow*, we played our first Asian dates outside of Japan. We'd been to Japan on a couple of occasions on our own in the early '90s, but with Pearl Jam we were able to play to thousands of grunge fans in places like the Philippines, Thailand, and Singapore for the first time.

The next six months would be dedicated to supporting an album that we loved, but that sank without a trace. Our relationship with Reprise was also changing. Though things had started out positively, some of the old guard at the label, who'd supported us as a developing artist, were gone, and the new guard was now looking for something with a more immediate payoff. When we first signed with Reprise, we had free rein, but now, for the first time, people at the label were starting to be like, *What are you gonna give us?* As far as they were concerned, we were yesterday's news.

We didn't think we were yesterday's news, obviously, but 1995 was tough. Kurt Cobain had died the previous year, and it seemed the English press in particular was over grunge. So going to England in '95 and getting some terrible reviews and smaller crowds was a little disheartening. In addition, after several years of touring I was starting to get burned out myself.

And at home, the things that were now popular coming out of Seattle were very different. It was a happier kind of sound. You had the Presidents of the United States (featuring my former housemate Jason Finn on drums), and you had "Flagpole Sitta" by Harvey Danger. And in underground music, punk was suddenly new again. The Offspring, Bad Religion (both on the Epitaph label), and Green Day (Warner Brothers) were starting to hit big.

Of course, just as grunge's star was on the descent, Hollywood called. Penelope Spheeris, who directed the incredible documentary of the Southern California hardcore scene, *The Decline of Western Civilization*, was working on *Black Sheep*, a buddy flick comedy with David Spade and Chris Farley. It was set in Washington, so of course we got the call to do a cameo in the movie. (Actually, we were the second choice; apparently Bad Religion turned it down before us.) Even though I had done a commercial as a kid, this was my first time on a Hollywood film set, and it was a weird experience. Thankfully it was only one day. We got a little screen time saying a few lines (mine was, "No, you jag, he ain't the governor!"), and we played "Poisoned Water." Gary Busey, one of the stars of the movie, was nuts, and for some reason he wanted to hang out with us. His part was a crazy Vietnam vet, and he seemed like one.

Unfortunately, the movie did nothing to further anyone's career—not Spheeris's, not Spade's, not Farley's, and certainly not ours. We got some money from it, but the movie was a total dog, and everyone hated it.

We had some mixed experiences with Hollywood when we were signed to Reprise and became part of the Warner Brothers family. On the plus side, we made some good money contributing songs to soundtrack albums. Some of those advances would be like $30,000 for one song, cash up front. We'd go into Egg and record for under a thousand dollars, and then get to keep the rest. We did a good number of them, and it was a great deal. However, in true Mudhoney fashion, we inevitably killed the cash cow when we were asked to do a song for a movie called *With Honors*.

With Honors was a college campus love story starring future heartthrob Brendan Fraser and Joe Pesci. Someone involved in making the movie—the music person or the director, I don't know—wanted us to do a song for the opening scene of the movie. It was Brendan Fraser running through the Harvard campus in the snow, training, like a *Rocky* thing. They wanted something anthemic, hip, and of its time. The song they were using as a placeholder to illustrate the vibe they were looking for was "Unbelievable" by EMF.

Since we'd done a few soundtracks already, we got a little cocky about it. I had this really cool instrumental (we almost always did an instrumental on our albums) that was a surfy thing. We submitted that to them, but they were like, *Yeah, but we don't want an instrumental.* So, we were going back and forth between our manager and them about it. One of us—maybe Mark, maybe a collective moment of evil genius—decided that if we wrote awful lyrics to it and submitted both versions, they'd be forced to use the instrumental. So, we

Super Team USA at the Little 100 bike race, with Eddie Vedder, his then-wife Beth Liebling, Caryn Palmier, and Steve Malmin, as our mechanic. Circa late '90s.

A Polaroid test shot for the movie *Black Sheep*, circa 1995.

I wasn't doing much skating circa 1995, but my nephew Rob Maxwell got me back on board!

The entire European Mudhoney crew in 1995.

submitted a song titled "Run Shithead Run." Which is an awesome song, but obviously not the right song for a scene with an athlete training. The people making *With Honors* were *not* amused. The woman we'd been dealing with was so mad. She told our manager, "They will never do a soundtrack again." And we never did; we never got offered another. We really were given the "you'll never work in this town again" treatment.

Dan once pointed out that we have a habit of shooting ourselves in the foot career-wise, and that was a big one. We should've handled that one better. Another way we inadvertently self-sabotaged was by leaving some of our best songs off our records because they were either too poppy or because they came so easily that they seemed like throwaways.

A perfect example is "Ounce of Deception." We left it off *Every Good Boy Deserves Fudge* because we came up with it in like three minutes, but that's one of the best songs of that era. We did put it on the B side of the "Let It Slide" single, and later Sub Pop made a video for it for the reissue of *Every Good Boy Deserves Fudge*. We should have kept a bunch of those, because I'm of the opinion that first thought is the best thought, so go with it. I like shit that just falls into place, and you power through it.

We steamrolled through '95 in much the same way we had the previous six or seven years: lots of touring, including our third appearance at the Reading Festival. We were on the main stage on Sunday, August 27, a couple slots behind our friends in Soundgarden, who now had their own number one, multiplatinum album, 1994's *Superunknown*. And instead of Nirvana being on the bill, Dave Grohl's new band, Foo Fighters, was on the smaller Melody Maker stage. One of our final shows of '95 was opening for the Ramones in front of twenty thousand people at Seattle's Bumbershoot Festival that September. Those last two gigs were the highlight of a tumultuous year.

One personal highlight was an interview I did that year. Wez Lundry, a Spicoli-type dude who'd worked at Fallout Records in Seattle in the '90s, wanted to do a Mudhoney feature in *Thrasher*. I agreed on the condition that he publish a picture of me skateboarding from back in the day. He was into it, so when the issue hit the stands, I'd fulfilled a teenage fantasy of seeing photos of myself skating in *Thrasher*.

This also helped rekindle my interest in skateboarding. I knew some guys who were still skating, so I asked my friend O (Otis Barthoulameu), a musician and skate photographer from San Diego, if he could get me a board from Foundation (a skateboard company). I discovered that skateboards had dramatically changed since I was last on one. The board he sent me was this tiny thing and I couldn't make sense of it, so I pulled out my old fat board from the mid-'80s. I immediately sprained my ankle badly, and that was that.

After touring and recording relentlessly for more than half a decade, I was exhausted. I told the band that I was done, that I needed to take some time off. I needed to take a break from Mudhoney and not do anything band related—no tours, no recording, nothing. It was starting to put a strain on my relationship, my ears were ringing, and I questioned if I really wanted to keep playing music at all. I felt like I'd rather be a *fan* of music than a musician. I didn't want to not like music anymore, and that's what it was starting to feel like. So, in 1996, Mudhoney went on a hiatus. The timing was OK, because while we'd made good money the previous four or five years, it had slowed way down.

My personal taste in music was also changing and evolving. In the '80s, I had dismissed the singer-songwriter craze of the '70s, because the *Creem* magazine vibe at that time was *Fuck James Taylor; he's the Antichrist of rock 'n' roll*. But in the mid-'90s I realized I actually *liked* all that stuff. So, doing what I do, I started digging to find more and more obscure singer-songwriters. This led me away from garage and psych rock because, after finally giving the more flowery and mellower psych stuff that I'd previously ignored another listen, I realized that I *liked* the more acoustic material. It took me a while, but I even found that I liked the Grateful Dead.

I argue about the Grateful Dead with a lot of people. I'm not a huge Grateful Dead fan (because none of them could sing), but I like *Workingman's Dead* and *American Beauty*, their more acoustic-based records from the early '70s. Jerry Garcia's later solo records are great, too, when he got back to doing almost bluegrass. He grew into his voice a little bit in later years.

During this Mudhoney hiatus, I was able to focus on doing Super Electro and reconnecting with what was going on in Seattle. Caryn had been enlisted by Rob Vasquez (of Nights and Days and Night Kings fame) and his girlfriend Dawn Johnson to join their band, Man Tee Mans, on bass. She'd never played an instrument in her life, but she learned enough to record a single for Bag of Hammers Records and play some shows. After that, Dave Holmes from the Fall-Outs convinced her to sing in his side project called the Wiretaps. The Wiretaps were a cool band, and Caryn was a great singer. I put out their first single, "Call Waiting," on Super Electro in 1997.

I've always been into vintage bikes (like old cruisers and the fat-tire Flyers), and I had a group of friends in Seattle who rode bikes from the '30s and '40s. Every year we would do a race called the Little 100, which was a hundred laps around a school track. (The name was homage to the Little 500 race in the movie *Breaking Away*—one of the greatest movies ever, in my opinion.) It was a lot of fun, with plenty of beer drinking and hilarity. There was even a contest for best costume. Some of the riders took the race seriously, others didn't. I did it several years in a row.

Caryn and I were still spending time with Eddie Vedder and his wife Beth when we could, but it was hard to do "normal" stuff due to Eddie's stardom. So, one year Caryn and I got Beth and Eddie on our Little 100 team. We were Super Team USA Number 1, and we all had vintage '60s and '70s red, white, and blue clothing on. Beth and Eddie had an old vintage '70s van that looked like Evel Knievel's van, so we were perfectly matched. And we had a roadie with us dressed in a red, white, and blue mechanic's outfit. We won for the best costumes that year, and miraculously, no one hassled Eddie. Honestly, I think half the people there didn't even know who he was. So, he still managed to do normal things sometimes, and he was always grateful for the chance to do regular goofy, fun things that people in their twenties or thirties do.

Even though Mudhoney went on a hiatus in 1996, and played very few shows in '97, we still owed Reprise a new record, our third full-length album for them. Things had changed dramatically at the label. Our A&R guy, David Katznelson, was still there, but all the other higher-ups at Reprise had changed. They'd gone through several different presidents by this point, and the days of leaving us to our own devices were long gone. No more recording on the cheap and pocketing the rest of the advance. They were insisting that we'd need to work with an actual producer for the next record. They even wanted to hear demos of the new material in advance for the first time.

The business had changed after the great grunge explosion. As far as major label problems go, we didn't have it too bad. They never tried to screw us, they just gave up on us. And I gave up on them.

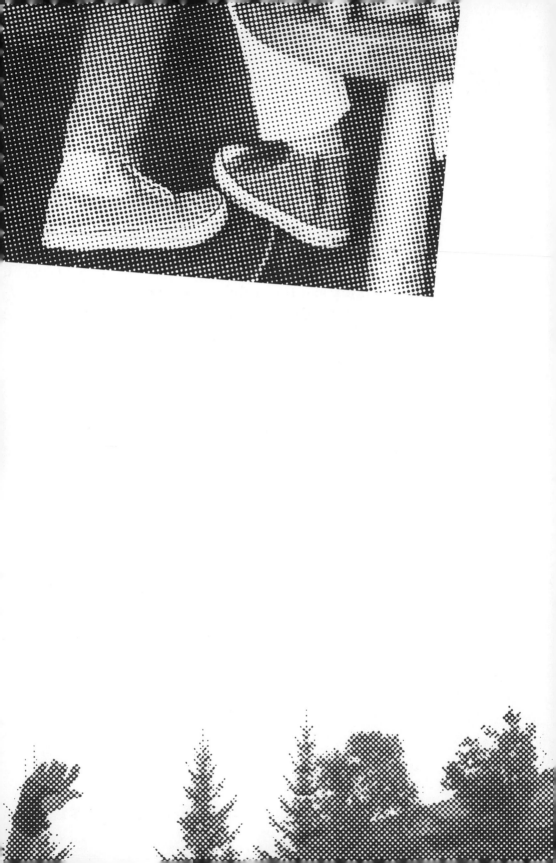

MAJOR LABEL BLUES

MUDHONEY DIDN'T HAVE TO MAKE *TOMORROW HIT TODAY*
for Reprise. We could have walked away from our major label
deal, paid for the recording ourselves, and released it via Super
Electro. And honestly, that's what I wanted to do. But the other
guys—Mark and Dan in particular—argued that we'd never used
an outside producer and worked in a more expensive way. *We're
never gonna get the chance again, so why don't we just do it?* They
won the argument, fair enough. So that's how we ended up working with Jim Dickinson. (And I don't regret it.)

Jim Dickinson may not have seemed like an obvious choice
for a grunge band. His resume was all over the place musically: Ry
Cooder, Toots and the Maytals, Albert King, G. Love and Special
Sauce. But he had also done records Mark and I loved, like the third
Big Star record and *Like Flies on Sherbert* for Alex Chilton. We liked
the chaos of them. When *Like Flies on Sherbert* was released in 1979,
it was such an angrily reviewed record because the people who liked
Alex Chilton from his Box Tops and Big Star days were like, *What
the holy crap are you doing?*

Jim had also produced the Replacements' 1987 album *Pleased
to Meet Me* for Sire Records, which wasn't my favorite record by the
band (a band I loved), but he claims that's the record they wanted

to make. There was no one twisting Replacements front man Paul Westerberg's arm to put a heavily gated reverb on the snare drum.

Jim flew from his home in Memphis to Seattle, and we started work on the album at Stone's studio, Studio Litho. It was wintertime and it was snowing, miserable, and cold. Let's just say that the weather didn't suit Jim's temperament. So, we decided to go down and do the rest at Ardent Studio in Memphis, which was a place he was very comfortable with. We did manage to record most of the basic tracks at Litho, and then wrapped it up in Memphis.

Working with Jim was a great experience and very different from making records with Conrad Uno and Jack Endino, who were more engineers than producers. Jim was getting paid to *produce*; he was not a knob-twiddler. He had an engineer do the engineering, while he listened, smoked weed, and had ideas and suggestions for changing the arrangements here and there. He was one of those guys who really digs in and listens hard. I think that's what he saw his job as. He was hired for his point of view and his ears more than anything else.

Matt was playing less and less bass (he was playing like two notes in every song, where he used to be a busy bass player), but I think that appealed to Jim. He just loved Matt's bass playing. Overall I think we made a great record together. I like *Tomorrow Hit Today*. No regrets.

Based on the direction that things seemed to be heading with Reprise, I didn't have high hopes that the label would get behind this record. One concession they made was to let me issue the vinyl version of the record on Super Electro. Major labels had mostly given up on vinyl, so I was all too happy to take care of that. I was able to sell four thousand copies with no problem. Reprise claimed they couldn't even sell ten thousand CDs, but that's because they didn't try. It was a write-off for them. They'd already given up on us. I knew that I could have sold twice as many CDs through Super Electro. No matter where we went on tour in support of *Tomorrow* following its release, there were no CDs in any stores. It was obvious that Reprise was done with Mudhoney. I knew that was it.

Despite our degenerating relationship with the label, we were still committed to touring. We did a late summer run with Pearl Jam, hitting stadiums and sheds and playing to thousands of people, before we did a headlining club run with garage/stoner rock band Nebula (who were on Sub Pop) and the Kent 3, a low-fi garage punk band from Bellingham, Washington, whose records I'd released on Super Electro.

I loved the Kent 3 and had been working with them since 1996, putting out their records. I thought they were an amazing band. As much as I loved them, however, the record-buying public didn't necessarily feel the same. They would draw big crowds in Seattle, but people outside the region didn't seem to get it. They didn't quite fit in. They didn't get close enough to the garage rock sound, and they were too scuzzy to be indie rock. But the tour we did with them and Nebula was a blast, except for when the Kent 3 got busted for marijuana possession in Texas and I had to spend $2,000 to bail them out. That's how dumb drug laws were in the '90s.

One of the pluses of touring with Nebula was that their bassist, Mark Abshire, was a great skater. So, when we were touring through California, he got me into a legendary skating place, a great backyard private pool. That was the first time I'd ever been able to skate in a pool. As you can imagine, skating in pools in the Northwest isn't really an option because, well, people don't have pools.

Though this tour was a lot of fun, and we loved the bands we were touring with, we couldn't help but notice that the crowds were getting smaller. In late 1998 there was a definite end-of-an-era vibe creeping in.

Me, Mark, and a skateboard, circa late '90s.

With Mark at a small cafe in South Seattle, circa 1995.

This compilation could have been the end of the Mudhoney story! We really weren't sure if we would continue after Matt left.

My label, Super Electro, had put out releases from bands I really loved—Thee Headcoats, Holly Golightly, Wellwater Conspiracy, the Kent 3, the Masonics, the Wiretaps, and others—but we'd had distribution problems with some of our later releases. Adding to the turmoil was the fact that my relationship with Caryn, my partner in the label, had been falling apart for a couple of years. It was a very slow, friendly breakup, no drama. I sometimes think if we'd had fire between us, and had gotten upset with each other now and again, it might've worked out better. But we just kinda went with the flow. So that was just it.

She had recorded an album with the Wiretaps, and I knew it wasn't gonna sell, but I felt like, *I gotta release it*. And that was the last official Super Electro release. It seemed like the time to wrap things up. It was 1999, and Super Electro came to the end of its run.

The theme of this era seemed to be relationships running their course. Matt's interest in Mudhoney had clearly been waning for a while. He was contributing less and less musically and never really had much of an opinion on band decisions. We were frustrated by his lack of interest in the band, and honestly, I couldn't ignore the fact that he seemed to fucking *hate* Mark and me, for whatever reason. (He still liked Dan, however.)

When Matt finally broke the news to us that he was leaving the band, Dan was heartbroken. He and Matt were a team, and Dan wasn't sure if he wanted to continue doing Mudhoney without him. Dan loves everybody and gets along with everybody; that's kinda his strength. But Matt quit because he didn't want to play music anymore, and you shouldn't play music if you don't want to. He hasn't played music since.

By 1999, most of us were back to working regular jobs when we weren't on tour, so everyone's time priorities were being considered. When we officially got dropped from Reprise, it cemented

Mudhoney's situation. We no longer had a bass player, we no longer had a label, and there was some question as to whether we would even be continuing as a band. Dan figured we should just throw in the towel altogether, as he couldn't imagine Mudhoney without Matt.

After years of taking our success for granted, I had finally started to appreciate what we had. I think we all did, because it was in danger of ending. We'd invested so much of our lives already in the band, I didn't want us to do anything rash. So, my suggestion at the time was this: "Why don't we put the band on the back burner, not even think about it for a while, and let's check back in in a year." So that's how we left Mudhoney: effectively in limbo. Rather than making any hard decisions, we kicked the can down the road. The only thing we knew definitively was that we were no longer on a major label. Our old friends at Sub Pop, however, were poised to soften that blow.

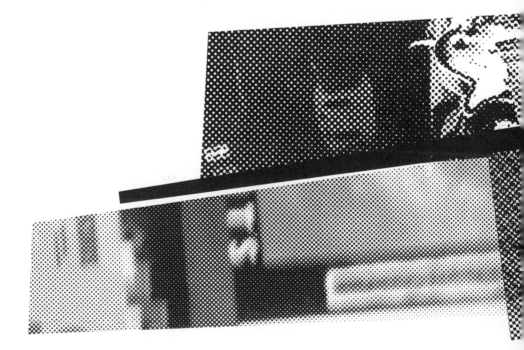

Not long after Nirvana hit big with *Nevermind* (which Sub Pop had points on, meaning they got a small percentage of every sale), Warner Brothers Records (Reprise's parent company) bought a non-controlling share of Sub Pop, so the two labels became friendly in the ensuing decade. Right after Reprise dropped us, Sub Pop had the brilliant idea of doing a Mudhoney "best of" compilation that would encompass not only our formative Sub Pop years, but the near decade spent with Reprise. Surprisingly, Warner Brothers was extremely cooperative, and they smoothed the path for what was looking like a (possibly) posthumous career-spanning retrospective. We didn't know whether Mudhoney were finished, but this seemed like a worthwhile project anyway. If *this* was going to be our swan song, I wanted it to be memorable—something we could all be proud of.

I ended up being the point person on *March to Fuzz*, a three-record vinyl (and two CD) collection of not only our greatest

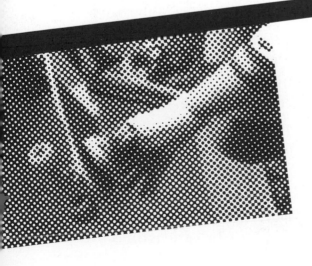

"hits," but also a ton of B sides and compilation tracks we'd done over the years. I worked on everything: I was down at Sub Pop, working with advertising director Tammy Watson and designer Jeff Kleinsmith, figuring out the photographs we'd use in the booklet, collecting memorabilia and quotes from the other members of the band, and dealing with the track listing. It was nice to be hanging around there again.

Working on the project at Sub Pop during that time, I got the sense that the label had come back from the abyss a little bit. In the mid-'90s, Bruce Pavitt had left, and they'd lost some of their focus. But now it seemed like they were returning to form. They were even starting to sign hard-rocking bands again—not exclusively, but it seemed like they were signing bands for the right reasons, because somebody at the company believed in them. Sub Pop was a trimmed-down machine, and the people they had working there were all really cool. It felt good to be working with them again, especially after our experience at the end with Reprise.

It was also bittersweet working on *March to Fuzz* and going over all the archives—the songs, the photos, the old posters—from the days when we were the top dog in Seattle. In 1999, everything was different. Seattle was a different city, and most of the bands we'd come up with—Soundgarden, Tad, Blood Circus, Swallow, Skin Yard, Feast, the U-Men, and others—were long gone, and grunge had become a word no one wanted to be associated with.

Where did that leave Mudhoney? We didn't even know if we were still a band, or what our future would be without a label. Mudhoney were on hold for at least a year. Where did that leave me personally? My long-term relationship was over, my financial future was unsettled, and I didn't really have a fallback plan. At thirty-four, I was four years past the age at which I'd promised my parents I'd have a college degree. I'd tried at various times over the years to finish, but in 1999 I wasn't close to fulfilling the promise, and I wasn't particularly motivated to.

At this point I'd been playing music professionally in some capacity for more than a decade, nearly a third of my life. If I walked away now, what would I do?

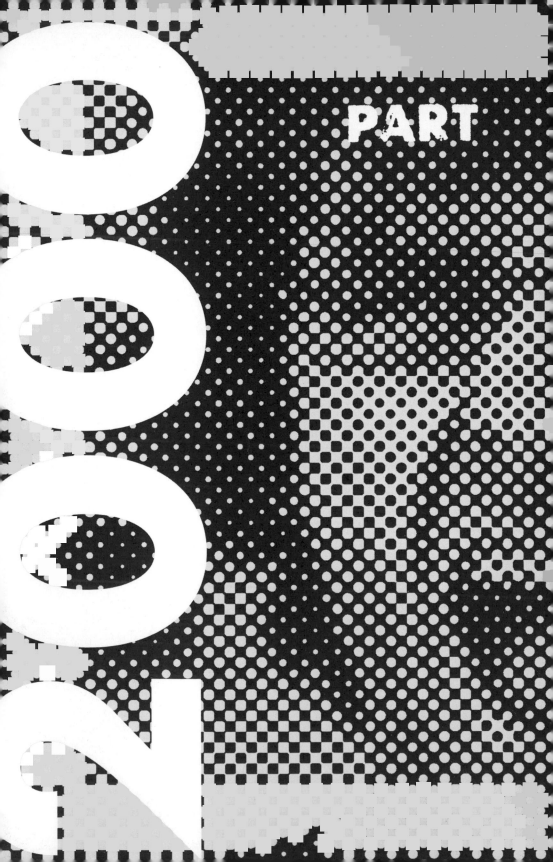

PART

0002

THREE

VANISHING POINT

THE LIFE OF A PROFESSIONAL TOURING MUSICIAN ISN'T exactly stable and settled, but in 2000 I was in some ways more unmoored than I had been in the previous decade spent touring the world with Mudhoney. For the first time in a long time, my job wasn't making music; I was now working as a landscaper. It was strange. I wasn't tied to a record label, and I had no commitments to record or tour. There had been a time four years earlier when, fried and burned out, I'd wanted to be set free. But now I *wanted* to be a musician, to keep playing music. Maybe not loud music, maybe not with Mudhoney, but I wanted to keep playing. And if it meant I'd just play acoustic guitar, that's what I'd do. I didn't really have any specific notions about what I'd be playing, or with whom. I just knew I wasn't done.

Around the same time I had this epiphany, I was approached by the Experience Music Project (EMP)—Seattle's own rock 'n' roll museum with a Northwest slant—which wanted to create an exhibit about how skateboarding and punk rock merged. I wrote a proposal, and soon after, I was hired to research and write an installation for the museum (today called the Museum of Pop Culture, or MoPop). I don't think I could have invented a better job for myself. The multimedia exhibit would feature archival videos, music, and skateboards,

225

as well as contemporary interviews, and much more. I would get to research and document the two things that helped launch my career.

The museum sent me and a crew down to California to interview old skaters, heroes of mine from back in the day: Tony Alva, Steve Olson, Duane Peters, Brian Brannon from JFA, and all the surviving members of the band T.S.O.L. Guitarist Ron Emory of T.S.O.L. is a legend in the underground backyard pool skateboarding scene from the late '70s and early '80s. Steve Alba, one of the Alba brothers, was another one. His little brother Micke Alba was one of my favorite skaters as a kid. I got to meet all these heroes of mine. We were way out in Ontario, east of Los Angeles, at an abandoned hotel with an empty swimming pool, and all these old dogs were skating there. (Well, they weren't *that* old, but they were a good twenty years removed from the glory days of the early punk and skating scenes.)

It was totally inspiring to me to see these dudes who were a bit older than me still ripping it up. All I could think was, *I really have to start skating again.* Serendipitously, when I got home, I learned that Seattle had recently built a skatepark, SEA SK8, right across the street from EMP. Since I hadn't been on a board in a while, I didn't know it had opened, but once I caught news of it, I stopped by to check it out. It was a full cement skate park, not just a half pipe.

I was admiring the setup when one of the skaters yelled at me. "Turner! Is that you?" It was Pat Quirk, a.k.a. Q-Man, this old Seattle punk rock skater dude from North Seattle. He was a good skater back in the day, but he got too into the fighting and the violence of the pit at punk rock shows. I hadn't seen him in probably a decade; I couldn't figure out how he even recognized me.

He shouted at me, "It's time to get a board!" and rode off.

He was right. I needed to start skating again. I mean, there was a new skate park in Seattle, and I'd just met all my skateboarding heroes, who were older than me and still skating. There was no excuse.

So, I got back on it. I started going down to SEA SK8 in the early mornings (at least when it was dry), and skating before I headed out to my landscaping job. The cool thing was, I hadn't been in touch with any of my skater buddies from back in the day, but as soon as the park was built, they started showing up. Some of them were just getting on their boards again after eight or ten years, just like me.

So, we'd be there at like seven or eight in the morning, just us old men—guys in our midthirties. I didn't really care what the modern skaters were doing—I just wanted to get back to where I was in 1982, and SEA SK8 was a good place to at least start. Later, once I started skating other parks, and going on road trips down to California, I realized SEA SK8 wasn't the best park around, but it was still better than anything I'd ever ridden as a kid.

Once I started skating again, I reconnected with the same community of oddballs that had always been there. Some of them were people I had admired back in the day. After I met Steve Olson, the original skate punk, during the EMP project, we became pals. He was *the* dude.

I still feel that connection to the skateboard world. I think it's arty, independent, and cool, and there's still a lot of music involved in it. There's this underground, offbeat sense of community to it. The weirdos find their people.

This connection is how I learned to skate bowls at one of the best places in Seattle. I'd befriended a local punk band called the Vaccines because their singer, Slim, was a skater. He and the band's guitarist were originally from Sacramento, and they were super influenced by Tales of Terror, one of my old hardcore favorites. Their drummer was a professional skater, a West Seattle dude, and he and Slim had some good connections in Seattle. Slim knew I'd been riding at SEA SK8, but he told me he knew of someplace much better. He'd have to make the introduction, because outsiders weren't welcome at this private, outdoor park in the Pigeon Hill area of West Seattle—basically no-man's-land. We arranged a time to meet, and he took me to what was known as the West Seattle Bowl.

The West Seattle Bowl had been built in the back of a rental house in the early '90s by some skaters who'd famously gotten busted trying to build a skatepark underneath the West Seattle Bridge. These guys were tenacious, though, and luckily, their old hippie landlord gave them the go-ahead to build a bowl on the property. However, they really didn't know what they were doing. It wasn't an ideal spot, because it was up a steep hill. They hand-dug an eleven-foot-deep hole in the backyard and filled it with cement, crafting it into a crude skateable bowl. It was gnarly.

Monk, one of the guys who lived at the West Seattle Bowl house, was also one of the crew who'd built the famed Burnside skatepark in Portland a decade earlier. He wanted to make something similar to Burnside in West Seattle. So, a few years after they built the West Seattle Bowl, they built a better bowl next to it, known as the Butter Bowl, because it was "smooth as butter." It wasn't exactly on par with Burnside, but the Butter Bowl was a huge improvement on the original West Seattle Bowl, and it was the perfect place for me to hone my bowl-riding skills.

Once Slim got me in there, those guys were super nice, and I could skate there whenever I wanted. Basically, if you brought a twelve-pack of cheap beer, you were in. They liked my skating buddy Chris Manaras and me, because we were a little bit older, and the first time we went there, we were still on our mid-'80s skateboards, which they thought were cool. Riding bowls for the first time at age thirty-five, I realized I could still learn some new things.

During the year we agreed to not think about Mudhoney, Mark and I had the idea to do another Monkeywrench album. We figured it would be fun to reconnect creatively with old friends and keep

Skating at Jeff Ament's Treasure Bowl in Missoula, Montana, 2002.

Monkeywrench in my front yard, 2000. That's my bike in the background.

In the batting cage with Stone, circa 2001.

With Steve Olson, skate punk legend and all-around cool guy, 2002.

playing music, without the pressure and commitment. The change of scenery, musically, was also good. Mudhoney had played with the same lineup since 1988, so the Monkeywrench were a comfortable place musically without any baggage.

Our Texas-based guitarist, Tim Kerr, was spending a lot of time in Seattle producing bands for Estrus Records, so he was around and available with some regularity—he'd even stay with me sometimes. Things seemed to be winding down with Tom Price's band, Gas Huffer, as well. Like a lot of my musical peers from this era, they were doing less touring and were settling down and getting more domestic, so the timing seemed good all around. Once we got everyone on board, I made cassettes for them of some weird, obscure songs that maybe we could cover, and we started formulating ideas.

We couldn't get together that often, but the idea behind the Monkeywrench was to do something loose and garage-y with a retro vibe, so being precise and well-rehearsed wasn't a priority. We recorded a quick session with Jack Endino at Private Radio studio in Seattle, and since Tim had been doing so much work with Estrus, we decided to go with them to release our second album, *Electric Children*. Mudhoney were on good terms with Sub Pop, after putting together the *March to Fuzz* compilation, but they weren't our label of record, so to speak. They kept our earlier records in print and paid us regularly, but we weren't connected to any label, so Estrus, which focused specifically on trashy garage rock, was a better fit for the Monkeywrench.

Electric Children was released in April 2000, and we had the opportunity to do some touring to support it. Because of everyone's various schedules and jobs, we didn't exactly tour in normal fashion. We played a handful of record release shows in the Northwest, headed down to Texas for a few gigs, and then met up with our friends in Pearl Jam in London for a couple of dates at Wembley

Stadium and a couple of club shows on our own. Later that summer we bounced from Japan to Spain and finished out the year with some gigs in the Midwest. It was super random. We thought our itinerary was so funny, we put the dates on the back of the T-shirt we were selling on tour. This tour was all about having fun, enjoying the music, traveling, and playing with some bands we liked.

In my year away from Mudhoney, I surprisingly made a lot of music, and I found it was fun for me again. I rediscovered the feeling of creative freedom, and I liked it. We still hadn't made any definitive decisions on Mudhoney when we got an offer in late 2000 that forced a move: Wayne Kramer of the MC5 called and asked if we wanted to record a new track for a compilation he was putting together. And when Wayne Kramer of the MC5 calls and asks if you want to record a new track for a compilation he's putting together, you don't say no. The MC5 were one of the original proto-punk bands, and they had a profound influence on a lot of Seattle musicians, us included. Wayne Kramer is a legend.

The problem: With Matt gone, we didn't have a bass player. I'd played bass with the Monkeywrench and other bands, so I thought maybe I would play both bass and guitar, and we could write some songs and record them. While we couldn't perform that way, we could record just fine.

That left us with one more pressing issue: We needed to crank out a song for Wayne. The album, *Wayne Kramer Presents Beyond Cyberpunk*, would be a compilation of modern and old punk bands. I suppose we were the former, though that was a bit of a stretch. Anyway, we told him we had a song idea, so he said he'd fly up to Seattle to hear it. There was apparently a big budget for this project, but I have no idea where all the money came from. He came over to Mark's house and we played the song for him. Obviously, I couldn't play guitar and bass, so I just played guitar.

"So, who's playing bass on this?" Wayne asked.

"I figure I'll play both guitar and bass when we record," I told him, hoping the fact that we weren't a complete band wouldn't quash the deal. Thankfully he wasn't fazed.

"Well, what if I play bass right now, just to fill it out?"

We gave him a bass, he plugged it in, and we kicked into "Inside Job." It's hard not to feel a bit of a fanboy thrill when you're playing with Wayne Kramer in your band's practice space. And not surprisingly, he instantly came up with a bass part that was way better than what I had in my mind. His version is the one we took to the studio when we recorded the track with Jack Endino, and that's how we got MC5 legend Wayne Kramer to play on a Mudhoney song.

Reconvening Mudhoney for Wayne's project turned out to be an effective way to see if it felt OK to continue without Matt, or if it was time to let it go. After the session with Wayne, I think we all felt like there could be life left in the band. There was no denying the chemistry that the three of us—Mark, Dan, and I—still felt. Matt had been an important part of the band, but three of us still had a lot to offer.

Though Matt was officially done with Mudhoney, he hadn't played his last gig. He'd graciously agreed to do a handful of West Coast dates we'd booked and said his final farewell at a packed house at Graceland in Seattle at the end of January 2001. Mark, Dan, and I had tossed around ideas for potential replacements once we knew we were going to continue, and we had two candidates. Steve Dukich was from beloved Seattle band Steel Wool and was a skate buddy of mine (we'd hit the West Seattle Bowl together sometimes). He's a natural musician—the guy's *good*. We'd known Steve forever; he'd even been our roadie for one tour. The other was Guy Maddison, an Australian expat who'd played in Lubricated Goat, Monroes Fur, and Bloodloss. Guy had moved to Seattle in the '90s, and Mark had played with him in Bloodloss (which issued an album via Reprise in 1995, and many others on different labels since). We'd known both these guys for a long time and thought either could be a good fit. While we were contemplating all of this, we received an offer to go to Brazil, a place we'd never been before.

We wanted to do it, but we couldn't ask Guy to come with us because he was in nursing school at the time, though he seemed excited about the prospect of playing with us. Instead, Steve came along, and I was really thrilled he did. He seemed like a perfect fit for Mudhoney. The catch was that he didn't want to join the band full-time, but he was happy to come to Brazil with us. I don't think he'd wanted to play much after Steel Wool had split.

We had a great time in Brazil. Steve and I brought our skateboards, and when we were there, we mentioned to a couple people that we wanted to go to some skateparks that we knew about. Somehow word spread, and it turned into this thing where all these skateboard magazines and press people came with us, because they thought we were really *good* skateboarders.

After the tour, Steve played his one and only Seattle show with us at the Crocodile Cafe's anniversary party in May 2001, and that was the end of the brief Steve Dukich era of Mudhoney. We still needed to find a permanent bass player if we were going to keep going.

I'M 37

AFTER RECORDING A TRACK WITH WAYNE KRAMER AND
touring Brazil with a bassist other than Matt for the first time in
thirteen years, it seemed like there was a consensus that we could
still do this and, in fact, still enjoyed doing it, and wanted to keep
going. We also got the news that Dan's wife was pregnant with their
first child. He showed us all a picture of the ultrasound when we
were recording with Wayne. It was amazing to see, and we were
all excited for him—the first Mudhoney dad! We knew this would
change things, but I always felt that personal lives are more important than the group, by far. Dan made his peace with continuing
without Matt (a compromise on his part), so we would, of course,
make it as easy as possible for him to stay in the band by working
around his family's needs.

I think it helped that the person we got to replace Matt, Guy
Maddison, was someone we all knew and liked. Guy was excited to
play in Mudhoney, and since we'd known him for more than a decade,
he knew what life in the band would entail. If we were embarking
on a new, post-grunge-era arc of our career, it made sense that we'd
have an updated lineup—some fresh blood. We broke him in with a
gig on July 6, 2001, at "Tex Games 2001," an extreme sports festival

held on the Omak Stampede Rodeo Ground, in rural Omak, Washington. Welcome to Mudhoney, Guy.

One of the other things we forsook when our major label deal went south and Matt left was our management. We sort of decided to self-manage once we made the decision to keep doing Mudhoney. We fumbled around with that initially, but the combination of our years of experience and the relative simplicity of how we were now operating made it easy enough for us to handle. While we obviously had a booking agent for touring, we had the logistics of touring down pat. We'd been shrewd about touring from very early on. We'd always tried to tour real bare bones. I mean, we realized early on that the most important person to bring along is someone to operate the club's sound system's mixing board, because the people running the sound at the clubs you're playing don't always have your best interests at heart—in fact, sometimes they just plain hate you. If you have someone who actually knows what you're *supposed* to sound like, that's the most important part of a good mix when you're playing live. That's why I tell young bands, if you hire anybody to go on tour with you, make it a soundperson. And hey, that person can do other stuff too. They can lug the gear. Just make them an equal partner—give them an equal cut. As our tours got bigger over the years, we would still only take, at most, four people along with us—a tour manager, stagehand, soundperson, and merch person. We were good at keeping things simple.

We also didn't have a label to deal with, which eliminated the need for any sort of managerial wrangling. But once we started thinking about recording new material, we knew that if we wanted to release it, we'd need to at least explore our options with a record label. From the start, I wanted it to be Sub Pop.

It had been a decade since they'd released an album of new material by Mudhoney (*Every Good Boy Deserves Fudge*), but we still had a good relationship. We'd put together *March to Fuzz* with them, plus I'd known them personally long before Mudhoney existed. So, once we as a band decided we wanted to work with them again, Dan had a conversation with Jonathan Poneman, who said he'd be happy to put out our next record. It was a real homecoming, and everything had come full circle.

The first record we delivered to them in 2002, *Since We've Become Translucent*, was exactly the record we needed to make in the new millennium. It was a fresh start in nearly every way: the music we wrote, the way we recorded, and who we recorded with. Going forward, we didn't know if we were going to tour much or what we were gonna do, really. We were all back to working day jobs, so the pressure was off to make the band our sole source of income.

It was nice not to have a major label wanting to hear demos and providing us with a recording advance that we *had* to spend on the recording. Instead, we had a supportive label that was cool with letting us make the album we wanted to make, however we wanted to go about it. We could even bring in other people to play other instruments (horn section!). There were no rules. It was fun to do it that way.

We'd already recorded that track with Jack Endino ("Inside Job," featuring Wayne Kramer playing bass) that we knew we wanted to use for *Since We've Become Translucent*. That gave us the idea to record multiple sessions, late in 2001, with different engineers at different studios. We spread the love around and recorded three sessions of three songs each: one with Martin Feveyear at Jupiter Studios, one with Johnny Sangster at Egg, and one with Scott Colburn at Gravelvoice. That way we could work around everyone's schedules, family lives, and outside projects, by spending a weekend here and there, doing a few songs each time, over the course of a few months. I liked the fact that we only had to focus on a small number of tunes in each session, and that there would be a little bit of variety in the tones and sounds.

We were happy enough with the results that we did our next album, *Under a Billion Suns*, that same way. We thought that the varied sounds were the strength of our new process, but in retrospect, it might not have worked for everyone. These records weren't quite unified enough sonically. We'd also turned a lot of people off by starting *Since We've Become Translucent* with "Baby, Can You Dig the Light?," which is eight and a half minutes long. I wasn't worried, though. We were getting our musical bearings in this new incarnation of the band, and we really didn't feel like we owed anybody anything.

Christmas Day 2001 I spent alone. My parents had relocated from Mercer Island to Yakima, Washington, where my sister lived, but I opted to stay in Seattle for the holidays. For some, the idea of being alone on Christmas Day might seem kind of sad, but in 2001, being alone on Christmas suited me. The house was quiet, it was a beautiful, sunny day in Seattle—almost warm, I remember—and I went outside and did some gardening. As I was working in the yard, I decided I was going to teach myself how to sing and play guitar—no band, just me and an acoustic. It was the kind of thing I didn't *want* anybody around to hear. So, when I got back in the house and cleaned up, I sat down with my Gibson and gave it a shot. I can't remember what song it was—maybe a Townes Van Zandt tune—but I mumbled my way through and figured out some chords. It came easier than I thought it would. This was the start of developing my folkie aspirations, something I'd tried and failed at in my first attempt back in 1991. This was music I loved, but I'd never seriously tried to play.

My part-time job as a landscaper had me up at 7 a.m., but I decided to rise an hour earlier every day to teach myself to sing and play. Since I was no longer drinking, getting up early was now easier for me to do than it had been in the past. I had stopped drinking around the turn of the millennium largely because I was poor—there's not much money to be made as a landscaper, and Mudhoney weren't very active. Sobriety seemed like a good idea for my health (and wallet), and I was dating a woman who didn't drink either.

I'd roll out of bed, have some tea, and spend an hour practicing. I did that for a few months, and I progressed so quickly, it kept me going. It was the first time I felt like I was improving at something musically. My whole theory with punk rock and guitar in Mudhoney was that I didn't *want* to get any better. I thought that was my enemy. But this was a totally different thing. I was learning how to finger-pick a little bit, and I could feel myself getting better at playing and singing at the same time. That was really encouraging, so I kept at it, not knowing where it would lead. I just liked what I was doing, and I liked getting better.

By this point, I had been listening to the kind of music I was now trying to play for maybe twenty years, though you wouldn't know it by listening to Mudhoney records. I guess I had compartmentalized my musical interests for a long time. Like all my deep dives into music, I was always looking to go beyond the obvious stuff.

I credit Goodwill for turning me on to a lot of music. Back in the '90s when I was first getting into the "children of Dylan" sort of music—the obscure '60s and early '70s songwriters—I could find all kinds of cool records in that vein at Goodwill for next to nothing. I was finding Townes Van Zandt records at Goodwill back then. The real dealers didn't care about them and weren't buying them, so they weren't demanding collectors' prices yet. Now those same records are worth a lot of money. Even as I was collecting all those rare punk records, I was *listening* to the two-dollar folk records I was picking up at the thrift store.

Though Mudhoney had been up and running again since late 2001, we were doing things in fits and spurts, whether it was

In my living room, 2002. I did this every morning for an hour until things started sounding like songs.

Skate punk is over; make way for skate folk!

Sittin' on the porch with my banjo, circa 2001. Photo by my neighbor, Vern Green, a retired *Seattle Post-Intelligencer* photographer. He sadly passed away before I moved to Portland.

recording or playing live. It was just as part-time as my landscaping job, and I was fine with that. I didn't have kids yet, and I lived by myself, which I found essential to my songwriting process. That was the only way I could do it—I needed weeks alone without anybody anywhere near me to hear the horrible folk songs I was coming up with (before I wrestled them into shape).

One poignant moment in this process happened on my thirty-seventh birthday. There was a new wave-y Seattle band from the early '80s called the Macs that had a song on the first *Seattle Syndrome* compilation called "I'm 37." The day I turned thirty-seven, first thing in the morning, I learned how to play that song. It was about a thirty-seven-year-old who's working a shitty job. I could relate!

I decided to further dip my toes in the singer-songwriter waters and record the songs that I had come up with so far. So, I booked time at Egg with Johnny Sangster (one of the engineers we worked with on *Since We've Become Translucent*) and laid down the first twelve songs I had. It was just me and a guitar (with a little accompaniment from Johnny). I was nervous going into Egg, but I'd been practicing those songs relentlessly every morning before work for months, so I felt confident. The process of recording on my own went smoothly, and I was happy with the results.

Stone and I had continued to get together regularly, when our Mudhoney and Pearl Jam schedules would allow. Sometimes we'd go out to dinner; other times I'd go over to his house and we'd jam. He was really getting into playing drums, so I'd usually play bass or something, and we'd just fool around and blow off steam. At one of these sessions, I mentioned to him that I'd recorded these folkie-type songs, and he was really intrigued. I played the Egg recording for him, and he offered to re-record it for free at Studio Litho, the studio he owned. As a bonus, he'd also play bass. Great!

Soon I had Dan on drums, Stone on bass, and Johnny Sangster on second guitar. From there, things progressed quickly. Having Stone's support to go into a nice studio helped a lot. Not that Egg isn't great—we could have done it there. But since I didn't have to worry about the cost, I was able to be more leisurely about it. So, the four of us went in for a few days and recorded my first solo album, *Searching for Melody*.

Recording the album was a great experience—very different from making a Mudhoney record—and it got me energized. Now I just needed to find a label to release it. Mudhoney were working with Sub Pop again, but I didn't really consider running it up that flagpole. I never discussed it with them, and I don't think I even gave them the recording. I didn't see my solo career amounting to much more than what it currently was—a little side project thing. I knew where I fit in, because there was already a small underground acoustic/folk scene percolating at the Sunset Tavern in the Ballard neighborhood. It was the Seattle old guard, though.

Ballard was where a lot of people my age had bought their first houses and started families, so the demographic at the Sunset skewed toward middle-aged. Everybody was over thirty; it was an adult music scene. Kurt Bloch from the Fastbacks was always there, as was Scott McCaughey from Young Fresh Fellows. There were certain days of the week where everyone congregated at Sunset Tavern and played a few songs each.

Emboldened by seeing my peers perform, I finally decided to do my own brief set, opening for Jesse Sykes and the Sweet Hereafter. It was terrifying—suddenly I was the sole focus of attention, and I was singing! But Johnny Sangster volunteered to sit in with me on second guitar, so that helped ease my nerves.

Music publicist Barbara Mitchell was a constant at these Sunset Tavern shows. She'd been part of the Seattle music scene for quite a while, so she knew everyone. Inspired by all the great music she was hearing at the Sunset, she decided to start a record label, Roslyn Recordings, and asked if she could put out *Searching for Melody* as one of her first releases.

Working with Barbara appealed to me. It felt akin to how Mudhoney got on Sub Pop. Just like how Bruce and Jonathan put out records by their friends' bands in the small grunge scene, one of the supporters of the small Sunset Tavern scene was putting out records by *her* friends. Before *Searching for Melody* was released, Kwab Copeland (who worked at the Sunset and had his own label, Burn Burn Burn Records) offered to put out a split 7″ with Jesse Sykes and me. It was a smaller thing, but I felt comfortable working at that level.

It seemed like both Mudhoney and I had found the right people to put out our records. We were working with labels that cared about the music, not just their bottom line.

NOTHING BUT THE BLUES

IN THE PREVIOUS DECADE, WHEN MUDHONEY RELEASED an album, I could be reasonably sure that the rest of my year would be booked. We'd been road dogs for much of the '90s—playing the United Kingdom, Europe, Australia, Asia, even Brazil—and had made good money doing it. With the release of *Since We've Become Translucent* in August 2002, the only significant chunk of live dates we had mapped out were eight shows in the United Kingdom and Europe in September.

Unfortunately, I returned to Seattle to some bad news from my sister, Mary-Virginia. Mom was having some weird health problems (including a couple of seizures), and her doctors didn't know what was causing them yet. Mom had had a benign brain tumor in the late '80s, which had been diagnosed after she'd had some seizures, so it was hard not to feel alarmed. Following a series of tests, she was diagnosed as having a very aggressive malignant brain tumor, and she was deteriorating quickly. This time, there would be no operation. There was nothing that could be done to help.

She knew the prognosis, but she didn't appear anxious about it. It was oddly painless for her, as far as we could tell. Whatever part of her brain the tumor was affecting made it so she didn't seem to suffer. In fact, she was rather childlike in the final weeks.

Her thoughts were simple, and her memory was compromised. For example, she no longer remembered how to eat edamame when we went to a sushi restaurant. She kept trying to eat the rough exterior.

Two weeks before Thanksgiving, I got a call from my sister around 3 a.m. telling me I needed to come to Yakima, because Mom was likely not going to survive the night. I drove eastward across snowy Snoqualmie Pass and then south over two more passes; the whole time it felt like I was going downhill. She died that morning surrounded by her large family. It was six weeks from her diagnosis to when she passed.

That year, 2002, I spent the holidays with my family in Yakima. It felt important to be there, gathered with everyone. Dad was living alone and had started looking ill himself—he was turning orange. He was a heavy drinker, and the orange color was a signal that his liver was starting to fail. Tests were performed, and he was diagnosed with liver cancer that had metastasized to his organs. The prognosis was not good.

After his diagnosis, I spent a lot of time taking care of Dad in Yakima, traveling over from Seattle to stay with him. Since I was living alone, I wanted to spend this time with him while I could. My siblings and I divided Dad's care among us, with Patrick flying out from the East Coast from time to time, as well. My sister pitched in as much as she could, even though she was pregnant at that time and had five young kids to look after.

My father received some chemo treatments, but not for long. They were just extending his life by a few weeks, maybe a few months. I didn't think he should have done the chemo (because it was quite painful), but he wanted to try treatment, and I supported him. Toward the end he couldn't get around the house easily, so we had a hospital bed installed on the ground floor of the house.

Dad passed at home, with Patrick tending to him, eight months, nearly to the day, after Mom did. I was in Seattle at the time, though I'd seen him two days before. He was still quite alert and communicative to the very end, so I don't think I understood how sick he was at that point. I was glad that Patrick was there with him.

Once Dad was gone, we all felt a little shell-shocked. Mom's death happened so fast that we had no time to really grieve, and then Dad got ill so soon after. It had been a hard year.

During my dad's illness, I had to fulfill some solo touring commitments in Europe. I knew that Dad's prognosis wasn't good, but it also didn't appear to be immediately imminently dire, and my siblings were there to help, so I didn't cancel the appearances. I would only be gone for a week in February and then a little more than two weeks in May, so I felt comfortable leaving.

They were good trips and gave me something to focus on in a sad time. Barbara from Roslyn Recordings had licensed *Searching for Melody* to Loose Records in England and Houston Party Records in Spain, so I actually had product to support. Naturally, I brought Johnny Sangster along to accompany me. I'd played a couple of solo shows outside of Seattle, but this was a much different endeavor, made possible by a lot of help from friends overseas who provided gear and support.

Our first two shows were in Spain, and unfortunately I discovered that the promoters had been leaning hard into the Mudhoney connection when promoting the gigs. I'm not sure what the crowd was expecting, but they didn't get any grunge. We next went to London for three shows, where ex-Screaming Trees drummer Mark Pickerel, now doing his own folkie singer-songwriter thing, joined us on the bill. Holly Golightly, whose records I'd released on Super Electro, played at two of our shows. She and Bruce Brand from Thee

Headcoats helped me out with gear (an amp if I needed it) and were super supportive.

Another source of encouragement—one I did *not* expect—came from Bruce Dickinson, the lead singer of Iron Maiden, one of the biggest heavy metal bands in the world. In addition to flying commercial jets, fencing, writing books, making solo albums, being a TV presenter, and generally ruling the heavy metal world, Bruce also somehow had the time to record a regular BBC 2 radio program, "Masters of Rock," in the early '00s, on which I was invited to be a guest.

If we can rewind about twenty years (or twenty chapters), you might recall that I hated Iron Maiden during the Green River years. I felt like the influence of Iron Maiden was taking the band completely outside of where I thought it was going to go. I had built up a certain amount of animosity toward Maiden, but when I was offered the chance to promote my solo album and shows on BBC Radio 2, I wasn't gonna say no. As much as I didn't necessarily like his band's music, meeting Bruce Dickinson was like meeting Superman. I was thrilled.

Bruce seemed excited too. Very excited. He's a very enthusiastic man. When I arrived at the BBC at noon (very hungover, because my temporary abstinence from alcohol was over), he met me outside the studio. He had things to talk about right off the bat.

"I made a record with one of your buddies," he said as he shook my hand. Then he did a spot-on Jack Endino impression, which was a good icebreaker. When Bruce left Iron Maiden in the mid-'90s, he tabbed Jack to produce his first solo album, *Skunkworks*. When Mudhoney recorded with Jack in 2000, he told us all about being picked up by Bruce in his helicopter—with Bruce piloting said helicopter—and being flown to Bruce's castle for that recording. Bruce clearly had knowledge of the Seattle music scene, but I would

Playing at my sister's fortieth birthday in Yakima, Washington, 2002.

Italian artist Photocoyote did two illustrations of me—folk Steve and punk Steve—so I used them on a 7" record.

have assumed it went no further than, say, Soundgarden or Alice in Chains. But no, he knew about me, and Mudhoney, and was genuinely excited about meeting me.

He ushered me into the studio for the interview and started off with:

"I love your record, Steve. It reminds me of James Taylor," he gushed. "It's so good!"

In my young punk rock days, this would have been the ultimate insult. But I actually *like* James Taylor. (Well, not everything he's done.) I think "Fire and Rain" is one of the greatest songs of all time.

After the initial shock of that comparison, I felt OK, and the rest of the interview went really well. It was fun, and we had a good chat. It wasn't just an assignment to him; he was clearly familiar with *Searching for Melody*, and he asked me questions about specific songs. Plus, he's Bruce Dickinson; he can probably do whatever he wants on the radio, so I don't think anyone told him he *had* to interview Steve Turner from that grunge band Mudhoney. He actually wanted to.

After we wrapped up the interview, he broached the idea of heading off and grabbing a pint. My hangover said, *Yes, that's a great idea*, but I had to be at the club for sound check, so I walked away, still in some disbelief that that whole thing had happened. I felt certain that there had been some sort of mistake—that it would have made much more sense if he'd interviewed Mudhoney. But, whatever—he loves James Taylor. That's the takeaway: Bruce Dickinson loves James Taylor.

THE STRAIGHT LIFE

IN 2003, I DID THE MOST UNROCK 'N' ROLL AND UNCOOL thing a single man in his late thirties can do: I bought a minivan. There's really no way to justify it, and it certainly didn't do anything for my punk rock cred. But for practicality, it suited my needs.

I had been borrowing my sister's beat-up minivan for a while, and I found that it worked well for hauling gear when I started doing solo shows. It's not like I was bringing a drum kit and a bunch of amps, so the minivan easily accommodated the equipment I brought with room to spare if, say, Johnny was accompanying me. Plus, it got the same gas mileage as a car.

Despite myself, the minivan won me over. So, I succumbed and bought my own, because I planned to do some solo touring in the United States, and I needed something more reliable than my sister's beater. It was perfect. I've become a minivangelist and have even convinced some other reluctant parents to get one. I even wrote a song, "I-5 Corridor," about driving my sister's minivan on the interstate from Seattle to Portland.

It was a good time for me to have my own touring setup too. For the most part this was a mellow time for Mudhoney. Mark had gotten married, Dan and his wife were having kids—all the usual stuff that inevitably happens. Of course, we were all a little behind the curve on all that because we'd spent our late twenties and early thirties touring relentlessly. I was the least encumbered member of the band, so since I had a solo album out and material in the works for a second, I was going to take advantage of the freedom and hit the road. Not only that, but I was going to find times to play solo shows on off days or while on tour with Mudhoney. This had a twofold benefit: I could promote my record in locales further afield, and it kept me from whiling away my free time partying on a free day and ending up with a hangover on a show day. In the past, free days had been particularly hard on Dan and Matt for this reason. If I had something to keep me busy, it kept me out of trouble. So, I'd book gigs around any gaps in our Mudhoney schedule.

I booked this one show at a record store, M-Theory, in San Diego, when Mudhoney were doing a California tour and we had a break between appearances. One thing I hadn't considered, though, was that I'd have my Mudhoney gear with me instead of my standard solo setup. This meant I had to stand when performing. I don't like being a standing-up folk guy—I want to sit down, because it's easier for me to sing and play at the same time. Lesson learned.

Later that fall, when Mudhoney went down to San Francisco to play a couple of dates, I continued down the coast playing dates on my own and then worked my way back up north to Seattle in the minivan. Mudhoney didn't really have any tour dates lined up for early winter, so in November I loaded up the minivan for a two-week tour out to Chicago and back.

One more thing about minivans: They have a special power that I didn't know about, that I've warned people about since I discovered it, and I'm not talking about horsepower. Listen to me: If you buy a minivan as a single man, the children will arrive. Guaranteed.

Less than nine months after I bought mine, I had a pregnant girlfriend who had a three-year-old son.

I was introduced to Desiree at the end of 2003 by my good friend Michael Maker, the lead singer for the Makers, a notorious Spokane, Washington, garage rock band. Desiree, who was eleven years younger than me, was originally from Bakersfield, California, but had lived in Seattle since she was eighteen. Less than two months after she and I started dating, she got pregnant, and she and her son Aldous moved into my tiny two-bedroom house on Capitol Hill. Instant family! Desiree was a charming woman, and I developed a quick bond with Aldous. Just like that, I was no longer the unencumbered member of Mudhoney. It was my turn to become a parent, and I was ready.

My days of loading up the minivan and hitting the road in it to play solo shows would soon be effectively over. And writing new material would be challenging, if not impossible, as I'd no longer have the solitude that suited my writing process. But I had a new album already recorded, *Steve Turner and His Bad Ideas*, that Barbara would once again release on Roslyn Recordings and license overseas. I just wasn't going to be able to pop over to Europe for a few weeks to promote it this time. A couple of years earlier, it was like, if the trip paid for itself, I'd get a little fun holiday to Spain with Johnny Sangster—why not? With a child on the way, I couldn't do that. I had to make money, a lot more money. The priorities changed, and if I was going to be gone on tour, I had to really make it worth it—and the only way to do that was with Mudhoney.

Mudhoney could still make a sizable chunk of money on tour. And we needed to as the kids started piling up. We had to pay for family expenses, especially if we were going to be gone for any length of time. We were now earning for our families, not just ourselves, and everyone's family dynamics were different. Desiree stayed at home during those early years, so at least I didn't have to pay for childcare while I was on tour. But Dan was the primary homemaker in his

Mudhoney, circa 2005.

Cover of my 2006 solo album. It's from an old punk badge I found on the floor at the Showbox, circa 1980.

With Aldous in our Seattle front yard, 2005.

With Milo, 2005.

family. His wife, Donna, worked as a lawyer, and he was a stay-at-home dad. So, when we were on tour, he had to make sure he could cover childcare costs. Same with Guy, once he had his daughter.

My son Milo arrived on November 27, 2004, deep into the Pacific Northwest's dark, cold rainy season. When it came to choosing his name, I told Desiree that whatever name we picked, it had to link somehow to skateboarding or punk rock. I was aiming for Knox—I thought that was a rad name. It would have suited him because he's turned out to be such a gnarly kid. We instead landed on Milo, inspired by Milo Aukerman, the lead singer of the punk band the Descendents (who released the classic album *Milo Goes to College* in 1982). I've since discovered lots of little Milos, named by people like me, moms and dads who grew up listening to the Descendents.

I had to curtail my solo touring when Milo was born, but I was still really into skateboarding at the time, and *that* I could do locally. I was trying to skate as much as I possibly could, as I figured I only had a couple of years left, due to my impending middle age-dom, fatherhood, and whatnot.

Milo grew up around skaters and skateparks. As soon as he could toddle along, I'd drag him to the skatepark with me. He always carried a tiny little skateboard around with him.

Even though I enjoyed Seattle's decent skate scene, I was tiring of the city and had been for a few years. The tech boom of the late '90s had changed the character of the place dramatically. By the time that first dot-com crash happened early in the new millennium, the tech culture that pervaded the city was getting ridiculous. There were all these young soon-to-be millionaires with their start-ups and IPOs. I remember going out one night and these twenty-two-year-old assholes (who should have been baristas at Starbucks) were talking about their hundred-dollar cigars. That's when I thought, *I gotta get outta here.*

I had had my eye on Portland, which was still behind the curve on the whole high-tech thing. I always loved going down there. It was cheaper and more rough and tumble, like Seattle used to be. The TV show *Portlandia* was right about one thing, the dream of the '90s *was* alive in Portland. My crazy plan was to buy a house on a double lot and put in a cement bowl next to it. This dream had been hatched when I was still living on my own, *before* Desiree, Aldous, and Milo came along.

Life as a family man happened in such a fast and dramatic way that it was a huge adjustment for all of us. Desiree and I really didn't know each other that well before we started a family together. We hadn't been able to go through much of a dating or courting process before we were living in the same house and raising children, and we didn't have the opportunity to ease into these huge life changes. So, it wasn't always smooth sailing.

We had a son together and I was raising Aldous with her, so nearly two years after Milo was born, we made it official: She and I got married on Poipu Beach on Kaua'i. Since Aldous has lived with me from the time he was three, I've always considered and raised him as my son. He doesn't call me Dad (he already had a dad), but he's my son.

Unfortunately, Desiree didn't share my passion for moving to Portland. She was open to moving—neither of us was particularly anchored to Seattle—but she wasn't sold on Portland the way I was. I already had plenty of friends who were living there, like Michael Maker, Scott McCaughey, and R.E.M.'s Peter Buck. There was a West Coast skateboarding mecca, the Burnside skatepark, located under the Burnside Bridge downtown. Mudhoney were obviously based in Seattle, but me being three hours down the I-5 corridor wouldn't be a deal-breaker, as the band wasn't really anyone's sole priority anymore.

Desiree didn't have a traditional career at this point, either. She worked as a vintage clothes picker. She and her friends would find cool clothes in the pay-by-the-pound Goodwill bins and sell them to vintage clothes shops for a few hundred bucks cash every day. She could do that in Portland, if I could help her to see that she'd like it there.

She'd been to Portland with me when Mudhoney played there, but only to, say, Dante's on Burnside in downtown (a shithole club, really). I knew I had to show her the good parts of the city. It helped that Stone had a condo down there in this new, beautiful building in the up-and-coming Pearl District, and he let us stay there. Plus, the city was a great place for kids.

We ended up with a compromise that would work for all of us: We'd move there, but not until Aldous had finished first grade. He was in kindergarten at the time and thriving in the classroom with a teacher he loved, and who would be his teacher for first grade too. So, we held off until he'd completed both years.

I managed to record one more solo album during my early years as a father, *New Wave Punk Asshole* (my least folkie solo album), but it was only released in the United Kingdom. Barbara's label (Roslyn Recordings) had become insolvent, so she couldn't afford to put it out. Simon Keilor, one of our oldest UK friends, had a couple of labels, and he put out my album on his Funhouse Records. It's the only one of my solo albums that was never released on vinyl, which I was bummed about.

I wasn't playing many solo shows, so I wasn't in the position to really support or promote a new record. I'd play the odd show on off days when Mudhoney were touring—including a couple dates in Melbourne and Sydney, Australia, and two in London—but it was becoming less feasible, because I was at home a lot, busy with a young family.

Still, when Mudhoney were offered lucrative tours, such as a two-week run opening for Pearl Jam in South America at the end of 2005, we said yes. We could play to tens of thousands of people on any given night, and we were always treated like kings by our friends in the band and their crew.

After Pearl Jam went through several different drummers over the years, their lineup solidified with the addition of former Skin Yard and Soundgarden drummer Matt Cameron—another one of the Seattle grunge old guard. Matt joined Pearl Jam in 1998 following Soundgarden's breakup. Between Mudhoney and Pearl Jam, there was quite the musical legacy stretching back twenty years. Grunge's heyday had long since passed, but both bands continued to put out relevant music, and people still showed up when we toured. Every now and then Stone, Jeff, Mark, and I could even relive our Green River days onstage.

We'd been having informal mini reunions since the '90s, when Pearl Jam would take Mudhoney out on tour with them. With four of the original five members—Mark, Stone, Jeff, and me—on the road together, we could jam on a Green River classic or two during a Pearl Jam encore here and there. It was fun to play with those guys, and nice to be able to perform some of the old Green River tunes for Pearl Jam fans, who may have been unfamiliar with that chapter of Stone and Jeff's musical career. So, when the idea was broached by Sub Pop of a *complete* Green River reunion, which would include drummer Alex as well as my replacement in the band, Bruce Fairweather, we were all excited to give it a go.

The "official" Green River reunion happened in 2008, spurred by Sub Pop's twentieth anniversary celebrations that summer. We loved the fact that it would be a combination of the two eras of the band and that it would be the first time all six of us—a three-guitar army—would share the stage together. Still, there was some irony in the fact that Sub Pop's twentieth anniversary celebrations coincided with the twenty-year anniversary of Green River's demise.

There had been some bad blood back then, especially surrounding Green River's posthumous 1988 swansong, *Rehab Doll*—the push-pull tension between some members wanting to go commercial and others wanting to stay underground—but that was long gone. We'd all mended fences and were excited to play together again. The tricky part would be putting together a setlist that we were all happy with. We all agreed that whatever the setlist was going to be, it shouldn't include much from *Rehab Doll*. We did end up playing the song "Rehab Doll" (which was written by one of the guys who inspired me to play hardcore, Paul Solger), as well as "Together We'll Never." We also played some deep tracks from my era, like "33 Revolutions" and "Leech." For both Bruce and me, there was a learning curve, trying to lock in songs from each other's respective eras. But I came away with a better appreciation for some of the material Green River wrote after I left.

We played a packed, sold-out warm-up show at the Sunset Tavern in Seattle, and the next day we performed at the big Sub Pop anniversary gig at Marymoor Park in Redmond, a Seattle suburb. We all had such a good time that we got together for a handful more gigs, both in Seattle and Portland, over the next six months, and we left the door open for future shows when we could all find the time. This was a much better ending than how I left things with Green River back in 1985, and I was glad that we all still got along so well both musically and personally. The acrimony I felt as a teenager quitting his first real band seemed so distant and unimportant compared to the friendship and closeness we'd built and maintained over the many years since.

THE DREAM OF THE '90S

THOUGH I HATED THE DOT-COM, TECH-BRO CULTURE THAT had replaced Seattle's gritty, blue-collar edge in the early 2000s, I significantly benefited from it when I sold my dinky, falling-apart house on Capitol Hill and made a tidy profit. (So did the people who bought it, no doubt—they immediately knocked it down and built two tall, skinny modern houses on the lot. Whatever.) I took the equity and used it to buy a bigger five-bedroom house in Portland, one that could comfortably accommodate my family. I didn't get the double lot I'd dreamed about years earlier as a single man (nor did I put in a cement bowl), but it had a basement the kids could use as a rec room, and I had my office and space for my records down there too.

I was still skating as much as possible, and one of the best things about living in Portland was being able to skate at the Burnside skatepark, a defining feature of Portland's skate scene. The Burnside skatepark, underneath the Burnside Bridge on the east side of the Willamette River, is a destination for skaters from all over the world. The park was built entirely DIY. In the early '90s, some of the local skaters just started pouring concrete and building it without permission. It started small, with just a vertical transition obstacle. It was in an area that was of no commercial

261

value, and it didn't interfere with anything, so the city turned a blind eye.

Having played in Portland plenty of times over the years, I knew that a lot of the city was pretty rough, and it was especially sketchy in that part of town. Before the skatepark was built, the area was inhabited by prostitutes, drug addicts, and unhoused people. But there were some legit businesses in the area, too, mostly warehouses and food distributors. They liked the skaters being there, figuring a skatepark and its visitors was better than who was there before.

So, a deal was made: The city wasn't going to tear down the skate park, nor was it going to pay for it to be more developed. The park was funded by donations, and the skaters provided the labor. They started digging bowls and pouring cement (which was free, leftovers courtesy of a local cement company). The structures were rough initially, but as the construction grew and improved, the park became legendary. In fact, it became so legendary it was featured as a location in one of the early Tony Hawk skateboarding video games.

The Burnside park has a worldwide reputation for real street-level skateboarding. And it has influenced the Portland skateboarding scene to be a bit rougher than most, a reflection of the gnarly homespun way it grew. Portland has its own flavor, compared to other West Coast cities. In California, you'll find first-wave skaters who wear pads, but nobody wears pads or helmets at Burnside. It's just not done. And if you land on the cement, it's like a cheese grater—you'll definitely lose some skin. It's a proving ground for amateurs and pros alike.

The locals have kept the park going for thirty-plus years, and it hasn't been shut down yet. On any given day you might even see the Q-Man, Pat Quirk, down there proselytizing about the "skate army." There's also an annual Halloween party that's absolute mayhem— an all-day affair, with people skateboarding in costumes, bands playing, and people shooting fireworks at each other. The hottest Halloween skate session with the local pros is usually earlier in the day, before the crowds show up. As the day progresses and more people arrive, the crowd gets drunker and wilder. It's a real party.

One of the reasons I wanted to move to Portland is that it's the most punk rock city I've ever known. But it's the kind of punk rock city where an old-school California hardcore band like MDC, who had relocated to Portland, would only play acoustic shows. Their reasoning? They refused to tap into the electrical grid. That summed up Portland perfectly to me. That's the Portland I moved to in the summer of 2007, after Mudhoney did a brief trip to Brazil in June and Europe in July. Desiree and I wanted to get settled in our new house before Aldous went off to school in September.

Mudhoney were due to make a new album in the fall of 2007, and this would be the first test of how it would work with me living in Portland. We'd recorded our last album, *Under a Billion Suns*, in 2006 utilizing three different engineers—Phil Ek, Tucker Martine, and Johnny Sangster—in three different studios, the same way we did 2002's *Since We've Become Translucent*. While it suited our schedules to do multiple short, quick sessions for those records, it didn't make for cohesive albums. So this time, we tried an entirely new approach.

Mark always really liked the four of us jamming in our practice room for hours, sometimes on the same riff. We'd be playing a riff or two, and he'd spend what felt like quite a long time slightly changing his guitar part. On *Under a Billion Suns*, this took forever, and we just weren't finishing any songs, which effectively bottlenecked the writing process. What we felt we really needed at the time was Mark working on vocals and lyrics, not guitar.

So, when we were writing the songs that would end up on *The Lucky Ones*, we said to Mark: *Why don't you put the guitar down and sing along with the riffs we have and see if it unblocks the flow of*

lyrics? Just make shit up and see where vocals might fit with the riffs?
And it worked really well. We were writing all these songs and he
was coming up with lyrics, and at some point we realized we didn't
need him to play guitar on that album. We kept thinking we would
eventually figure out guitar parts for him to overdub later, but when
we went into the studio to record, it sounded really cool the way
it was. At the time I called it our midlife hardcore crisis: We were
rocking out, and we recorded it all in three and a half days. Some
people didn't like it and said it sounded rushed or unfinished, but
I dug that record.

When we moved to Portland, I had to make some hard choices as
to what I had room to keep. Before my new life as a family man, I
had spent a lot of time in previous decades collecting guitars, amps,
fuzz boxes, and records. Some of the stuff I could (and did) put into
a storage locker, but the bigger, bulkier items—like a lot of musical
gear—I sold, because there wasn't room. In Seattle I had an absolute wall of amps in my basement and too many cheap guitars. I'm
down to about ten guitars now, two of which are Guild Starfires, my
main guitars I play live with.

I still have a pretty good collection of vintage fuzz boxes, since
they don't take up a lot of room. I had obsessed over collecting fuzz
boxes from pawnshops and music stores in the '80s and '90s. On the
early tours, I always sought out any guitar stores near the venue. And
once Mudhoney got going, I would bring a lot of different fuzz boxes
into the studio when we were recording, much more than my basic
live setup. This was right when fuzz boxes were starting to creep up
in value (calling our record *Superfuzz Bigmuff* might have incited a
little bit of the vintage craze), so some of the ones I sought out while
on the road, I never got. The first notable one I found, however, was
from a music shop employee who gave it to me for free. It was one

With Milo on Cannon Beach, Oregon, August 7, 2009.

Milo and Aldous, first day of school at Winterhaven School, Portland, Oregon, September 6, 2011.

With Aldous before one of his School of Rock concerts, September 23, 2012.

The Thrown Ups reunion, August 28, 2010. I should probably have regrets.

Skating in Canada while on tour with Pearl Jam, September 17, 2011. I can't even look at my skateboard without putting wrist guards on.

Mudhoney cramped in a van reading while on tour in Europe, July 12, 2011.

of the original Maestro Fuzz-Tones, and it looked like a little piece of pie with a cord attached to it. Gibson originally put it out in '62, and it was the first fuzz box ever made.

Oddly enough, a fuzz box wasn't thought of as a "rock" thing when they were first marketed. Country musicians used them to replicate the sound of pedal steel or the sound of saxophones on a guitar. Then the Rolling Stones came out with "(I Can't Get No) Satisfaction," and that was a game changer. One of my fuzztone inspirations, Davie Allan (of Davie Allan and the Arrows), was sponsored by Mosrite guitars in the '60s, and he used the Mosrite Fuzzrite. I spent seventy-five dollars on one in '89; I just had to have one, and I still own it. If you listen to any of our instrumentals, it's all fake Davie Allan and the Arrows; that was my primary influence on those.

For some reason Electro-Harmonix, the Big Muff maker, licensed the manufacturing to a Russian company, Sovtek, for a period in the '90s. People obsess over the Russian ones, and they're worth hundreds of dollars. Over the years, I've sold two of them and traded a third for a 1971 Guild acoustic twelve-string. I'd paid fifty dollars for that pedal in 1990.

My crate digging for obscure records—going back to the '80s— also started to look more like a good investment and less like a weird obsession. I definitely brought my now-mammoth music collection when we moved to Portland. My entry to all this started innocently enough in the '80s, checking out the selection at the thrift stores where I was mostly looking for vintage clothes. My secret to accruing such a large stash of valuable records was that I'm always seeking out obscure bands and "digging deeper," but also that I was buying stuff for cheap that nobody but me cared about at the time. There's a reason the magazine *Ugly Things* exists. It's for the people who have to keep digging.

I have always obsessed over rare punk records. Often the music didn't even matter, I just needed to get those records into my collection. But I'd also buy anything for a dollar if it looked interesting. I remember buying Love's *Forever Changes* at Goodwill. I didn't even know what it was; I just thought the band's logo was so cool. I found a sealed Chocolate Watchband album in a Value Village on Lake City Way in 1985. I knew and loved the band—they were an underground proto-punk, garage-psych band from the '60s—but I couldn't bear to open it. So, I took it to a record convention and sold it to a dealer for $175.

There was a bus stop in downtown Seattle that happened to be in front of a record store/skate shop/comic shop called Time Travelers. It was a great record store for a while, but they seemed to be clueless. Back when I lived with my parents, I found some of the rarest records of my collection there for a dollar or two—7″ singles by Cleveland garage punk pioneers the Pagans. These are like gold. I think the owners of Time Travelers just lost interest in them and were clearing out the back room.

In the '90s when Mudhoney were touring, I had friends in different cities take me to their local record stores. Sometimes I'd get the VIP treatment, where I'd get to go in the back room and look through unsorted records. I had realized that record stores—both in the United States and the United Kingdom—would sell stuff for cheap if it had been sitting around too long or was no longer hip. I've always been really into 7″ records, and at the time, a lot of record stores didn't really give a crap about them, so they wouldn't really have any out for sale. So, I'd ask, and occasionally they'd have some in the back. That's how I found a lot of my most valuable, rarest, coolest punk rock records, just sitting collecting dust in a box in the back of the record store.

My knowledge of and interest in weird, obscure artists frequently paid dividends. Moby Grape cofounder Skip Spence—sort of America's Syd Barrett—put out a bizarre solo album called *Oar* on Columbia Records in 1969 that sold nothing and went out of print almost immediately. For whatever reason, it wasn't in the price guide of rare records, so even the old hippie guys didn't know what it was. If it was for sale anywhere, it was often out for like five bucks. But it is the rarest Columbia record ever released, due to the small number sold and printed, and it's almost impossible to find. Over the years, however, I found several of them while on tour, simply because it wasn't widely known about. I even found a *sealed* copy of it once, which I sold for $500. You can never predict what will become valuable, but if it's weird and rare there's a good chance that someone will pay good money for it.

That's how I ended up selling a lot of Christian hippie records around the time I moved to Portland. The psychedelic rock collectors ran out of other records to buy, so they were like, *Well, there's one little moment of fuzz guitar on this one track on this terrible hippie folk record about God, so I guess that's worth some money now.* One of the most famous Christian heavy psych bands was called Wilson McKinley. They put out two albums, and even when I was a kid in the '80s, they were already hundred-dollar records.

There are some weird Mormon records out there too. I found one that's sort of a folk-psych record about Jesus for children: *And a Little Child Shall Lead Them . . . Vol. 1* sung by the Children of Israel. Some of the songs are remarkably cool though. It's got a weird psych vibe, but it has children singing these weird Mormon stories about death and damnation. And it's worth a good bit of money. Go figure.

An additional, unexpected source of income has been some of the ephemera I accumulated from the grunge era. If you have an original flier with Nirvana on it, it's worth a lot of money. Not long ago, I pulled out a spare copy of the *Sub Pop 200* vinyl box set I was going to list on eBay. When I opened it up, I found four posters for the *Sub Pop 200* record release shows from December 28 and 29, 1988. I didn't even realize they were in there. It just so happened Nirvana played that gig.

I have some Nirvana collector friends in Portland who I've sold stuff to in the past, and they didn't know posters of this particular gig even existed; they'd never seen them offered for sale. One of my collector friends made me a generous offer and was over at my house within thirty minutes with a wad of cash, and then I was off to buy a bottle of bubbly to celebrate. Those four pieces of paper were worth so much more than the boxed set of records I was about to sell.

The mania for grunge collectibles—and the music—so many years later is eye-opening. There are still fans out there and, even though playing in a band hasn't been my sole source of income for a while, Mudhoney continue to be a draw around the world.

BAD IDEAS

AS THE PARENT OF TWO YOUNG BOYS, I CAME TO HAVE A better appreciation of what my own parents experienced raising Patrick, Mary-Virginia, and me. You can imagine what parenthood is going to be like before you experience it, but you can never account for the little individual people you end up with. My parents had three very different children who challenged them, and their Catholic faith, in every way imaginable. But they adapted, and we were, and remain, tighter as a family for that attitude and approach. So much of parenting is simply about acceptance, and my parents accepted us unconditionally no matter what we threw at them.

Now that I was the parent, I knew that I'd have to let Milo make his own choices for his life. That said, I also wanted him to like the things I liked, and that's natural too. So, when he was a toddler, I started taking him with me to skateparks. I would put all the pads on him and set him loose. And by the time he was five, he was really into skating. This lasted for about a year, and then he declared, as only a six-year-old can, "I don't want to skate anymore; I'll skate again when I'm eight." I told him that was fine. He never offered a reason, and I didn't want to push it. He just seemed to have an on-again, off-again interest.

When he turned eight, he said he was ready to skate again. He was already a natural—much better than I was at an early age—and now he was fully committed and dove right in. The moment when he took his skating to another level, however, happened to be in Walla Walla, Washington, while he and I were driving to Jeff Ament's house in Montana. Jeff has two bowls in his yard in Missoula—one indoor and one outdoor—and we were looking forward to skating them. In the summertime in the Northwest, there are a lot of forest fires, and as we were driving east, it kept getting smokier and smokier. I couldn't figure out why I-84 along the Columbia River Gorge was even open—there were literally fires on both sides of the highway, with flames twenty feet away from the road! By the time we got to Walla Walla, Washington, the smoke was so thick, I decided we weren't going any further east and we got a hotel room for the night.

We discovered there was a killer skate park in Walla Walla that had been built by some Seattle skaters. Even though there was a lot of smoke in the air, we still managed to skate for an hour. I'm glad we did, because that's where Milo crossed the barrier, so to speak, and pulled off his first frontside grinds against a Jersey barrier in the park, something I've never been able to do. And just like that, he *had* to skate every day. He went crazy for it.

Back in Portland, he quickly became one of the best young riders in the area. He could do any trick on mini ramps—he'd just nail it. He was obsessed with skate videos and learning every single trick and variation and naming them all. He had an encyclopedia in his brain of skating facts and techniques. I started learning some new things through him.

I loved watching him skate new tricks. He was not only talented, but he also looked good—he has amazingly cool style. Since I had the free time, we went to a lot of places to skate. Skating was everywhere in Portland—there was even a tiny indoor skatepark two blocks away from where we lived. Milo was there every day after school, for hours, for two and a half years. It made him so good that he was skating at Burnside before he was even a teenager (during certain times when younger kids were allowed to skate). He was passionate and got amazingly proficient quickly.

A little road trip to California in 2016, however, shook things up a bit. In the summer of 2016, Mudhoney had a couple shows to play: one at the Psycho Las Vegas Festival, and then another at Ohana Fest in San Diego that Eddie Vedder puts together every year. There were a few days in between the two gigs, so Milo, me, and one of my skate buddies decided to drive down there, hitting a bunch of skate parks on the way to Vegas, and then heading over to California.

My SoCal skate buddy O had been roommates with skate legend Tony Hawk back in the '80s, and he knows everybody in the Southern California skate scene. When he heard I was heading down to Ohana Fest, he messaged me that he was at Tony Hawk's house and invited us to come over and skate at Tony's private skate park. I'd met Tony before at a couple of different skate-related events down in California, and he's super cool. So, we went over to his place and got to ride with Tony at his private park—it was surreal. So surreal that when Milo posted a picture of him and Tony Hawk on his Instagram account, his buddies thought it was a fake.

Though Milo had a blast riding with Tony, the Southern California scene turned him off in a big way. It wasn't like Portland. It was way more jock-ish; the kids all had coaches, and their dads were all trying to relive their glory days through their kids. It was like Little League. We were at this park in Encinitas, and Milo stopped and watched the kids for a while, recognizing a few of them who were famous for their ages. It wasn't personal; he just didn't like the vibe. But that's probably because he's a Portland skater, and a Portland-raised ne'er-do-well.

Milo has never cared too much about music, but because of skateboarding, he and his Portland skate buddies started listening to early '80s hardcore. I thought that was cool. It's gratifying to see there's still an appreciation of that subculture within skateboarding. Some of Milo's buddies even formed hardcore bands and started wearing Lockjaw T-shirts (a Portland hardcore band from the early '80s). It's like, *What year is this?* There's this sense, especially in the gritty Portland skating scene, that through the generations here it'll continue to be 1982 forever.

The phony, money-obsessed culture in Seattle may have driven my family and me out of town in the early aughts, but I have to give the city credit. Seattle may not have embraced grunge beyond the initial explosion in the early '90s, but it has at least acknowledged the impact the grunge scene had on the city.

In 2013, Sub Pop was celebrating its twenty-fifth anniversary, so of course they had big plans to mark the occasion. And what looms larger over the city, both figuratively and literally, than the 605-foot-tall Space Needle? It's the defining feature of the city's skyline, just as grunge is Seattle's defining musical style. So, someone at Sub Pop had the brilliant idea to have Mudhoney, their relentless standard bearers of grunge, play a gig *on top* of the Space Needle. Not only that, but it would be recorded and filmed by local radio station KEXP, made into a limited-edition live album, and afterward, we'd all be "knighted" as Seafair "royalty" as part of the city's annual summer Seafair celebrations. It was possibly the most Seattle thing ever.

The day of the gig, July 11, 2013, did not go easy, though. The first challenge was what to do with Milo. He was eight and wanted to be there for the momentous gig, but when we arrived, we discovered there was no way he could go up to the roof where we were playing, because he was young and wild and there were no childproof barricades up there. We had to scramble to make a plan, and in the end I had a friend look after him in the restaurant at the top of the Needle, watching our set on a giant TV screen.

With Milo in good hands, we headed up to the roof. Now, you can take elevators to get to the restaurant in the upper part of the Needle, but getting to the roof requires traversing a couple of long stairways and then a vertical ladder that leads to a hatch in the roof itself. The hatch was small, so they had to devise a pulley system to get our amps up there. Guy's amp was so big that it wouldn't fit through the hatch, so he had to play through a smaller one. And then, once we were up there, there was only a small platform, surrounded by a waist-level barrier—barely enough room for us, our gear, the camera crew, and a small audience, which included Sub Pop cofounder Bruce Pavitt. Kim Thayil from Soundgarden made it up the stairs, but when he got to the ladder, he took a few steps and was like, *Oh hell no.* So, he stayed below in the restaurant with his friend and Sub Pop's other cofounder, Jonathan Poneman.

It wasn't our best gig. Mark didn't play guitar, and I stood relatively still, because there wasn't a lot of room to move. I was closest to the edge, and when I got up to the platform that was our stage, I noted the ridiculously unhelpful structure around it—a couple of cables (several half broken) and a sort of fence. Dan was afraid of dropping a drumstick and killing somebody down below, which seemed a reasonable concern considering the height. Our buddy Charles Peterson was taking pictures from a helicopter that was cruising around, which was distracting. But in the end, no one got hurt, and it turned out to be fun. Afterward, the Seafair King and Queen gave us cheap plastic necklaces and made us honorary Seafair royalty. It was such a weird experience.

After the seat-of-the-pants way we recorded *The Lucky Ones* with Tucker Martine, Mudhoney decided to reunite with Johnny Sangster for the follow-up, *Vanishing Point*. By this time, we were all familiar with Johnny and liked his demeanor as much as his engineering and producing skills. We all had personal responsibilities in this era (and I was living in Portland), so recording under the circumstances could be stressful, but Johnny helped reduce that. He's so mellow, and we needed someone like that in the studio. He was also a trusted pair of ears, because he knew us so well, and he had good ideas, especially for backing vocals, which he loves. So, he'd chime in, and we'd listen.

Unlike a lot of bands in the Pro Tools era, we still record our rhythm tracks as a band. So for every song, if Dan, Guy, and I can get through a take with almost no mistakes, and we think the vibe is good on it, that's a good take. We can fix a little bass or guitar flub. But we always want to have our three instruments together live. Mark rarely plays a live guitar track, because typically we don't all know the songs very well initially. He'll sing to our rhythm tracks to guide us, and then once we have solid rhythm tracks, we'll go back and put down final vocals and additional guitar overdubs.

When it comes to mixing, I stay out of it these days—I don't feel like I have anything to add. Also, I don't want to be there for six hours or whatever. After a certain point, you can't even tell what it sounds like anymore, and you can get lost trying to build a song up. So, I have a listen once they're done, and I usually think they sound great.

Living in Portland left me with a lot of free time musically, as long as Mudhoney weren't recording or touring. And we'd been doing less of each over the years. Portland has a thriving music scene, so it was easy enough to meet like-minded musicians. I already knew plenty before I moved down there myself but hadn't yet entertained the idea of doing anything outside of Mudhoney at that point.

That changed when I had the chance to play bass in a band with two like-minded guitarists (CJ Stritzel, formerly of the Drags,

Backstage at a Soundgarden reunion show, February 2, 2013: L-R: Ben Shepherd, Krist Novoselic, Kim Thayil, and me.

With Desiree and the kids at Enchanted Forest, 2017. We love that place!

Milo skating with Phantom Ships, 2014. I split my chin open and cracked my ribs a few minutes later.

Aldous with Milo at Cannon Beach, Oregon, 2017. The long-suffering big brother. Halloween, 2017.

Possibly our weirdest gig! On top of the Space Needle, July 11, 2013!

and Scott Derr, also ex-Drags and ex-Monoshock) and drummer Michael Hendrickson. Cheap Flight were billed in Portland as a garage punk supergroup, but other than writing some songs and playing some gigs, we didn't really accomplish much. CJ and Scott were good friends (and also played in a country band together), but they couldn't agree on anything, not even how and where to record a demo. So, there's no audio evidence of my time in the band, because we never did any recording. But I dug the music and liked playing with them.

After Cheap Flight fizzled out, a friend in Portland kept suggesting that I meet Matt Brown, a local singer-guitarist who also owned a restaurant called Bunk. I wasn't necessarily looking to form a new band but was open to the right situation. This is how I came to play in Phantom Ships. I had been playing around on that Guild twelve-string I had traded the Russian-made Big Muff for, so I thought that this would be a good opportunity to put it to use. I hadn't played a twelve-string in a band, and for the first time I experimented with some pedals other than fuzz boxes to augment my sound. I'd read that using a chorus pedal accentuated the twelve-string's best qualities, so I bought some pedals like that and a few others to play around with.

Phantom Ships played sort of fuzzy Americana-leaning indie rock, and the band included Brent Rahja, one of my skating buddies, on bass. I shared some of the lead vocals with Matt, and our drummer was Evan Railton. We played locally and recorded an album's worth of material over a couple of different sessions. Most (if not all) of that material came out via a series of 7″ records and split singles released on Valley King Records out of San Francisco, and one on Tym Records in Australia. As of this writing, you can also hear and download the tunes from our Bandcamp page. We all had other more serious obligations and endeavors in our lives, so it never progressed beyond a hobby band, but that was all I wanted out of it anyway. I already had a serious band, and Matt had his growing restaurant empire.

Desiree had found her way into the Portland restaurant scene as well. She'd been a vegan since I'd met her, and she continued to get more interested in cooking over the years. She was asked to be the second chef in an *Iron Chef*-type competition for vegan chefs in Portland, and her team won. After that, all the other vegan chefs in town had their eyes on her, and she got great jobs in a couple different vegan places. She worked at Harvest at the Bindery, which was opened by Jon Paul Steuer, who was famous because he was an actor on *Star Trek: The Next Generation* for one season as a kid. Super nice guy, but he had some serious health issues and took his own life. His mom had been running the restaurant with him, and she shut it down in 2018 immediately after his death. Desiree also worked at Holiday (closed in 2019), which was started by the guy who started Stumptown Coffee, Duane Sorenson.

What wasn't working, however, was our marriage. Something needed to change.

SEARCHING FOR MELODY

DESIREE HAD BEEN ABSENT A LOT OVER THE YEARS, AND she hadn't really been all that present when she was home, either. I felt like I had been raising my sons as a single dad for years, and it was starting to wear on me.

I would sometimes have to leave the boys with my sister in Yakima when I went on tour, because Desiree couldn't be relied upon. Home life for all of us wasn't great, but it was especially hard on my sons. And in a lot of ways, they were forced to grow up fast. Aldous had a bad stutter for a while when he was younger and suffered from such severe social anxiety that he didn't want to go to school. It was a daily battle to get him out the door, into the car, and then out of the car and into the school. It was hell—for all of us.

Aldous had always been a smart and well-read kid, and he even skipped ahead a grade while we were living in Portland. By tenth grade, he was a math tutor for seniors. But as smart as he was, he wasn't attending class, so he was expelled—a scenario that reminded me all too well of my own experience in high school thirty-five years before. I was on tour with Mudhoney when all this went down, so Desiree made a unilateral decision and sent him to live with his biological father in Olympia, Washington. Though I would have preferred that Aldous stayed in Portland, his dad and stepmom enrolled him in a smaller alternative school that turned out to be perfect for him. It was a bunch of oddballs and outcasts, and he did really well there. He had two great years of high school in Olympia and got his diploma.

During the years Aldous was in Olympia with his father and stepmom, Milo and I were spending a lot of time skateboarding together, especially when I wasn't touring or working part-time doing general warehouse work—quality control, packing orders, etc.—at the Cascade Record Pressing plant. Every Friday night, he'd have three or four of his friends staying with him at our house, and we'd all head out to the skatepark Saturday morning. It was an every-weekend thing. When he was eleven or twelve, it was still OK to hang out with me. But then he got older, and it became like *Maybe I'll go to the skate park without you.* I totally got it. I wanted the kids to have their own scenes, and I was fine with them getting into *some* trouble.

Once Aldous finished high school, he stayed in Olympia for a few more months before moving back in with us, because it wasn't going well with his father. I'd had to sell the house I bought when we first moved to Portland, so at this point we were all living in a rented duplex. Desiree was technically living with us as well, but she and I were both seeing other people, so, as I mentioned, she wasn't around much.

In the late fall of 2018, I left town to do a monthlong European tour with Mudhoney in support of our latest Johnny Sangster–produced album, *Digital Garbage*. Aldous was eighteen and Milo was about to turn fourteen, so the plan was that they would be staying at the duplex, and Desiree would stay with them every other day. Unfortunately, it didn't work out that way. Desiree checked in on them a few times, didn't stay a single night, and spent the money I left for groceries very quickly. Aldous had a job, so he used his money for groceries until I returned from tour. I was furious when I got home and heard all the details from the boys.

As if that wasn't bad enough, 2018 had one last indignity to deliver. In December, a couple weeks after I returned from tour, Aldous and I were at home in the duplex when we smelled smoke. We determined that it wasn't coming from our unit but from the neighboring one—it was on fire. I went next door and pounded on the door. There was no response, so I broke a window to see if our neighbors were home, and then called 911. Luckily no one was there, and neither Aldous nor I was injured, but our unit suffered smoke damage and we had to move out. The duplex was the last place Desiree officially lived with us.

Aldous, Milo, and I moved into a house together (where we still live), and I took full custody of the boys. There was no legal battle; they just chose to be with me full-time. They could see Desiree whenever they wanted to, and Desiree was welcome to come by the house and see them anytime. I wanted them to be able to have a good relationship with her (and Aldous with his biological father and stepmom), but I try to stay out of it and let them figure out what that looks like. Desiree and I are friendly; it's all water under the bridge at this point. When I stopped expecting much from her, things got easier.

The fact is, I'd already been a single dad for a while, and I could count on my sister Mary-Virginia for support if I needed it. She not only has the experience of raising her own large family, but she also holds an advanced degree in child psychology. She's been my go-to for parenting advice. Luckily, Yakima's not too far from Portland—about the same as the drive to Seattle—so my boys have been able to spend time with and get to know their many cousins over the years.

As a single dad with two kids and a minivan, the obvious next move was to join a "dad rock" band, right? Sunday State were, again,

Mudhoney's first pandemic rehearsal, June 14, 2021.

With Andrea showing off my pandemic moustache, June 2020.

Milo and Aldous at Cannon Beach, Oregon, March 2021.

not a serious endeavor, but a way to be creative in my time away from Mudhoney. It was easier than trying to write solo material with two teenage boys around. I joined the band on bass and played on their first EP, *Mono*, which they self-released in a very limited run in 2019. Unfortunately, Mudhoney got busy that year, as we did a lot of touring supporting *Digital Garbage* and the EP of leftovers from that session, *Morning in America*, released a year later. I just didn't have a regular night of the week to devote to Sunday State, as much as I enjoyed the music.

Mudhoney had big plans for 2020. There would be a monthlong North American tour in May (including some dates with Meat Puppets), as well as a month in Europe in the fall. Before that, however, we played a one-off show on leap year day, February 29, in a small California town near Joshua Tree National Park, way out in the desert. Before we headed back to the Northwest, though, Mark and I recorded a session in Los Angeles with Melvins, where we did Neil Young and Black Flag covers for an Amphetamine Reptile release called *White Lazy Boy*. Mark returned to West Seattle, and I went to Portland, oblivious to the fact that everything in the world was going to change in just two short weeks.

When the pandemic hit in early 2020, I, like every professional musician in the world, was out of work. Even though playing in Mudhoney was no longer my full-time job, we still recorded and had been touring regularly, and it brought in money. Unfortunately, that source of income was gone for the foreseeable future. The two tours we had booked for 2020 were both "postponed" until 2021, because no one knew what lay ahead. Not long after, I learned I'd lost *all* my jobs, as Cascade Record Pressing laid me off too. Bands and labels were canceling their orders for vinyl because they didn't know when they would be able to tour. So many of the jobs we did at Cascade were for small indie bands, and if they can't tour, they can't sell records. Mudhoney were in the same boat. Didn't know when we'd be touring, didn't know when we'd see each other next, didn't know when we'd record a new album.

The answers to some of those questions arrived in 2021. Even though vaccines were becoming available in early 2021, bands still weren't really playing live and touring, so our postponed 2020 tour dates were once again moved forward to 2022. However, we were all brought together in April 2021 for the most Mudhoney thing ever. Seattle Public Utilities had purchased an eighteen-foot-tall tunnel-boring machine to create a giant storage tunnel to help reduce sewage overflow during the rainy season, and they decided to let the public name it. The winning name: Mudhoney. So, after being apart for more than a year, the four of us reconvened for a photo shoot in front of this red behemoth, painted with our name, all sporting matching "Solidbrown" shirts (designed to mimic the '80 Polish trade union *Solidarność* logo). If anyone ever questions our underground cred, this settles it. You can't get much more underground than having a tunnel-boring machine named after your band.

This is when we began to consider the possibility of recording a new album, though how that would be done was up in the air. We'd have to write and rehearse new material, which would be challenging, because Guy and his family were planning to move to Australia in the fall. So, however it was going to happen, it would have to be done fast, and we're not always good at fast, especially thirty-plus years in. That's why five years would lapse between albums, pandemic or no. But at least we would have something creative and productive to work on, some goal to shoot for.

In June 2021, I spent a couple of weeks in Seattle so we could get reacquainted and start jamming on everybody's ideas to see what we could come up with. We knew we wouldn't get the whole album written, but we were flying by the seat of our pants, per usual. We had recording time tentatively booked in September with Johnny Sangster at Crackle & Pop Studio in Seattle's Ballard neighborhood, so we had something to aim for.

Mark doesn't like working fast because he doesn't want to write throwaway lyrics. Which I get, but I always liked to say to him, *Remember when you were young, and you'd form a new band, and you'd have to come up with a whole set in like a month or two? You just go with whatever's happening.* I thought we should tap into that vibe and just get it done. I love to mix things up a little bit, and having to run into the studio real fast was invigorating. Luckily, we had a backlog of riffs that we'd accumulated leading up to the lockdown—stuff left over from previous writing sessions. So, we just had to go back and remind ourselves what they were. Mark had come up with several riffs and songs, and Guy and I did most of the rest. Even Dan brought in a couple songs. We continued to get together weekly in West Seattle at Mark's place over the summer, and I felt like we had plenty of material that was coming together nicely for our upcoming recording session.

Because of Australia's strict approach to COVID containment, Guy's move to that country was ultimately delayed, and we were relieved that we wouldn't have to rush the album and possibly record part of it without him. Our recording dates were pushed back to November, and we were able to lay down most of the tracks—what amounted to a double album's worth of material—in a week. We were all vaccinated and there weren't any of the hyper-transmissible variants flying around, so we were able to comfortably record like we always had in Johnny's studio. And because we weren't up against any hard deadlines, we were able to book another bit of time in January 2022 to tweak and further finish things. It looked like we'd be back to touring in 2022—making up most of the postponed dates from 2020—but the new record wouldn't be scheduled for release until 2023.

Mudhoney will be celebrating our thirty-fifth anniversary when that album lands. It will be our eleventh full-length studio album, and our eighth for Sub Pop. Our second chapter with the label has been a perfect symbiotic relationship. They don't expect a whole lot out of us other than the music, and touring when we can. We expect them to make a great product for us and to get us in the studio when we want to get in the studio. Beyond that, there's no pretense that we're expected to have a hit or anything like that. They like the connection to the early days, the Sub Pop history. We grew up together, so it's nice that in our doddering old age we're still linked.

I think it's a great label: They do good, quality work. I'm not going to like all the records they put out, but that doesn't matter—what they make, they make well. Besides, Seattle's obviously not a small, tight-knit music scene anymore, and the grunge era ended a long time ago. Times change. They've done great by us for over twenty years. (And now that Mark works there, they can never *not* put out our records!)

In 1988, I figured this whole grunge thing would be over in a couple years, and I'd go back to college and get a degree after I'd had my adventures. I was thankfully wrong about that. What Mark, Stone, Jeff, and I started—along with Melvins, Soundgarden, the U-Men, and others—has resonated with more people, for a longer time, than I could have ever imagined.

I've had more crazy, weird experiences than most have had in a lifetime: I met Lemmy when we opened for Motörhead! I hobnobbed with Iggy Pop at a festival in Australia! I befriended Kim Salmon from the Scientists! I put out a Billy Childish record! I toured with Sonic Youth, many times! I recorded with Sir Mix-a-Lot and got a gold record! It goes on and on. I never did get that degree, though, and I think my parents were OK with that.

As someone deeply interested in rock music history, I'd argue that most bands are only good for two or three years, and then they're less relevant. I suppose I contradict my own argument by sticking with Mudhoney for thirty-five years (and counting). Are we less relevant today than we were in 1988 or 1989? I still think we make solid records and we're still a great live band, and beyond that, our ongoing relevance is for other people to assess.

We are who we are, and we did what we did. In many ways I never really embraced the idea of making a career in music. I was kind of indifferent. At the same time, Mudhoney were making good money; we were all living off of it. So this gave me the impression that my indifference worked well. If we were more serious, would we have made better records? I don't know. Mudhoney did get more serious as the years went by. As the grunge explosion faded, we got more serious. Kind of funny. We also got older and appreciated what we did, what we achieved, in a different way. We helped create grunge. I don't have any regrets about that.

EPILOGUE

MUDHONEY'S FUTURE HAS ALWAYS BEEN INSCRUTABLE, AT least to me. There were several points along the way in our now-thirty-five-year career where I thought I was done and that the band was too. I've been repeatedly wrong on both counts. I'm writing this in the middle of a US tour, unfortunately the last we'll do with Guy as a resident of this continent. When this tour wraps up in June, he and his family will relocate permanently back to his home country of Australia—a place Mudhoney love so well. What does that mean for us? I'm not really sure.

There's a European tour booked for the fall of 2022. Guy will meet up with us in the Netherlands for a few days before the tour starts to rehearse, but it's going to be more difficult to keep making records and touring with Guy living in Australia. But we've considered some of the possibilities. We could always record down there. We already have an Australian tour potentially in the works for spring of 2023, so it's likely we'll be there regularly, just as we've always been.

Luckily, we were able to complete our latest album, *Plastic Eternity*, before Guy left. Well, it's almost complete. Guy's parts are done, but it still needs to be mixed, and Mark is thinking about resinging a few songs. He recently put vocals over a song Dan wrote that was going to be an instrumental. It's currently called "Little Dogs," and it's really funny—all the dogs in the land of Mudhoney are tiny. Another song Dan wrote is going to remain an instrumental, and we got Ed Fotheringham's son, Joe, to play on it. It's got a bit of a mariachi vibe to it, so Joe plays some Herb Alpert–style trumpet. (He did a great job.) We have twenty songs in total, and I'm happy with all of it. There's nothing that seems like an outtake to me.

We've tried some different things musically over the years, but Mudhoney have our own palette. We add elements here and there, and our individual influences come through, but there's just a certain chemistry that happens—our inherent DNA—when we get together. We try to make sure new music isn't a carbon copy of something else we've done, but it ultimately always sounds like Mudhoney. This album is the same. Right now, we don't know all the details—how many songs will be on it, what the cover will look like— and that's OK. That's Mudhoney—we figure things out as we go.

It's hard to say what we'll do until we do it. Regardless, we've had a good ride.

Mudhoney like little dogs! 2022.

SELECT DISCOGRAPHY

Green River (guitar)
Come On Down EP (Homestead) 1985
1984 Demos LP (Jackpot) 2016
Live at the Tropicana, Olympia, WA, September 26, 1984 LP (Jackpot) 2019

Love + Respect (guitar)
Record LP (Penultimate) 1990

Mr. Epp & the Calculations (guitar)
Ridiculing the Apocalypse LP (Super Electro) 1996

Mudhoney (guitar)
"Touch Me I'm Sick" b/w "Sweet Young Thing Ain't Sweet No More" 7" (Sub
    Pop) 1988
Superfuzz Bigmuff EP (Sub Pop) 1988
Mudhoney LP (Sub Pop) 1989
Every Good Boy Deserves Fudge LP (Sub Pop) 1991
Piece of Cake LP (Reprise) 1992
Five Dollar Bob's Mock Cooter Stew EP (Reprise) 1993
My Brother the Cow LP (Reprise) 1995
Tomorrow Hit Today LP (Reprise/Super Electro) 1998
Here Comes Sickness: Best of the BBC Recordings LP (Strange Fruit/BBC
    Music) 2000
Since We've Become Translucent LP (Sub Pop) 2002
Under a Billion Suns LP (Sub Pop) 2006
The Lucky Ones LP (Sub Pop) 2008
Vanishing Point LP (Sub Pop) 2013
LiE LP (Sub Pop) 2018

Digital Garbage LP (Sub Pop) 2018
Morning in America EP (Sub Pop) 2019
Plastic Eternity (Sub Pop) 2023

Phantom Ships (twelve-string guitar/vocals)
Phantom Ships LP (self-released, digital only) 2015

Solo
Searching for Melody LP (Roslyn Recordings) 2003
Steve Turner and His Bad Ideas LP (Roslyn Recordings) 2004
A Beautiful Winter EP (Houston Party) 2004
New Wave Punk Asshole LP (Funhouse) 2006

Sunday State (bass/guitar)
Mono EP (No Night Travel) 2019
Sunday State LP (No Night Travel, digital only) 2021

The Fall-Outs (bass)
The Fall-Outs LP (Super Electro) 1992

The Monkeywrench (bass)
Clean as a Broke-Dick Dog LP (Sub Pop) 1992
Electric Children LP (Estrus) 2000
Gabriel's Horn LP (Birdman) 2008

The Sad and Lonely(s) (guitar)
The Sad and Lonely(s) LP (Super Electro) 1991

The Thrown Ups (guitar)
Melancholy Girlhole Box 7" box set (Amphetamine Reptile) 1990
The Thrown Ups LP (Amphetamine Reptile) 1990
Seven Years Golden compilation LP (Amphetamine Reptile) 1997

ACKNOWLEDGMEN

STEVE THANKS

I would like to thank everyone I have ever played music with. First and foremost Mark Arm, Dan Peters, Guy Maddison, and Matt Lukin. Also Stone Gossard, Jeff Ament, Alex Shumway, Johnny Sangster, Tim Kerr, Tom Price, Ed Fotheringham, Dave Holmes—the list is long. I'm a lucky guy.

Adem Tepedelen deserves much praise for suggesting this project and seeing it through. This book would not exist without his efforts.

All my fellow record/music freaks have made my life better with their enthusiasm and love of obscure oddball music. I learn from them all the time. The hunt continues.

My family, of course. My parents and my brother and sister—Patrick and Mary-Virginia—never made me feel like a weirdo, even if I was one. MV's kids and their kids are the best, and I'm lucky to know and love them all.

Milo and Aldous are the center of my world, and I'm so lucky to be their dad. Our cat Sunna must not be left out.

Andrea, for putting up with me for the last three years. I hope it's forever.

All the fans who still show up—we feel incredibly honored and will continue until the proverbial wheels come off.

My skateboard pals—we will continue until the actual wheels come off.

Everyone at Chronicle and Omnibus who has helped make this happen, as well as my agent, Peter McGuigan.

ADEM THANKS

Steve, for entrusting me to help tell your story. Dawn Anderson, for transcribing a lot of that story, but most importantly for playing a crucial part in supporting and promoting the Seattle music scene via *Backlash* and giving Mudhoncy their first cover feature. My wife, Susan Kerschbaumer, for doing all that you do to make it possible for me to do what I love to do most; you are our family's MVP and are an amazing wife, friend, and mother. Samuel, for being the best son/mountain biking partner a guy could ask for. Everyone at Chronicle Prism (past and present)—Mark Tauber, Eva Avery, Cara Bedick, Allison Adler, Pamela Geismar—for your relentless, unwavering enthusiasm for this book. Laura Mazer, for your positivity, encouragement, and ace editing skills and advice. My best friend, Jeff Kleinsmith, for bringing it all full circle—thirty-five years later—with your incredible cover design. Patrick Barber, for adding that extra bit of Stymie magic with your ace interior design skills.

PHOTOGRAPHY CREDITS

Jeff Ament
Skating at Jeff Ament's Treasure Bowl in Missoula, Montana (page 229)

Mark Arm
Skating in Canada while on tour with Pearl Jam (page 265)

Vern Green
Sittin' on the porch with my banjo (page 240)

Lisa Johnson
With Jeff Ament, on stage with Pearl Jam (page 198)

Libby Knudson
Playing guitar in Mr. Epp at the Metropolis (page 51)
With Alex Shumway and Mark Arm (page 51)

Michael Lavine
First Mudhoney photo shoot (page 126)
Mudhoney photo shoot at the Pyramid Club (page 139)
Mudhoney on tour in NYC (page 139)

Caryn Palmier
With my favorite rose bush (page 198)
Super Team USA at the Little 100 bike race (page 207)

Dan Peters
Mudhoney in Europe (page 139)

Charles Peterson
Mudhoney outtake from "You Got It" 7" (page 139)
With Krist Novoselic at Mark's wedding, 1994 (page 189)
In my bedroom at Rock Mecca, circa 1992 (page 189)
Monkeywrench in my front yard, 2000 (page 229)

Annie Philipsen
In the batting cage with Stone (page 229)
In my living room, 2002 (page 240)

Photocoyote
Italian artist Photocoyote did two illustrations of me (page 249)

Sydney Taylor
Mudhoney show at the Alamo (page 119)

Photographs copyright © by their original photographers.